$4.

11/21

The Glass House

John Hix

THE GLASS HOUSE

The MIT Press

Cambridge, Massachusetts

First published 1974 in Great Britain by Phaidon Press
Limited, London. All rights reserved.

No part of this publication may be reproduced, stored in a
retrieval system or transmitted in any form or by any means,
electronic, mechanical, photocopying, recording or otherwise,
without the prior permission of the copyright owner.

Second printing, 1981
First MIT Press paperback edition, 1981
First MIT Press edition, 1974

Library of Congress catalog card number: 74-5201
ISBN: 0 262 08076 1 (hard)
        0 262 58044 6 (paper)

Printed in the United States of America

Contents

Preface

Many persons have contributed information to this study, and as far as possible they are listed below: to all of them I am most grateful.

I would like to thank the students at Cambridge who built the experimental glasshouse with me, Clare Frankl, Brenda and Robert Vale, Jean-Paul Porchon, Dan O'Neil, Murdah and particularly Mike Goulden who later wrote a paper on early glasshouses and helped me in research. Allan Baird and Richard Winterton produced a beautiful historic brochure of the experimental idea. Graham Smith, former student in the Department of Architecture, University of Strathclyde, gave me excellent information on John Kibble.

The University of Cambridge helped finance our experiment and Professor Leslie Martin and my fellow teachers at the Department of Architecture provided a Brancusi Travelling Fellowship for which I am very grateful.

I am particularly indebted to the directors of the Botanic Gardens who sent me photographs and information: Belgian Botanic Gardens, Meise; Jardin des Plantes, Paris; Hamburg Botanic Gardens; Missouri Botanic Gardens, St Louis. Longwood Gardens, Brandywine, Pennsylvania; Milwaukee County Botanic Gardens; H. J. Van Hattum, Director of the Leiden University Botanic Gardens; Aidan Brady, Director of the National Botanic Gardens, Glasnevin, Dublin; and Professor T. Eckardt, Director of the Berlin-Dahlem Botanic Gardens. Gilbert Daniels, Director of the Hunt Botanical Library, Pittsburgh, and Director John Gilmore and his staff at the Cambridge University Botanic Garden gave me free

6

run of their rare books which was most helpful. R. Desmond, formerly librarian at the Royal Botanic Gardens, Kew, generously gave me his valuable references and advised on the section about Richard Turner.

Garden author Miles Hadfield also kindly sent me important references and advised on the manuscript, as did Professor G. F. Chadwick. Professor Reyner Banham, has inspired me from the very beginning when he suggested that perhaps nineteenth-century horticultural environment could be as interesting as nineteenth-century architecture.

Persons involved in horticultural and phyto-engineering today who gave invaluable help are: A. E. Canham, Reading University; Carl O. Hodge, Environmental Research Laboratory, University of Arizona; William A. Bailey, Phyto-engineering laboratory U.S.A. Department of Agriculture. The Instituut voor Tuinbouwtechniek, Wageningen; O. Ruthner, Ruthner Co., Vienna.

Many London Libraries have been of assistance; I am indebted to the staff of the Guildhall Library and Art Gallery; Chiswick District Library; Westminster City Libraries; London Borough of Lambeth, Minet Library; the British Museum; the Royal Horticultural Society; Victoria and Albert Museum; the Science Museum; Rare Prints Library of the Greater London Council; Leyden University Library Map Department; The National Trust for Historic Preservation, Lyndhurst, U.S.A.; the Library of Congress Prints Department; Historic American Building Survey; Bibliothèque Nationale, and in Cambridge, the University Library and the Department of Architecture and Fine Arts Library.

Architects Ib and Jorgen Rasmussen gave me initial ideas and photographs; Bruce Goff, Frank Newby, Frei Otto, Ted Happold of Ove Arup; Gillinson, Barnett and Partners; Kevin Roche and John Dinkeloo and Associates all sent me valuable information.

The Belgium Embassy in London organised a visit to the Royal Garden at Laeken and my State Senator from Iowa, Harold Hughes, helped me in Washington D.C.

Several companies contributed information and assistance. Pilkington Brothers Ltd., Howard Cross of Lord and Burnham sent me invaluable photographs as did Michael Hope of Crittal-Hope. Elisabeth Bayles of Ickes-Braun Glasshouses Inc., and the Cambridge Glasshouse Company gave me contemporary literature.

I am indebted to the Staff at the Department of Architecture and particularly Christine Allbut who struggled through my rough notes.

I am also indebted to Frank Lipsius for advice on editing the work and for the encouragement from my colleagues at the Department of Architecture and Alison MacDonald.

Introduction

I became interested in glass structures while searching through material found by my students at Cambridge University. We were assembling a brochure explaining to industrialists why they should contribute to our experimental 'Maximum Space Glass House' which we built in 1969. This book grew from this fascinating material.

I was concerned by the fact that architects had become increasingly involved with seemingly esoteric matters. I felt that they were abandoning to other specialists the very purpose of architecture—the control of man's environment. As Reyner Banham has written in *The Architecture of the Well-Tempered Environment:*

> . . . it is probably true that an intelligent commercial glasshouse operator today, judiciously metering temperature, moisture and carbon dioxide levels in the atmosphere around his out of season chrysanthemums, has more environmental knowledge at his fingertips than most architects ever learn.

This problem is not a new one to architects. I discovered that even in the early nineteenth century, architects and horticulturalists were in conflict over how the new glass gardens should be made.

Though *The Glass House* is not a history of all glass buildings, it shows contemporary designers that their thin-skinned plastic and pneumatic structures have a fascinating heritage. In the seventeenth century, the desire to nurture exotic plants in a foreign and often hostile climate led to the development of the glasshouse with its sophisticated mechanical servicing that created its own artificial climate; while the botanist could adapt to changes in his environment, his hard-won exotics could not move closer to the fire, and would wither and die. Consequently fascinating equipment was developed for plant environments, which were more advanced than those for man. This functional approach created buildings as rich in form as they were in scientific control.

Though this book is not a chronological study, I have discussed one building type, the glasshouse, to show how the needs and tastes of different periods have created different built forms. *The Glass House* is divided into two parts. The first part deals with man's growing ability to use the forces of nature. It ends with the 'Industrialization of Horticulture', demonstrating that low-energy, non-toxic technology can fulfil some of the world's food requirements by taking advantage of the 'glasshouse effect' to trap solar energy. These environmental machines, run by scientists, environmental and phyto engineers, will surely affect future food production and land-use planning.

The second part begins with 'The Private Conservatory', the exotic glass garden that man created for his plants only to take over for himself. When it became man's house, it was enriched in eccentric and diverse ways. In short, these chapters describe glass buildings that provide enclosed habitable space, and are a complement to recent studies of arcades, markets, and associated buildings.

The story of the Crystal Palace is told from the constructional point of view. The techniques used in its modular construction would humble any builder today. A short chapter on the German Expressionists is presented as a sequence of quotations from a spirited language difficult to duplicate. Their story would form the basis of another book, and an English translation of Scheerbart's *Glasarchitektur* would be a most exciting beginning.

Since I wrote *The Glasshouse*, the world has experienced a rapid rise in energy costs; solar energy has become a household word and solar houses have been built everywhere. The early 18th and 19th century glasshouse designs, in Chapter one, are fundamentally similar to contemporary passive solar glasshouses proposed to save energy today. The efficiency of these 19th century glasshouses, such as the McIntosh vinery on page 55, should be studied by all students interested in passive solar and energy efficient design. Because of the high cost of energy, the glasshouse principle, as described in Chapter 5, has become as useful today as it was then. My own low energy double envelope home with its large glasshouse heating system, built near Toronto, finds its inspiration in many of the designs found in this book.

The images of arctic cities covered with large pneumatic enclosures are certainly too energy intensive for the 80's. However, they exemplify the inspiration conjured by the glasshouse that provides summer at all seasons.

University of Cambridge
June 1972.

1 A wintering gallery in Leyden University Botanic Gardens.

I   *Early Beginnings*

The use of artificial climates for plants in the fifth century B.C. in Greece is hinted in references to the 'gardens of Adonis' made by writers of that time. On the other hand Plato may only be describing a good natural micro-climate when he describes, in the *Phaedo,* that 'a grain of seed, or the branch of a tree, placed in or introduced into these gardens, acquires in eight days a development which cannot be obtained in as many months in the open'.

By the first century A.D., Pliny the Naturalist and Columella describe the use of a forcing house much like that of the eighteenth century. Columella writes of growing cucumbers in very large vessels:

> It is also possible, if it be worth the trouble, for wheels to be put onto the larger vessels so that they can be brought out with less labour. In any case, the vessels ought to be covered with slabs of transparent stone, so that in cold weather when the days are clear, they may be brought into the sun. By this method Tiberius Caesar was supplied with cucumbers during almost the whole year.

This 'transparent stone' according to Seneca and Pliny was *lapis specularis* (talc). It was split into thin sheets and also widely used at the time for glazing. The hot water and flue systems that the Romans used in their houses could easily have been modified for the forcing of vegetables. In Pompeii archaeologists have identified *specularia* (stoves) complete with masonry tiers for plant display and heating flues in the walls. Seneca took a sceptical view of this when he asked whether it was not 'contrary to nature to require a rose in winter and use hot water to force from winter the later blooms of spring?'

It was not until the Renaissance that there was a methodical approach to the study of nature and in particular the growth of plants. In 1543 the first botanical garden was started at Pisa, and by the end of that decade they existed in Padua and Florence, with Bologna and Leyden in Holland starting theirs by the end of the century. In Padua, a wintering shed for the more delicate species of plants was built and called *viridarium*, or greenhouse. It was no more than a masonry shed with a brazier to supply additional heat. Leyden also had one in its Botanical Gardens before its plant gallery was built in 1599.

In England, as in Holland, the sixteenth-century plant environments were closely linked with the expansion of international trade and commercial exploration. The Eastern trade through Venice and Genoa brought many new plants into the gardens of the North Italian merchants and the new university botanic gardens. Here they could be seen by other European travellers. William Turner, considered the first original botanical author in Britain, visited Italy at the time. Between 1580 and 1588 during Elizabeth's reign, many new plants were introduced into Britain by Raleigh and Cavendish. The first known orange seeds brought to Britain were given to Sir Francis Carew by Raleigh. Planted at Carew's estate in Beddington, Surrey, they were killed by frost in the harsh winter of 1739–40.

In the mid-seventeenth century botanical knowledge was disseminated by printing and copper-plate illustrations. In 1654, Sir Hugh Platt published practical advice and general reflections on forcing and greenhouse gardening under the title *The Garden of Eden.*

9

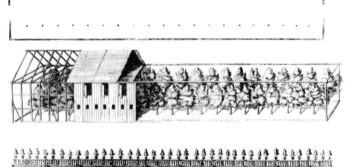

2 Portable wooden orangery constructed for the Elector Palatine in Heidelberg by Salomon de Caus.

3 Permanent stone orangery built for the Elector Palatine in Heidelberg by Salomon de Caus.

4 The Apothecaries' Garden at Chelsea, London, was established around 1673. This plan, made in 1751, shows the architectural conservatory with the glass wings built by Philip Miller. Near the statue of Hans Sloane are the bark stoves and glass cases for exotic plants. The gardens, near Cheyney Walk, are now cut off from the Thames by the Embankment.

I hold it for a most delicate and pleasing thing to have a fair gallery, great chamber and other lodging that openeth fully upon the East or West, to be inwardly garnished with sweet Herbs and Flowers, yea and fruit if it were possible.

Greenhouse gardening still had overtones of profane conjuring, as Platt reveals in his defence of Ripley, an alchemist, 'who suffered death,' he says, 'as the secret report goeth for making a pear tree to fructify in winter . . . But it was the denial of his medicine and not the crime of conjuration with killed him'.

The aristocracy came to have a great interest in their gardens and competed to get the best gardeners in their employ. Very often it was these gardeners who made valuable contributions to botanical science by keeping small physic gardens for their private use where they could study and experiment with 'herbs and simples'. For them the dung bed and oiled paper or green glass frame were sufficient to temper the climate. But the central preoccupation of their patrons was with citrus fruits, for the table and for their decorative qualities. Their environmental requirements were not great but the size of the trees necessitated buildings of some magnitude. In his book, *Upon the Garden of Epicurus,* published in 1685, Sir William Temple, diplomat and traveller, wrote with pride of his own oranges and of the trips he made to see others.

Temple would have seen ambitious projects on the Continent. In 1620 Salomon de Caus described his design for a portable wooden orangery to the Elector Palatine in Heidelberg; the building was to be 280 ft long (Illustration 2).

It covers thirty small and four hundred medium-sized trees and is made of wood which is put up every year about Michaelmas and the orange trees are warmed by means of four furnaces all the winter, so that in the time of the great frosts one can walk in this orangerie without feeling any cold . . . At Easter the framework is taken away, to leave the trees uncovered all summer.

The success of this structure led to Salomon de Caus's suggestion of a permanent freestone orangery (3). He explained to the Elector that with a permanent wooden roof it was necessary only to close the windows in the winter. This masonry conservatory was an early example of the many garden banqueting halls *cum* orangeries enjoyed by the aristocracy in the seventeenth, eighteenth and nineteenth centuries both on the Continent and in England.

By the end of the seventeenth century, the botanic search was on. Wealthy private collectors and institutions like the Oxford Botanic Garden financed plant and seed hunting expeditions round the world, requiring better performance from the stoves, pits and greenhouses to cope with the new climate demands. One of these travellers, Sir Hans Sloane (1660–1752), knighted by George I on his return from the West Indies, wrote an important treatise on the botany of that area. He bought the Manor of Chelsea in 1712, near Wren's Royal Hospital, and gave a freehold to the Company of Apothecaries in 1722 on condition that they donate to the Royal Society fifty new plants a year for forty years. Under the hand of Philip Miller, hired by the Worshipful Company in 1722, the Apothecaries' Garden at Chelsea was excelled by

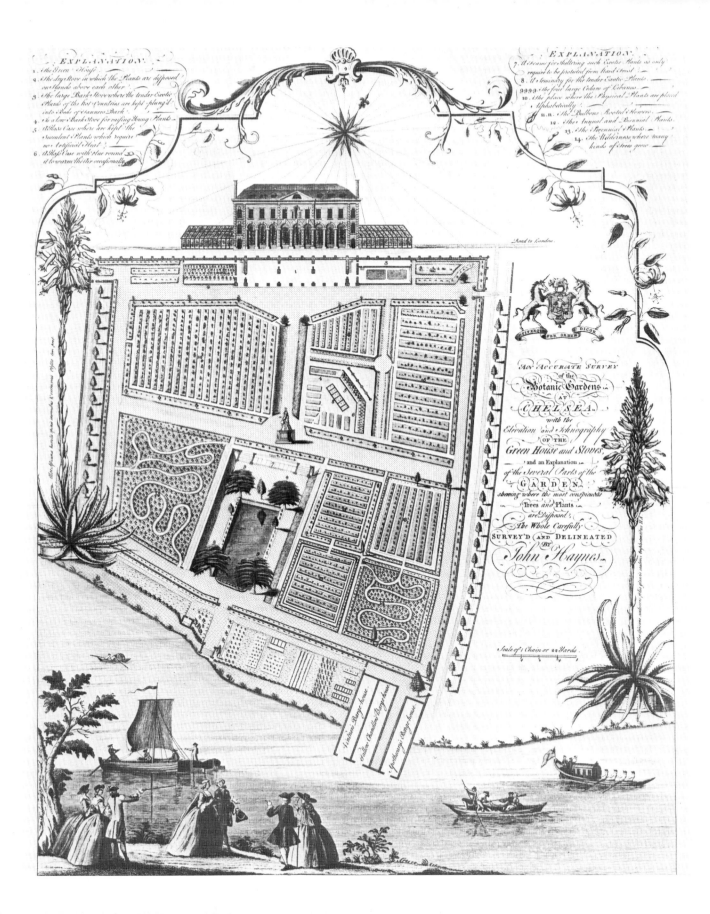

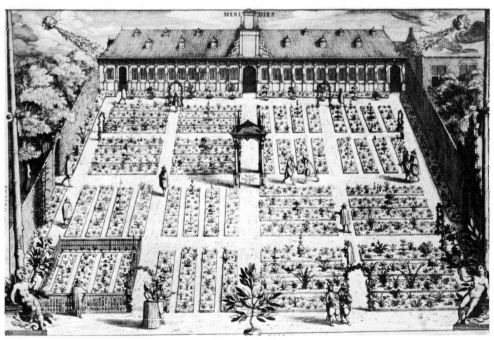

MERIDIES

5 Leyden University Botanic Garden in 1610. The wintering gallery was unfortunately sited on the south of the Garden, facing north and received little sun: there was still much to be learned. The gallery was 36·5 m long × 4·65 m wide, with glazed windows.

6 Winter place in the gardens of Pieter de Wolff. Tubs of orange and lemon trees were moved out into the sun each summer.

perhaps no other institution by the number of curious exotics it contained (4).

Miller was a professional gardener noted for his practical abilities in keeping all those exotic plants alive. The son of a Scots market gardener from Deptford, he started as a florist in St George's Fields, where he combined an encyclopaedic knowledge of plants with an extraordinary skill in growing them. His work was important, not from an ornamental point of view as in Victorian times, but for the medical use to which it could be put. At a time when naturalists were making the first accurate descriptions and classifications of the natural world, Miller gave plants to Linnaeus, the great Swedish naturalist, who himself visited the famous Chelsea Gardens in 1736.

Over a hundred years before, in 1587, Leyden University Botanic Garden was founded with a similar scope and ambition to the Chelsea Gardens. In 1599 the University's Senate Curatores built a gallery to serve as a conservatory, ambulacrum and lecture room. One of the earliest wintering buildings, it was decorated with maps and Indian curios, and filled with plants and animals. Before the completion of the building, a letter of the States of Holland to the East India Company transmitted a request from the Burgomasters and Curatores to allow a person going to the Indies to collect plants, seeds, spices, drugs, and minerals to enrich the garden. For in the seventeenth century it was one of the duties of the Professor of Botany to build up the collection through expedition or exchange with the other botanic gardens emerging at this time. It was said that a merchantman

never left the ports of Holland without the captain being asked to procure seeds and plants from exotic foreign shores (1; 5).

During this period, the Dutch winter places (or as they were often called, 'Dutch stoves') were built to a plan similar to the gallery at Leyden. In the book *Nederlantze Hesperides* (1676) by Jan Commeleyn, we can see the winter place of Pieter de Wolff (6) Jan Commeleyn and Joan Roeters. These houses have brick floors, solid back walls, high double-casement windows with small glazed panes towards the garden and a high exposed timber ceiling that supports a storage loft under a shed roof. Not only was this loft used for the storage of tools, seeds and flower bulbs, but it also provided insulation for the chambers below, being filled with buck wheat chaff as is still the case today at the Leyden Orangery. Ornate cast-iron fire boxes on legs with dampered metal smoke pipes going through the roof were placed equidistant along the back masonry wall. It was most probable that in winter these stoves were filled throughout the night by servants with peat or charcoal (10).

Plant houses of many sizes and types began to crowd around the Leyden Garden during the seventeenth century. From a description of the plants collected, it was clear that by 1680–7 (under the directorship of Clusius), the garden had proper glasshouses, though they might have had only very small frames. During Herman Boerhaave's directorship between 1709 and 1730, the garden was surrounded by numerous glass forcing frames, large heated stove houses with casement glass windows and another large gallery.

The Garden was basically an environmental machine producing plants. Boerhaave, Physician and Professor of Medicine, Botany and Chemistry, used it as a laboratory, where he carried out experiments that are described in his voluminous correspondence. Under him, the botanic collection became one of the finest in the world (7).

By the beginning of the eighteenth century, the Dutch had already developed forcing frames with sloped glass roofs, producing oranges, pineapples and grapes. The sloped-front forcing-frame was engineered to control the environment. The back wall was always massive masonry that would absorb the sun's rays and retain the warmth into the night. Within the back wall or under the floor, heat and smoke from the furnace wound its way in a circuitous flue discharging at the top of the wall. The front south wall was constructed entirely of glass set in wooden frames, with hinges on the sides or the top. The frames were large enough to allow plants to be removed and replaced. The windows were often left open in the summer for maximum ventilation and sun, but in the winter they were well sealed against draughts and only opened to the air on a warm winter's day. Oil paper in frames was often fixed under the windows to act as double glazing against the cold. One house shows a simple system of several canvas curtains in front of the windows, insuring three layers of winter clothing against the cold. Another mechanized frame had a series of wood shutters hinged at the top to be let down by pulleys and ropes at the back wall. This allowed the gardener to expose the glass on a sunny winter's day. There was also a sliding wood panel perpendicular to the house that pro-

tected the whole device from the cold prevailing winds; but the panel could also be pushed back for ventilation, an early use of mechanized micro-climate control (8, 9).

Although these control devices may now appear crude, they produced admirable gardens for George Clifford, which Carl Linnaeus described in the *Hortus Cliffortianus* (1737).

Clifford, a very rich Anglo-Dutch financier and a director of the Dutch East India Company, was an enthusiastic horticulturist and zoologist. The gardens and a private zoo at Hartekamp, his country estate on the road to Leyden, were famous throughout Holland. Linnaeus, the Swedish naturalist, took charge of the gardens, its hot houses, the fine library and herbarium, which were later to make an invaluable contribution to his classification of all known plants.

The gardens where he worked, Linnaeus says, were 'masterpieces of Nature aided by Art', with their 'shady walks, topiary, statues, fishponds, artificial mounds and mazes'. The zoo was 'full of tigers, apes, wild dogs, Indian deer and goats, peccaries, and African swine', with a variety of birds 'that made the garden echo and re-echo with their cries'. But most exciting were the 'houses of Adonis', or hot houses; which Linnaeus describes in the dedication he wrote to Clifford. They included cloves, poincianas and mangosteens; 'monstrous' plants from Africa, the mesembryanthemums, carrion flowers and euphorbias; American plants like cacti, orchids, passion flowers, magnolias and tulip-trees. Clifford's collection obviously stimulated Linnaeus, who goes on to say . . . 'I desired above all things that you might let the world

13

7   Leyden University Botanic Gardens in 1718, during Herman
Boerhaave's professorship. The original gallery is still here, more
glasshouses and another gallery have been built.

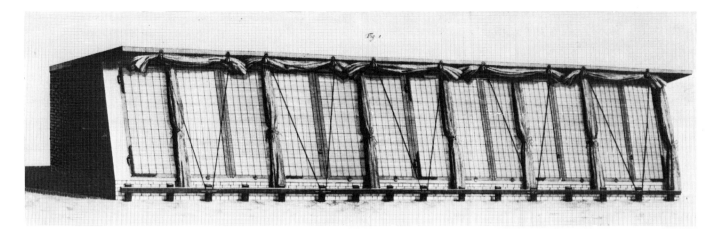

8　Dutch eighteenth-century forcing-frames had many sophisticated environment control devices.

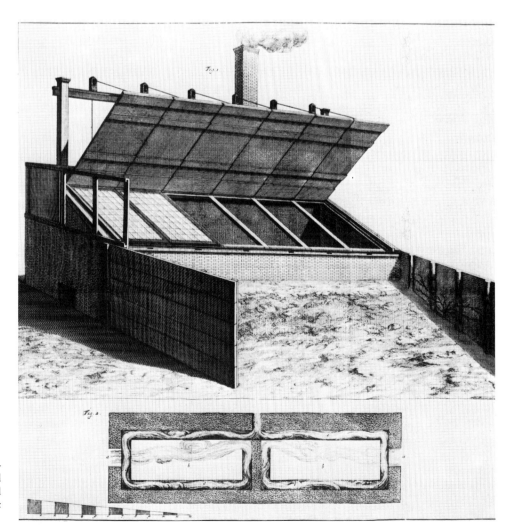

9　The flue-heated Dutch forcing-frame, with its mechanically-operated cover panels and sliding wind-shield is an early example of micro-climatic control.

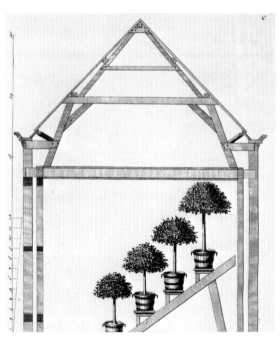

11 Hothouse with small casement windows. Along the back wall ▷ are tiled Dutch stoves.

12 Hothouse illustrated in a later edition of the same book, *Neue Garten-Lust*, showing casement windows extending to ground level for more light.

have knowledge of so great a herbarium, and did not hesitate to lend you a hand'.

Late in the seventeenth century, gardeners, in a quest for light, began to use more glass and to slope their building for more sun. John Claudius Loudon says the orangery at Wollaton Hall in Nottingham was one of the first to have a glass roof, but upon inspection of a painting of the Wollaton grounds by Jan Sieberechts in 1696, this appears untrue. In 1699, the Swiss, Nicholas Facio de Douiller, fellow of the Royal Society, designed the first sloped walls, which he presented in *A Way to build Walls for Fruit Trees, whereby they receive more Sunshine and Heat than ordinary*. These developments anticipated the important observation of Stephen Hales in 1727: 'may not light, by freely entering the expanded surfaces of leaves and flowers contribute much to enabling principles of vegetation?'

A German book, first published in 1696 and revised several times (Heinrich Hesse, in *Neue Garten-Lust*) gives a dramatic example of this developing awareness of light. The first edition shows a house with lattice casement windows from the roof halfway down the wall, while a later edition shows a similar house with windows down the whole wall, facing south (11; 12).

Similarly, Philip Miller at the Chelsea Apothecaries' Gardens gradually came to understand the importance of sunlight and redesigned the Garden's greenhouse accordingly. The first greenhouse was built at Chelsea in 1680, some forty years before Miller started working there. From the beginning, the ground floor of the house was used for plants with apartments above, as was to be seen

in all of Miller's *Dictionary of Gardening* illustrations. The plan shows an architectural house in the centre with a shed wing on each side. In 1731 the wings had tiled roofs, but by 1751 they had vertical glass faces and 45° pitched glass roofs. Miller described his reason for this change to glass roofs:

The most tender exotic plants ought to have their glasses so situated as to receive the sun's rays in direct lines as great a part of the year as possible: For which reason the stoves which have upright glasses in front and sloping glasses over them, are justly preferred to any at present contrived.

Landscape gardener Stephen Switzer was also to experiment with sloping glass and the glazed lean-to which eventually became the standard form of the forcing house. He had been an apprentice to London and Wise, the great nurserymen and garden architects who were presumed to have designed the glass covered orangery and gardens at Wollaton Hall. Switzer describes in his book *The Practical Fruit Gardener* (1724) a lean-to house with a 45° sloping glass front and brick back wall for the Duke of Rutland at Belvoir Castle. This early vinery was heated from behind by internal flues fed by small stoke holes. After this experiment, Switzer remarked that though the sun acted with more rigour on the 45° slope when it was in its solstice than on a perpendicular glass wall, it took an hour longer for the morning dew to evaporate from the slope so that what was gained at one time was lost in another. Orientation of the houses seemed more important to him, and he advises a south wall declining 20° to the east.

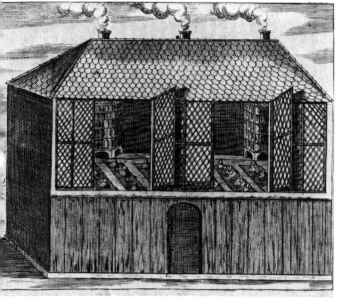

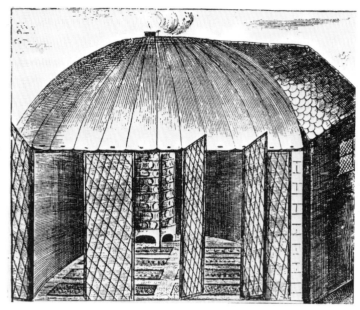

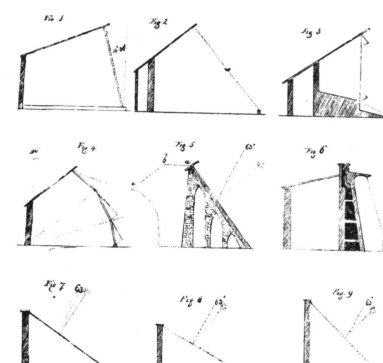

13   J. C. Loudon's sections through hothouses comparing the front glass angle at various latitudes. 1. Boerhaave at Leyden, 1720. 2. Linnæus at Uppsala, 1740. 3. Adanson, 1760. 4. Adanson, 1760. 5. Nicolas Facio de Douiller at Belvoir Castle, 1699. 6. Typical Dutch vinery, c. 1730. 7. Thomas Knight's vinery. 8. Thomas Knight's peach house. 9. Slope recommended by Philip Miller and Rev. Wilkinson. 10. M. Thouin in the Jardin de Semis, Paris. 11. Sir George Mackenzie's semi-dome, 1815. 12. Mr Braddick of the L.H.S. for Mr Palmer, Kingston, Surrey.

14   Carl Linnæus's famous Trädgard, the Hortus Botanicus of Uppsala, Sweden, for several decades the botanical centre of the world. In the back of the garden is the wood-burning caldarium.

In 1817, J. C. Loudon, one of the most important influences on nineteenth-century horticulture, reviewed different theories on the angle of forcing frames to the sun. His *Remarks on Hothouses* referred to a great variety of sources, including Boerhaave, Linnaeus, Adanson, and Nicolas Facio de Douiller. Their common goal was to maintain perpendicular sun penetration for a maximum period. Loudon claims that Boerhaave was the first to establish the principle for determining the slope of glass in his *Elementa Chemiae* (1732), an angle of 14 deg. 30 min. for $52\frac{1}{2}°$ latitude north. Linnaeus, no doubt consulting the laws of Boerhaave, described the caldarium or dry-stove constructed in Uppsala and the advantages of the slope that he fixed for the glass roof. The celebrated French botanist Michel Adanson in *Familles des Plantes* (1763) countered all the angle studies, recommending perpendicular glass, to avoid drops of condensation on the plants, but having a sloping back wall. He also gives rules, tables and diagrams to suit every possible latitude from the pole to the equator (13; 14).

2   'This Liberal and Improving Age'

By the dawn of the nineteenth century, a culture of environmental fantasy had developed in Britain. The eighteenth-century colonial legacy had brought the wealth, the plants and the patrons; the emerging industries, new resources and technology. Victorian writers at the end of the century were to describe the 'mania' of this period, which spread contagiously. Already, in 1810 Walter Nicol wrote that 'a garden is not now reckoned complete without a green house, or conservatory with flued walls and with frames and lights'.

The major experimenters in glasshouse design were professional gardeners, who learned the techniques of artificial climate by rigorous empiricism and presented their innovations in their newly-founded forums, horticultural societies, and periodicals.

John Claudius Loudon in his introduction to *Remarks on Hothouses* (1817) described the new era of horticultural interest which infused London's societies. The variety of members, including 'men of rank and influence', as Loudon calls them, scientists and amateur gardeners, were all welcome and, Loudon says, 'give a degree of *éclat* and salutary consequence to the study'. As Loudon was taken with the spirit of what he called 'this liberal and improving age', so he enthused about his own field of glass horticulture, now able to 'exhibit spring and summer in the midst of winter . . . to give man so proud a command over Nature'.

Another man of the age was Thomas Knight, elected president of the London Horticultural Society in 1811. In his inaugural address, he discussed a subject that was to occupy his fellow members for years to come—the construction of glasshouses. He blamed the members for the 'generally very defective' construction of forcing houses, for, he said, 'not a single building of this kind has yet been erected in which the greatest possible quantity of space has been obtained, and of light and heat admitted, proportionate to the capital expended'. He himself was something of a perfectionist, and had presented a paper in 1808 on the subtle and specific art of angling the glass of a forcing house. He calculated that an angle of $34°$ at latitude $52°$ would produce a highly flavoured, rather than early, crop of grapes. He was convinced that control of the environment was capable of producing a 'peach . . . ripened in greater perfection in St Petersburg, in a house properly adapted to the latitude of that place, than in the open air at Rome or Naples'. Clearly, Knight was bringing the art of horticulture into the realm of science, and in this spirit he challenged his colleagues when he told them in the inaugural address that 'the proper application of glass where artificial heat is not employed, is certainly very ill understood'.

In a bold attempt* at hothouse improvement, Sir George Mackenzie sent a letter to the London Horticultural Society in 1815 suggesting that one should 'make the surface of your green house roof parallel to the vaulted surface of the heavens, or to the plane of the sun's orbit'. This was the first proposed curvilinear glass roof for horticulture. The letter and drawing described an elegant

---

* On the form which the glass of a forcing-house ought to have in order to receive the greatest possible quantity of rays from the sun, sent to Sir Joseph Banks and read to the Horticultural Society in 1815.

15   Sir George Mackenzie's quarter-sphere hothouse.

cast-iron and glass quarter-sphere backed by a brick wall on the north. The radius of the dome was set at 15 ft 'as anything less would be too confined and anything greater would render necessary an inconvenient height'. A vertical trellis for grapes was placed along the back wall. In a postscript to the letter, Mackenzie suggested that his semi-dome 'could be made in two moveable parts, in the manner of an observatory dome so as to expose the whole of the plants in the interior to the direct influence of the sun'. Loudon, though impressed by the beauty of Mackenzie's semi-dome, attacked its deficiencies. He objected to the distance from the skin to the trellis, and suggested a trellis that would follow the curve of the vault. He noted that when the sunlight was perpendicular at one point, it would not be perpendicular to the rest of the surface. He thought that Mackenzie's house was too high relative to its length and width, and suggested that the semi-dome become a segment of a much larger sphere of 25 ft radius. He also thought that there were too many bars at the top of the dome and that its flat top would collect condensation that could fall on and injure the plants. He therefore proposed an alternative design to Mackenzie's, incorporating improvements to answer Loudon's own complaints. Its 'acuminated apex', as Loudon called it, would not collect condensation and the 'spread out' base gave a special place to small plants close to the glass. Loudon was obviously very impressed by Mackenzie's iron construction and suggested that although it could not be adopted as a forcing house without considerable disadvantages, it could be used for maturing fruits (15; 16).

Its appearance is most elegant, and it admits of a happy combination of lightness with strength in the construction; it may be considered, with the improvements of which it is susceptible, as a most valuable acquisition to the horticultural architecture of this country.

In his *Remarks on Hothouses* (1817), Loudon also described an elegant improvement to the common lean-to which he called his 'forcing-house for general purposes'. Based upon the semi-dome ideas of Adanson and Mackenzie he added 'ridge and furrow' glazing to the skin. 'Ridge and furrow' simply means long bands of peaked glass roofing which could catch the 'two daily meridians' of the sun, as Loudon said. Thus with this pleated skin, the sun's rays would be caught perpendicular earlier in the morning and held later in the afternoon. The articulated skin also concentrated the condensation down the lower astragals (the iron bars holding the glass), which here were made to collect the water as well. Loudon was later to suggest the ridge and furrow for vast areas, an idea that later influenced Joseph Paxton (17; 18).

Loudon's conceptions had the sophistication of an engineer creating environment control machines. There was a louvre system connected to ropes to open the glass, and this system could be connected to the automatic thermostat which James Kewley patented in 1816. There were canvas blinds for retaining heat, and 'air valves' top and bottom to replace the stale, damp air (19).

Loudon was an avid proponent of iron construction while others still used wood. In 1816 he invented a wrought-iron bar that could be heated and drawn through a mould to a desired curvature. This sash bar opened a new

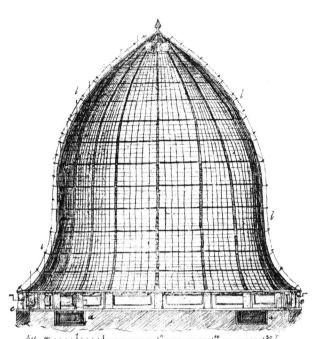

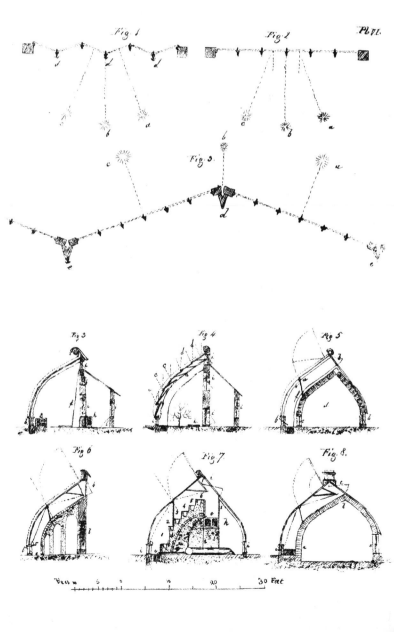

16   J. C. Loudon's improved glass dome, with 'acuminated apex' and 'spread out' base, was 50 ft high and intended for large trees in the centre. A system of glass louvres is connected with ropes to weights at the top and a handle, worm gear and drum at the bottom. Thus the whole of the glass could be opened to 'admit at pleasure air, wind, rain and the direct influence of the sun'.

17–19   Above, right: forcing house designed with first 'ridge-and-furrow' glazing to improve sun penetration, J. C. Loudon. Centre: Loudon's demonstration that 'ridge-and-furrow' glazing (Fig. 1) catches the morning and afternoon sun better than flat glazing (Fig. 2). At midday, Loudon argued, the sun was so intense that the angle did not matter. Fig. 3 shows a larger ridge and furrow, not unlike that later used by Joseph Paxton. Below: Loudon's design sections through forcing-houses read like environmental machines: curved ridge and furrow glass to maximize insolation; massive back walls to retain heat, smoke flues heating the glass front as well as tempering the back mushroom shed. Tempered air was drawn from the back shed when the air outside was too cold. The back shed could also be a fermentation chamber for heating a gardener's cottage.

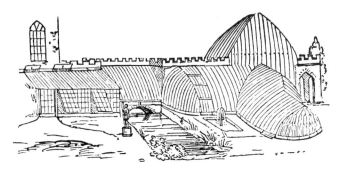

20   The curvilinear glasshouse at Bayswater was the prototype used
by Loudon to demonstrate the versatility of his wrought-iron sash bar.

era in curvilinear glass construction, replacing curved
bars made of several short pieces. Curving the bar outward improved its strength and, supported by cast-iron
columns, it could span large areas.

Loudon saw the commercial potential of his invention
and, with the construction facilities of W. & D. Bailey,
he advertised custom-designed glass houses in what
today would be called a 'package deal'. Loudon made a
remarkable prototype at his own London home, Bayswater House. The prototype, which spanned Bayswater
Brook, was built from thirteen sash bars and was covered
with seven types of glazing, plus corrugated iron and
special paper, to demonstrate the potential for building
covered markets, schools, theatres and even churches.
Loudon said that his new buildings could be designed in
almost any shape with 'every conceivable variety of glass
surface, without in the least interfering with the objects of
culture'. His operations were even sophisticated enough
to have a Mr McLiesch, a former pupil of Loudon, acting
as the rural architect and sales representative in Ireland,
Wales and Scotland, while Loudon himself covered the
London area (20).

Loudon obviously had a flair for salesmanship, even in
longer dissertations on the advantages of iron construction. In his *Remarks on Hothouses* of 1817, he compared
the prices of various materials and thought his method was
better than even 'the best constructed wood houses at
Kew, Kensington Gardens, and Chiswick'. His most
convincing argument had to be his bar graph comparing
the amount of light blocked by wood- and iron-frame
glass houses, where, he said, the dark area represented

the lack of light and therefore 'insipidity and tartness',
while the white was 'aroma and flavours'. Could any man
of taste have resisted this hard sell? (22).

He refuted major objections such as claims that glass
breaks from expansion and contraction of the metal, that
iron loses heat by conduction, that it rusts and attracts
electricity (lightning). To these he answered that most
expansion and contraction occurred with brass and copper, not iron; that the house should be covered with
canvas anyway to prevent heat loss, and that the bars
could be lined with wood. To prevent rust the bars could
be heated red-hot, then coated with coal tar or paint,
tin, lead, or pewter. As to electricity, iron foundries were
built completely of the material they produce, and had
been up for fifteen years without any damage.

He even came to envisage a new style of architecture
which 'may be beautiful without exhibiting any of the
orders of Grecian or of Gothic' design. This he wrote as
a challenge to architects, and, he continued . . . 'may not
therefore glass roofs be rendered expressive of ideas of a
higher and more appropriate kind, than those which are
suggested by mere sheds, or a glazed arcade'.

The alliance between Loudon and his manufacturers
produced the most elegant and beautiful curvilinear glass
and iron shells in Britain. But it is most probable that
Loudon did not enjoy the same lucrative remuneration as
the Baileys, who eventually worked without Loudon's
advice. Loudon transferred his design rights to them in
1818 to devote his time exclusively to writing. He was as
prolific in this as he had been in designing, and by his
death in 1843 had written some thirty books, including

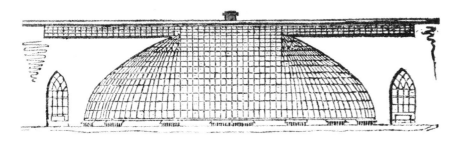

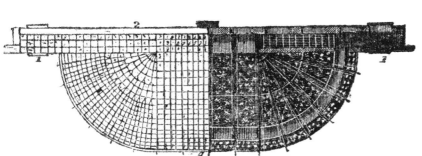

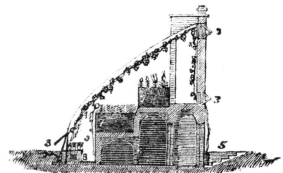

21   Pineapple pit and vinery at Langport, Somerset, built by W. & D. Bailey to Loudon's design in 1817. 'This house is fifty feet long by sixteen feet wide, contains a bark-pit for pine plants; a trellis for training vines; and space for 500 pots of strawberries or French beans. The house was entered by lobbies at each end which communicate with a back passage, having a glass roof and trellis for vines (2). In the back wall of this passage and also in the front of the house are glazed ventilators opening outwards through which the vines (5) are introduced and withdrawn at pleasure. The pine pits (7) are raised so as to be as near the glass as is desirable, by vaulting them beneath (6). Against the front of these pits, shoots of vines are brought down from the roof, and trained (9), and pots are placed over the front flue (8).'

22   The sweetness of the peach. A comparison by Loudon of light blocked by various glazing techniques, to prove the superiority of iron bars over wood.

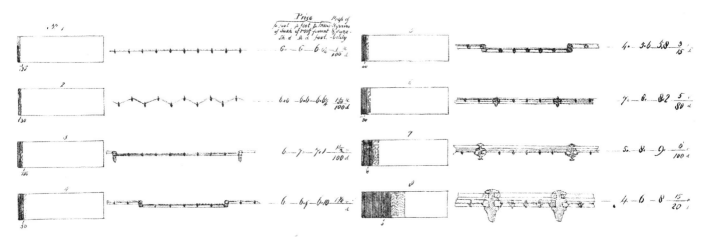

23 The Loddiges' Nursery, Hackney (1771–1854). The entrance led from Mare Street to the glass range including the Palm House (c) and the Double-Camellia house (e). To the right is the arboretum with its concentric walks and species arranged alphabetically. The section of the Double-Camellia House shows the flat, lean-to roof of copper sash by Timmins of Birmingham and the curved iron roof by Loudon and W. & D. Bailey. Loudon's curvilinear house was 120 ft long and 23 ft wide.

standard works like *An Encyclopaedia of Gardening* (first edition 1822), *An Encyclopaedia of Plants* (1829), and *Encyclopaedia of Trees and Shrubs* (1841).

Meanwhile, the glasshouses that W. and D. Bailey built around the 1820s with Loudon's glazing bar were numerous, elegant, and sometimes very large. One of the most elegant was a pine pit and vinery constructed at Langport, Somerset, in 1817 (21).

The Hackney Botanic Nursery comprised a series of hothouses arranged round a square filled with pits and frames. The nursery was a commercial operation begun in 1771 by the German gardener, Conrad Loddiges. Among the lean-to hothouses were, according to Loudon, the world's largest hothouse for palms (80 ft long) and a double-camellia house one side of the masonry wall roofed in copper sashes by Timmins of Birmingham and the other side, a curvilinear glass roof 120 ft long, with curved iron astragals, made by Loudon and W. & D. Bailey. The nursery had a walk 1000 ft long through the glasshouses round the square and the whole was heated by steam with rain-making devices for the palms. Joseph Paxton bought all the exotic plants in 1854 on the closure of the nursery and moved them to the Crystal Palace at Sydenham (23).

One of the most significant forerunners of the great conservatories to be built at Chatsworth, Chiswick and Kew was the detached conservatory built in 1827 for Mrs Beaumont at Bretton Hall in Yorkshire. The structure was 100 ft in diameter and 60 ft high, built with wrought-iron sash bars, on the Loudon principle. From these grand dimensions, one can easily understand why Loudon was not impressed with the dome at the Surrey Zoological Gardens which was also 100 ft in diameter but built three years later (24).

Loudon gives an extensive description of Bretton Hall in *An Encyclopaedia of Cottage, Farm and Villa Architecture* (1833). It seems to have had an ill-fated history, which involved Loudon's partner-builders, the Baileys.

. . . there were no rafters or principal ribs for strengthening the roof besides the common wrought-iron sash-bar . . . This caused some anxiety, for when the ironwork was put up, before it was glazed, the slightest wind put the whole of it in motion from the base to the summit . . . As soon as the glass was put in, however, it was found to become perfectly firm and strong, nor did the slightest accident, from any cause, happen to it from the time it was completed in 1827, till, on the death of Mrs Beaumont, in 1832, it was sold by auction and taken down.

A large model of Mrs Beaumont's short-lived conservatory made its way much later to Frogmore Gardens where it was presented to the Princess Royal by the heating contractors D. & E. Bailey with the intention of converting it into a Wardian case. Pieces of the actual conservatory were used on various patchwork greenhouses throughout the country, according to Loudon.

Besides the curvilinear conservatory built for the Horticultural Society at Chiswick, D. & E. Bailey, successors to W. & D., built the Pantheon Bazaar Conservatory and aviary in Oxford Street, London, in 1834. They most probably also built the delightful and extant Palm House at Bicton Gardens, Rolle Estate,

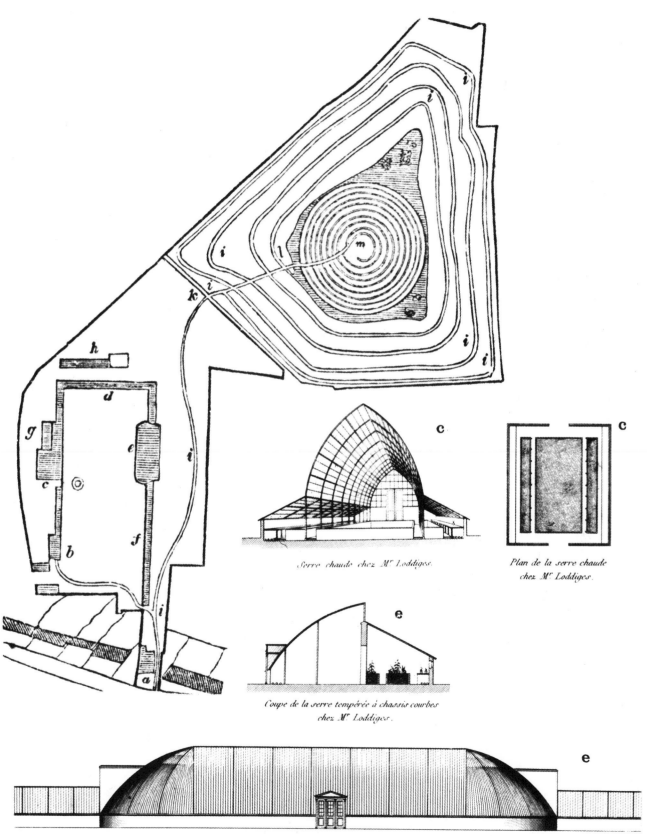

Serre chaude chez Mr Loddiges.

Plan de la serre chaude
chez Mr Loddiges.

*Coupe de la serre tempérée à chassis courbes
chez Mr Loddiges.*

*Serre tempérée à chassis courbes
chez Mr Loddiges.*

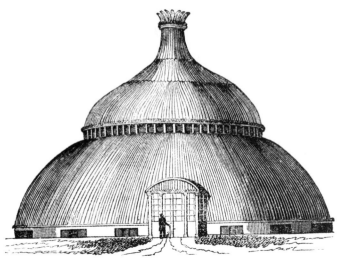

24 The first great glass and iron curvilinear conservatory was built for Mrs Beaumont at Bretton Hall, Yorkshire, in 1827, by W. & D. Bailey. The conservatory measured 100 ft in diameter and was 60 ft high. It was ventilated by horizontal shutters in the cast-iron base and upright windows hinged inward at the springing of the upper dome. At the top a glass light was swivelled under the gilt coronet.

25 Pantheon Bazaar Conservatory and Aviary, Oxford Street. D. & E. Bailey built a large iron and glass structure in 1834 which led from the Great Marlborough Street entrance into the Pantheon Bazaar designed by Sydney Smirke, on the site of the old Pantheon (now occupied by Marks and Spencer Ltd.). Inside the conservatory were fish in bowls and tropical birds, along with ornament and sculpture by Charles F. Bielefield, the *papier mâché* manufacturer whose catalogues display the flashy ornamentation so freely used in the 1840s and 1850s.

26   Bicton Garden Palm House, Rolle Estate, near Budleigh Salterton, Devon, has ironwork clearly descended from early designs by Loudon.

27   Interior wrought-ironwork at the Bicton Palm House. The back wall ventilators are opened in summer. The ridge ventilator swivels and is constructed in the same way as the ventilator for the curvilinear glasshouse at Chiswick of 1840 by D. & E. Bailey.

near Budleigh Salterton, Devonshire. Pevsner considers that it was built between 1820 and 1825. However, Loudon made a trip to Lord Rolle's Estate just before his death in 1843 and makes no mention of the curvilinear construction in an extensive description in the *Gardener's Magazine*. The detail of the elegant iron work of the skin is reminiscent of all the W. & D. Bailey constructions— for example in the camellia house for the Loddige's at Hackney. This unique design, halving the number of bars as the dome decreases in size, stems back to Loudon's early *Sketches* (1818). The ventilator at the ridge works exactly like the ventilator on the Horticultural Society's curvilinear conservatory at Chiswick, built in 1840 by D. & E. Bailey. It is, therefore, probable that the Bicton Palm House is a late and beautiful descendant of Loudon's early ideas and built after 1843 (25–27).

28   Interior of the Jan Commeleyn winter place. The stair leads to
the storage loft for tools, bulbs and seeds. Dutch stoves stand along
the back walls for winter heating.

29   Interior of plant-house heated by Musgrave's iron slow combustion stove. Stoves were used into the nineteenth century.

3 The Artificial Climate
I: Heating

ARTIFICIAL CLIMATE—RICHARD BRADLEY—PHILIP MILLER'S BEDS AT CHELSEA—OPEN FIRES—THE OXFORD IRON WAGON—IRON STOVES—UNDERGROUND VAULTS—JOHN EVELYN'S HOT AIR FURNACE—FLOOR AND WALL FLUES—THE IMPERIAL BOTANIC GARDENS OF ST PETERSBURG—EARLY STEAM HEATING—THE LODDIGES AT HACKNEY—LOUDON'S INDUSTRIALIZED STEAM POWERED FARM—THE IMPERIAL PINE PIT—MR HAGUE'S RETURN CONDENSATE SYSTEM—HENRY STOTHERT OF BATH—HOT WATER—MARQUIS DE CHABANNES—ATKINSON'S HOT WATER SYSTEM—THOMAS TREDGOLD AND THE SCIENTIFIC PRINCIPLE—THOMAS FOWLER AND JAMES KEWLEY: THE HOT WATER SIPHON—THE PERFECT BOILER—HIGH PRESSURE HOT WATER—THE WATER-JACKET BOILER—LORD AND BURNHAM—THE STANDARD BOILER

R. Buckminster Fuller's air-conditioned dome over New York City and Frei Otto's proposals for air-conditioned cities in the Arctic are a hint at our capabilities to create the 'artificial climate' today. Over a century and a half ago J. C. Loudon discussed the same idea in great detail in his 1822 *Encyclopaedia of Gardening:*

> Indeed, there is hardly any limit to the extent to which this sort of light [ridge and furrow] roof might not be carried; several acres, even a whole country residence, where the extent was moderate, might be covered in this way.

He made provision for artificial rain, steam heat and vents controlled by Kewley's automatons and a roof up to 150 ft high, to admit: '. . . the tallest oriental trees, and the undisturbed flight of appropriate birds among their branches'.

Later Loudon was to suggest that it might be preferable to begin with 25 ft, and to raise the roof by adding to the columns as the plants grow. In this controlled environment Loudon suggests that:

> A variety of oriental birds and monkeys and other animals might be introduced; and in ponds, a stream made to run by machinery, and also in salt lakes— fishes, polypi, corals, and other productions of fresh or sea-water might be cultivated or kept.

Then again, in more practical vein, Loudon says:

> In Northern countries, civilized man could not exist without glass; and if coal is not discovered in these countries, say, in Russia, the most economical mode of procuring a proper temperature will be by at once covering whole towns with immense teguments of

glass, and heating by steam or otherwise, the enclosed air common to all the inhabitants.

Loudon's confidence to create the artificial climate followed a heritage of experiments in environmental control dating back to the sixteenth, seventeenth and eighteenth centuries and pursued fervently in his own time.

In 1721, Richard Bradley, Professor of Botany at Cambridge, first described the relationship of plants to their environment, a realization that was to make horticulturalists the first real heating experts. Bradley said in his *Philosophical Account of the Works of Nature*: 'As every animal has its climate and food natural to it, so has every plant an exposure, temper of air, and soil, proper to nourish and maintain it in a right state of health'.

Practical problems in recreating indigenous climate began in the sixteenth century with the arrival in Europe of exotic plants. Experiments in heating and ventilation, both successes and failures, were passed back and forth among gardeners in letters and reports from travellers. By the beginning of the nineteenth century, men like Dr James Anderson, Walter Nicol, John Abercrombie and J. C. Loudon were able to compile this information in encyclopaedias of gardening and dissertations on hothouse design.

Because of their beauty and often dramatic dimensions, it is easy to lose sight of what glasshouses were all about: 'artificial climate'. I like this phrase, which was coined by Loudon, because it represents a positive, even arrogant, confidence in technology that was so prevalent in the nineteenth century. Today we call it air-conditioning and it represents to us, in architecture, the tempering of

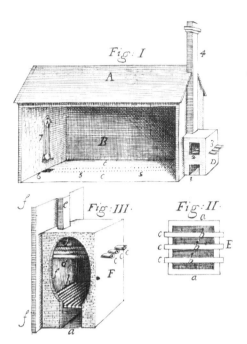

30   John Evelyn's greenhouse. In Fig. 1 the cold air, at the bottom of the house, is drawn down the floor extract duct (5) to the furnace, by the suction of hot air rising in the chimney (4). The house is replenished with air drawn through three crucible pipes (3), also heated by the furnace. A thermometer hangs above the registered extract duct opening. Figs ii and iii are details of the greenhouse. Evelyn suggested that the south wall be enclosed with glass windows, for 'the light itself, next to air, is of wonderful importance'.

31   Eighteenth-century Dutch forcing-frame with backwall flue. A balance between proper draw and the maximum length of the smoke path was difficult to maintain; smoke pollution on the glass was also a problem.

existing environment to allow for the activities of man. But in the nineteenth century, however, 'artificial climate' evoked the climate of the tropical colonies in contrast to the often cold and unpleasant climate of Northern Europe and the British Isles. It was a time of romanticism filled with the artifacts, stories and botanical exotics of lands some men visited but all men dreamed of visiting. It was a time when vast effort was marshalled to imitate oriental styles in garden pavilions (Brighton), and the conservatories of the colonizers. Loudon even looked to a time

> when such artificial climates will not only be stocked
> with appropriate birds, fishes and harmless animals,
> but with examples of the human species from the
> different countries imitated, habited in their particular
> costumes and who may serve as gardeners or curators
> of the different productions.*

Philip Miller in his *Gardeners' Dictionary* (1731) described some of the methods used at the Apothecaries' Gardens at Chelsea. The hotbed was simply a shallow trench filled with dung. It was covered with earth and enclosed in a glass frame . . . 'without which [Miller wrote] the English could not enjoy so many products of the warmer climates'. The tan bark hotbed, using bark instead of dung, was preferred for all tender exotics and fruits that required warmth for several months. By stirring and adding bark, the heat could last for two to three months. Miller's bark stove had smoke flues through the tan bark. The house was divided into various chambers, the farthest from the furnace being the coolest.

Smudge pots, one of the earliest forms of heating, are still used in the orange groves of Florida when frost is

expected. This form of open fire or brazier was used for orange trees as far back as the sixteenth and seventeenth centuries. Insulated by wood enclosures or masonry (which had good thermal capacity), the slow burning peat fires could maintain the plants in a smoke-filled room during cold and frosty nights. Refuelling these fires required much labour in a very noxious, unpleasant environment. An offshoot, but certainly not an improvement, to these crude fires was used at the Oxford Botanic Gardens until the end of the eighteenth century. The idea of using an iron wagon filled with burning charcoal is attributed to Jacob Bobart, a German, who was the first Keeper of the Garden in 1632. On a severe night, the wagon was drawn back and forth through the houses. Scorching and asphyxiation from these open fires must have been commonplace, as Richard Bradley noted in his *New Improvements of Planting and Gardening* (1718), while warning of a graver hazard: 'Several men have been choked by them and sparks from them have set fire to the house'.

Improvements were inevitable, and by the end of the seventeenth century, the iron stove was common in the winter places of the rich in Holland and Germany. 'Stove', in fact, became the common name for the wintering place or orangery. The stove itself was a free-standing, often ornate cast-iron box with a metal stack passing through the roof. The peat or charcoal fire was combined with a highly insulated attic and shuttered windows kept most of the house above freezing temperatures. Nonetheless,

* *Remarks on the Construction of Hothouses*, 1817.

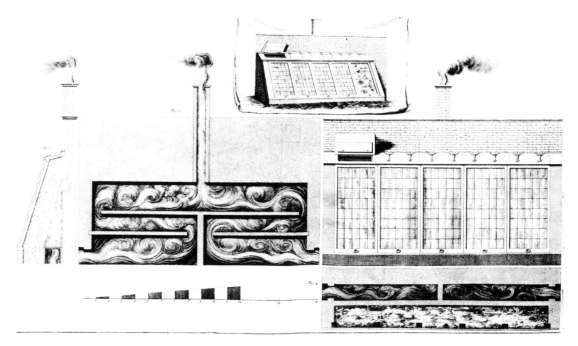

there was uneven heat distribution; plants near the stove were scorched and dried while the others were still killed by frost and damp. In the caldarium at Uppsala, Linnaeus used a portable stove moved to various locations for lowering the relative humidity when severe weather did not permit the opening of the sashes (28; 29).

Those without an upright stove may well have used one of the earliest forms of indirect heat—a vault under the house with a fire at one end and a flue taking smoke through to the other. John Evelyn, the eminent natural philosopher and diarist, saw an underground vault in 1685 at the Chelsea Apothecaries' Garden which protected 'the tree bearing the Jesuit's bark [Quinine] which had done such cures in quartans [a form of malaria]'. Evelyn was much impressed with the 'very ingenious . . . subterranean heat, conveyed by a stove under the conservatory, which was all vaulted with brick'. The system was so good that 'he leaves the doors and windows open in the hardest frost, secluding only snow, etc'. Evelyn designed his own hot air furnace, having consulted with Sir Christopher Wren and Robert Hooke, fellow members of the Royal Society. This was for his 'new conservatory or green house', as presented in his *Kalendarium Hortense, or Gard'ner's Almanac* in 1691. He first criticizes 'ordinary iron stoves', and 'subterranean caliducts' and their effect on the exotic plants, which he describes in almost human terms:

that even the hardiest among them, very rarely passed their confinements without sickness, a certain languor or taint discoverable by their complexions; many of their leaves parched about their edges, or falling, dry, and deprived of their natural verdure with other symptoms, which can proceed from no other cause as their being kept from breathing (as I presume to call it) the pure, and genuine air, impregnated with its Nitrous Pabulum, which is not only the nourishment and life of animals, but of all plants and vegetable whatsoever.

He believed that the trouble came from the

dry heat emitted from the common stoves, pans of charcoal, and other included heaters, which continually prey'd upon, wasted and vitiated the stagnant and pent-in air, without any due and wholesome succession of a more vital and fresh supply.

His 'contrivance, whereby to remedy this inconvenience' is one of the earliest known circulation hot air systems. Though doubtless very inefficient, the system works on the principle that hot air rising in the chimney draws internal air through the floor extract duct. This creates a negative pressure in the house that in turn draws fresh air through the three heated intake pipes. The temperature was most probably controlled by the extract system, for over the opening hung a thermometer, certainly one of the earliest.* In 1694 Sir Dudley Cullum of Hawstead, Suffolk, reported in the Royal Society's *Philosophical Transactions* the success of a house which he had had built and heated on Evelyn's principle (30).

* The Florentine liquid thermometer was introduced to Robert Boyle in 1661 and was formally disclosed to the Royal Society by Robert Hooke in 1694.

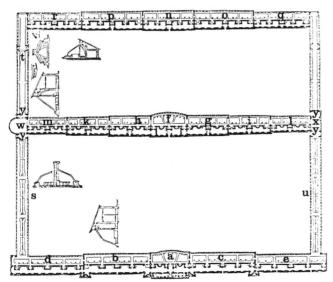

house with two sides of glass framework, 28 ft high, for oranges, magnolias, acacias, myrtles and the trees and plants of New Holland, etc. planted in the ground. c. Greenhouse of the same height with one side of glass framework, for the tallest plants of the Cape of Good Hope, China and New Holland. d.e. Greenhouses, 12 ft high, with two sides of glass framework, for Ericas, and other dwarf plants of the Cape of Good Hope and temperate America. f. Hothouse 32 ft high. g.h. Two hothouses 28 ft high, one of which is destined for the Bananas, and other plants of the same family. i.k. Two hothouses 22 ft high, one of which contains the succulent plants of the Tropics and representative specimens of all the different families of equinoctial monocotyledonous plants, which are cultivated in the garden. l.m. Two hothouses 18 ft high, in which the beds are raised to a considerable height above the level of the path. n. Hothouse for Chinese, Japanese and Nepal plants, 28 ft high, with glass framework on both sides. o.p. Two greenhouses, 21 ft high, for the plants of the south of Europe, of the Canary Isles and North America and for the succulent plants of temperate countries. q.r. Two hothouses, 12 ft high, for dwarf equinoctial plants. The beds in these houses are raised. s.t. Two houses, 12 ft high and glazed on two sides, forming passages of communication and containing half-hardy plants. u.v. Two houses . . . destined for the bulbous plants of the temperate climates and as reserve houses for hardy herbaceous plants. w.x.y. Entrances.

32   The glasshouse of the Imperial Botanic Garden, St Petersburg on the Apothecaries' Island in the Neva. Three major glass ranges, each of 700 ft, were described in detail by Loudon: a. Greenhouse 32 ft high, serving as principal entrance to the hothouses. b. Green-

In the eighteenth century, floor and back wall flues, or exposed flues within the house, were the most common form of heating. Gardeners still had to fill the stoke holes of many small furnaces throughout the night during severe weather. Flues drew with difficulty, and temperature control was often impossible and because they were so inefficient, the flue systems consumed vast quantities of coal and peat. When walls of the flues cracked, noxious fumes and smoke escaped into the house. Furthermore, there was a constant struggle to increase the length of the flues within floor or back wall and still get the flue to draw. By the end of the eighteenth century, an exposed flue system within the house was the accepted form. Loudon himself made a design for a flue which he presented to the nursery of Dickson and Shade in Edinburgh. Even at the age of 22, Loudon was inventive and enterprising, for he made models of flue and hothouse systems and sold them for one to three guineas each to nurseries in Edinburgh and in London from Chapel Street in Bedford Row, Loudon's improvements dealt mainly with fuel consumption, slowing down the flue gases, insulating the house at night, creating an artificial breeze, and tempering ventilation from outside. Soon, however, Loudon was to take an interest in steam heat, the next important development, which made him prophesy a whole new era in environmental control (31; 33–5).

Despite its defects, the flue system could support impressive botanical establishments such as the Russian Imperial Gardens built throughout the reign of Czar Alexander between 1801 and 1825. From the St Petersburg botanic gardens on the Apothecaries' Island in the Neva River, plants were distributed to Imperial Gardens all over the empire, as well as to private individuals. As the name of the island suggests, medical botany was practised in a large part of the grounds and the glasshouses were able to provide hospitals in 1828 with 4,560 lbs of aconitum napellus leaves (monk's hood, a narcotic and analgesic). By 1829, the St Petersburg garden contained 80,000 single plants of 11,000 species.

In the grounds, there were three major glasshouses each 700 ft long and between 20 ft and 30 ft wide, connected by double-glazed covered corridors (32). These corridors were filled with greenhouse plants and provided space for promenading. The three major glass ranges had sloped lights facing south, and were backed by masonry shed-roofed chambers to the north. The two periphery glass ranges were divided into five compartments for hardier plants with birch log furnaces in niches every 4 to 5 yards. The middle glass range was divided into seven chambers with furnace niches every 3 to 4 yards, providing more heat for the delicate tropical plants.

Russian glasshouses were usually narrower than those in warmer countries and were always backed by galleries, corridors, or walls, to combat the fierce winter winds. At St Petersburg, the sheds provided this protection and also were temperate chambers from which to draw air into the houses. An army of men was required to keep the hundreds of furnaces stoked. During the severe weather, the furnaces were filled with logs every twelve hours, one of those times being between one and two a.m. so that the highest temperature of the flues coincided with the coldest temperature at night, which could easily

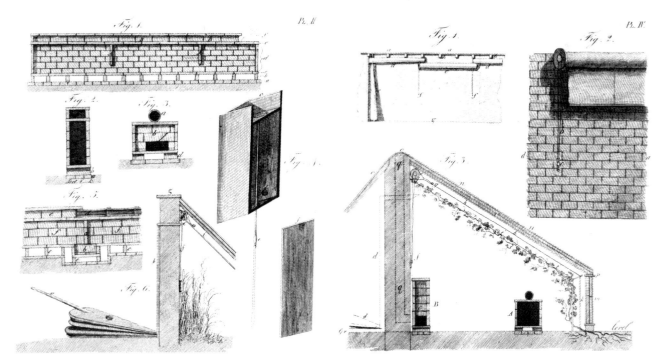

33, 34   Left: Loudon's smoke flue with partitions to slow down the smoke was under the earthenware air flue that discharged into the house (Figs. 1, 3). The air in the house could be replenished with air tempered in the back shed by means either of bellows through the back wall (Fig. 6), or of a box-like 'air pump' (Fig. 4) like those constructed in the sheds behind the houses for Dickson and Shade the nurserymen. Another form of the partitioned flue with the air pipe above (Fig. 5) is the weakness in Loudon's system, for the partitions slowed down the smoke and consequently the chamber became clogged with soot. Right: Loudon let coarse woollen curtains down under the glass at night (Figs. 1, 2) and a triangular sheet was pulled across the end of the house. Fig. 3 is a section through a vinery with a deep smoke flue at the back and a shallow smoke and air flue at the front. The dotted line in the back shed shows the position of the bellows for changing the air. At the apex is the wooden roller and the curtain which was fixed to a wooden rod which slid down over a wire supported top and bottom.

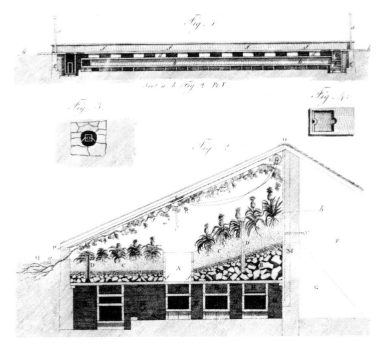

35   Loudon's vinery and pinehouse. Fig. 1 is a longitudinal section through the floor containing the smoke and air flues. This is more fully described in Fig. 2, the transverse section of a combination vinery and pine stove. The spaces around the flues were often filled with water to produce moist heat that would rise up through the rubble base into the soil and out the vertical steam and air tubes (D) into the house. The back shed was a mushroom house.

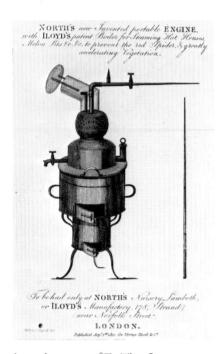

36   North's New-Invented portable Engine, 1802.

have been – 20°F. The flues were surrounded by a chamber which fed air into the houses. This system resembled Loudon's except that in this case the flues were constructed of thick brick, which retained the blasts of heat in their massive walls, providing a heat magazine that would be slowly transferred into the surrounding air. The central building was 40 ft high and contained a suite of apartments from which the Royal Family could look down on the plants. There were also apartments within this range for the director, Dr Fisher, an English botanist; his two chief gardeners, a Dane and a Frenchman; two secretaries, a Frenchman and a Russian; and a botanical painter from Germany. The total complex of conservatories, greenhouses, stoves and glazed corridors formed a rectangle of glass 500 ft by 700 ft, or as another English diarist, Dr Granville, reported more accurately in his travels,* the total length of houses measured 3,624 ft, nearly three-quarters of a mile, supposedly the largest in the world at that time. The lean-to houses were formed from glass and wood sashes either sloped to the parapet or with two angles to provide more volume for larger plants. These sashes were sealed with pitch and moss to keep out the severe winter cold. The poor quality of glass available in Russia at that time was of varying thickness, consequently it broke easily during frosts. It also contained bubbles and inequalities that concentrated the sun's rays, blistering the plants. Huge curved wood reflectors were attached to the back wall of the houses. These were rubbed smooth and painted white and their reflection produced astonishing growth and kept the plants from bending toward the windows. The wood reflectors were backed with hay and cotton wadding to improve their insulation qualities.

In his book *The Garden of Eden,* Sir Hugh Platt, observer of Elizabethan husbandry and gardening, had been one of the first to predict the use of steam for the forcing of plants. But it was not until the end of the eighteenth century that it was possible to use steam in any way. A Mr Wakefield of Liverpool is purported to be the first to use steam for forcing in 1788, and in 1791 a Mr Hoyle of Halifax took a patent for heating hothouses and other buildings (cf. J. C. Loudon, *Remarks on the Construction of Hothouses* [1817]). Hoyle's system actually returned the condensed steam back to the boiler for recirculation. In 1789 Boulton, the partner of James Watt, heated a room in his house with steam and then a bath. In 1793 the gardener to the Earl of Derby steam saturated tan bark and dung pits, and in 1807 horticultural architect John Hay of Edinburgh daily discharged steam into beds of stones that retained the heat through the nights.

Even in 1805 Loudon had no use for steam heat, which he considered 'is not only unnecessary but an immense expense'. But by 1817 in his *Remarks on the Construction of Hothouses,* he was praising it for its capacity to carry heat over long distances at even temperature, its cleanliness over the old flue systems, and its saving in fuel and labour. Loudon's original reservations pertained to early steam-heating devices, like North's engine (36) which simply boiled water into the houses and caused condensation on

* J. C. Loudon, *Encyclopaedia of Gardening,* 1835, p. 258.

Elevation of the
STEAM APPARATUS
for
HEATING HOTHOUSES &c.
at
HACKNEY.

37   The heating machinery drawn by George Loddiges in 1818 at the Loddiges' Hackney Nursery. The new equipment had a gravity-fed cistern, safety valves, mercury-filled pressure gauge. Steam was put under a pressure of 4lb/in² and distributed over half a mile of four-inch cast-iron pipe, maintaining winter temperatures of 80–90°F. A second boiler was kept as a back up, should the first fail.

glass and plants. This method had no perceivable advantage over pouring water on hot flues.

By 1817 however, steam was being contained in vaults and pipes, and heating masses of stones or being bubbled through water tanks below the plant beds. The Royal Gardens at Kensington and Hampton Court were heated by steam machines devised by an ironmonger and brazier, a Mr Fraser, and the 1,000-ft run of glass buildings at the Loddiges' nursery in Hackney had a modern steam apparatus (37).

Loudon's fertile imagination then forecast the use of central steam boilers as an all-purpose power source for small country estates; heating the glasshouses, the stables, the mansion house, the baths, laundries, malt kilns, cattle and poultry houses, while providing power for the mill, threshing machine, turnip and straw cutter, fire engine, in addition to pumping water to elevated reservoirs that would supply water closets and 'water cocks'.

The early volumes of the *Transactions of the Horticultural Society of London* provide beautifully illustrated examples of steam heating. James Brown, gardener to Richard Shawe in Dulwich, Surrey, presented in 1817 his steam apparatus for forcing pineapples in a pit and also a vinery. Gardeners at that time were still undecided between using the old flue systems and the new steam heating. Most steam houses were simply converted smoke flue houses. Brown's 24 gallon boiler was cistern-fed and equipped with that necessary device, the safety valve; for some gardeners had been killed by earlier steam machines exploding (40).

In 1819 an interesting pineapple and grape forcing house was built by Martin Miller Call for the Imperial Gardens in St Petersburg. Though a smoke flue system was retained along the front wall, the 100-ft long tan bark house was heated primarily by steam (41).

In 1820 Joseph Hayward presented to the Society a sophisticated hothouse heating system based upon a steam unit invented by Hague, an engineer from Spital Fields. Introduced into a factory run by Hayward in 1819, it was a patented system that distributed heat by radiation and convection and returned the condensate back to the boiler, saving on fuel and water consumption. Coupled with normal radiation, a convection system introduced outside air into the house, not different from methods used today (38).

By the 1830s, the variety of heat distribution systems was great. This is demonstrated in the work of Henry Stothert, a civil engineer from Bath, who built steam systems in South West England (39). Stothert is notable not only for the number of steam systems he designed, but also for the efficiency he introduced into them. A major problem posed by pipes directly exposed in greenhouses and conservatories was their inability to retain heat, so that the boilers had to be fired constantly. Stothert's main innovation combined the advantages of steam as a conductor of heat and water as a retainer. This system was first tried in a forcing-house belonging to a Mr Sturges near Bath, and later adopted in an iron conservatory belonging to the Marquis of Aylesbury at Tottenham Park.

In England today many houses are heated with off-peak storage heaters, which are simply a stack of bricks absorbing cheap night electricity and radiating it during the day.

35

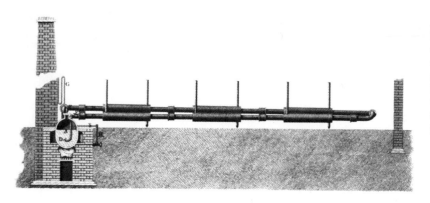

40 The vinery and pine pit, converted to steam by James Brown. The four-inch steam pipe was extended underground to the pine pit, the steam travelled along the front wall and was then discharged into the defunct smoke flue in the back wall. Several outlet valves in the pipe along the front wall steamed the pines. This was thought to be a superior way of watering plants, and to lessen the threat of scale and the bug.

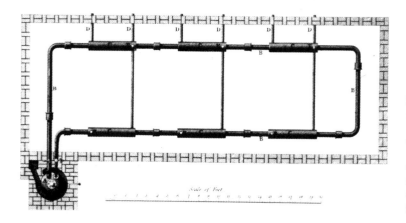

38 Section (top) and plan (centre) of Hague's Steam Apparatus presented to the Horticultural Society by Joseph Hayward who applied it to a hothouse. A 30-gallon boiler pressurized a three-inch diameter rising steam pipe and the declining return pipe. This closed system required sophisticated metering and safety devices, including an air cock at the end of the return pipe, a goose-neck steam gauge at the head of the rising main, a water gauge, and a safety valve at the top of the cauldron.

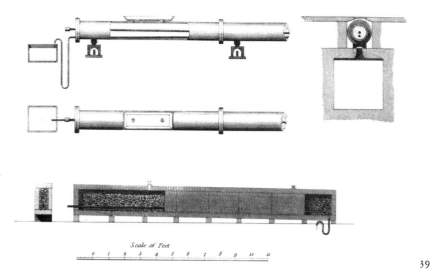

39 Henry Stothert's methods of heating by steam.

End Section.

41   The steam pits in the Imperial Gardens of the Taurida Palace, St Petersburg. Heat transfer was simple. A cistern-fed boiler developed steam at 3 lb/in² and forced the vapour into a horizontal pipe suspended over two fifty-foot water tanks made of caulked timber. Vertical pipes bubbled the steam into the water at six-foot intervals. The boiler was fired for six hours every week to maintain the tank water at 100°F to 145°F and the tan bark into which the potted pines were plunged at 88°F to 100°F. The front wall flue heated the house air in winter. In the summer it was used for cold air intake to prevent the tan bark fermentation from burning the plants when it went out of control, as it often did. It also drained the water from the wood tanks when they were being repaired.

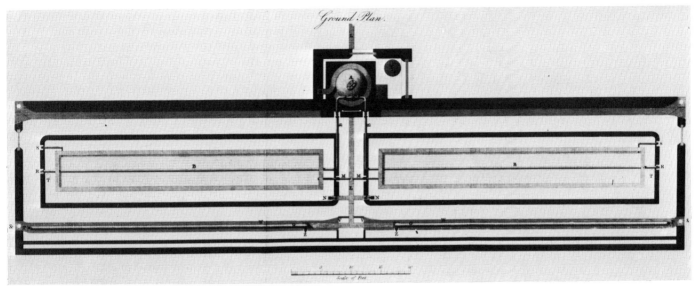

Ground Plan.

Scale of Feet.

42   W. Atkinson's hot water system applied to a hothouse in the gardens of Anthony Bacon, Aberamen, Glamorganshire, 1822.

43   Section of the architectural conservatory at Kew Gardens by Sir Jeffry Wyatville, heated by A. M. Perkins's high-pressure hot water system.

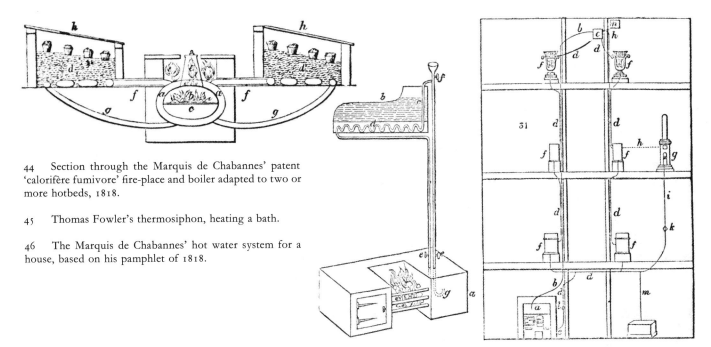

44 Section through the Marquis de Chabannes' patent 'calorifère fumivore' fire-place and boiler adapted to two or more hotbeds, 1818.

45 Thomas Fowler's thermosiphon, heating a bath.

46 The Marquis de Chabannes' hot water system for a house, based on his pamphlet of 1818.

Stothert's steam storage heater was also based on the same principle, except that a perforated steam pipe distributed vapour into a sealed stone chamber filled with rubble, and the condensate was drained off. Steam cocks at the top of the chamber could be opened for extra humidity and the pipe had more perforations towards the end of its run for even distribution.

Though extensively developed in the early nineteenth century, steam heat had only a short-lived popularity, for by the 1830s nearly every gardener was discussing the merits of hot water. Steam distribution systems could be extended for long distances from a central point but the fires had to be stoked constantly to keep the water boiling. The cauldron took several hours to come to the boil and a person had to be in constant attendance. Like any equipment that has to sustain pressure, it required constant maintenance, and there was an even greater than normal risk of explosion from boilers ill-managed by gardeners not used to such mechanical devices. Inventors, therefore, tried to find better ways to distribute heat and maintain an even temperature.

In 1818 the Marquis de Chabannes wrote a pamphlet* that contained an illustration of a hothouse heated by a water-jacketed boiler. It fed hot water to radiant pipes below the earth bed and the returning water entered at the bottom of the boiler to be recirculated. The most interesting plate, however, illustrated a complete hot water system for the home. A kitchen fireplace boiler

* On conducting Air by Ventilation and regulating the Temperature in Dwellings, with a Description of the Application of the Principles as established in Covent Garden Theatre, and Lloyd's Subscription Rooms. 1818.

supplied hot water to a bath on the same level and to urns on the three floors above (44; 46).

The first hothouse heated with hot water was designed by Chabannes at Sundridge Park, Kent, in 1816. W. Atkinson was mistaken in thinking that he was the first with the plans he made for the Bacon estate at Aberamen, Glamorganshire, in 1822. The boiler in Atkinson's scheme was simply a cauldron which could heat the chambers of the house throughout the night with one well-stoked fire. Water began to circulate as soon as the fire was lit. Hot water rose and flowed in the top tube through the house and into a cast-iron reservoir. When it became cool it flowed back to the boiler to be recirculated again. The water never turned to steam, and the level could be replenished by lifting the wooden lid that covered the boiler. The system must have been extremely efficient, for heat came from the hot water as well as the smoke and gases from the fireplace which circulated along the front wall, then to the back wall and out of the chimneys (42).

Chabannes' system was much more sophisticated and came into being ten years before a similar invention by Thomas Tredgold, and eighteen years before Alexander Cruikshank's water-jacketed boilers. In 1831 J. C. Loudon described a situation that should be observed by architects today:

We are not surprised that Mr Atkinson should not have heard of what Chabannes had done; for we have learned, from what we consider undoubted authority, that when in January last, some of the Bank of England directors proposed to heat a part of their establishment

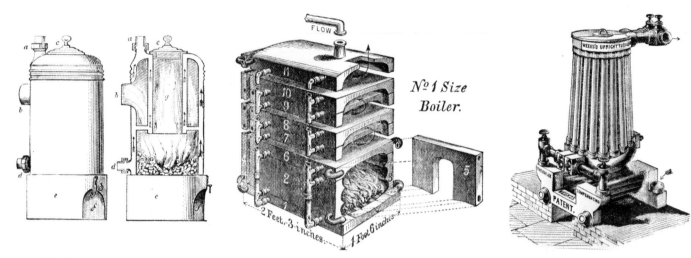

FLOW

N.º 1 Size
Boiler.

2 Feet. 3 inches.

1 Foot 6 inches.

WEEKS'S UPRIGHT TUBULAR

PATENT.

47   Stephenson's double cylinder boiler. An early example of a water-jacketed boiler.

48   English cast-iron boiler. Because of its weight, it had to be made in sections for shipping.

49   Weeks's Upright Tubular Boiler, exhibited by Weeks & Co., hothouse builders of the Kings Road, Chelsea, at the Great Exhibition in 1851. A circle of tubes round the fire gave a large surface area, which could provide instant heat at sudden drops in temperature. It was designed so that parts could be replaced while the boiler operated.

by hot water, their architect*, eminent though he is, had not heard of such a mode of heating.
Though the engineer Thomas Tredgold had developed a steam-heating method at Syon House, he was also instrumental in advancing hot water heating, for he read a paper on the new subject to the Horticultural Society of London in August 1828. In the paper he described how Atkinson's device worked, and presented some important hydrostatic principles and statistics, like the specific heat of various liquids, the coefficients of friction and expansion, formulae for heat retention, and boiler size in relation to the area of the glass. The art of heating was finally a science, based as it was on principles established as far back as 1701 when Newton presented the laws of heating and cooling to the Philosophical Society.

Hot water circulated by the principle of the siphon was invented separately by Thomas Fowler and James Kewley. Kewley used the method at Colvill's nursery in 1826 and later at the Oxford Botanic Gardens. Fowler acquired a patent for the siphon in 1829. While previous systems, except that of Chabannes, required that the boiler and the distribution pipes be at the same level, use of the siphon permitted a supply of water above and below the boiler.

Fowler published a pamphlet on his thermosiphon, which could heat a bath on the upper floors from a boiler in the kitchen. It created a complete circuit of water from the boiler to the water-jacket around the bath and back to the boiler again. The descending water drew the hot water to the bath in a never-ending circuit. Fowler provided a simple diagram of the siphon. The side of the

pipe system that was curved and therefore longer cooled the water first and drew it to the boiler while the hot water was siphoned up (45).

By the 1830s dozens of ironmongers, iron-founders, engineers and glasshouse merchants entered the new hot-water heating trade with their 'ideal' boiler and distribution systems. Charles McIntosh's *Book of the Garden* (1853) seems to describe and illustrate every one of them. Weeks and Co. of Kings Road, Chelsea, for example, produced just one of the choices (49).

In the 1830s, A. M. Perkins developed high-pressure hot water distribution by hermetically sealing the entire system and adding an expansion tube that allowed the expansion of the water as high-pressure steam. The system did not require a boiler, but several loops of half-inch pipe were embedded in a masonry core around the fire. The average heat of the pipes was $350°F$ which developed a pressure of 135 lb/in^2. Though mainly used in factories and dwellings, the system was also used in hothouses like those of John Hornsley Palmer, a bank director from Parson's Green, Fulham, and Jeffrey Wyatville's extant architectural conservatory at Kew (43).

The Chabannes boiler of 1816 was presented in a paper to the Horticultural Society in 1834 by Alexander Cruickshank, who described the boiler which a 'friend in France' used to heat his study. The cylindrical boiler, needing no masonry enclosure, was completely surrounded by a water-jacket similar to those on the high pressure steam engines being developed for transportation at that

* Sir John Soane.

50 Modest domestic hot water boiler on the thermosiphon principle, offered by Hitchings and Co. of New York, in 1889.

time. In his paper Cruickshank described other boilers that, along with Stephenson's double cylinder boilers, are forerunners of modern hot water systems (47).

Frederick A. Lord, carpenter and amateur greenhouse builder, established his glasshouse company in 1856. By the 1870s he was building very large forcing-houses, and glass ranges for private estates in Upstate New York, especially along the Hudson River, near his Irvington, New York plant. Lord took his son-in-law, William Burnham, as a partner and by 1873, they had their first boiler on the market. This was a cast-iron sectional, most probably similar to those used in England at the time but the first in the United States. The boiler had very little direct heating surface and was not adequate to heat a greenhouse throughout a cold New York winter night. Lord and Burnham's second attempt to design a boiler was in 1878. Giving up the 'sectional' because of leaks, they marketed a very expensive, but highly efficient, brass tube heat exchanger inside a cast-iron case. These brass tubes however burned out because of the electrolytic action of brass, cast-iron and water. In the 1880s

the company reverted to a cast iron water-jacketed boiler, which they sold in hundreds to florists and private gardeners. But by the 1900s, because of the shipping and installation difficulties of the huge one-piece boiler, a new 'sectional' replaced the standard. This was similar to the sectional boiler of Hitchings & Co. who merged with Lord and Burnham in 1905 (48).

In the 1880s Hitchings & Co. had developed the 'camel back' cast-iron boiler with a corrugated fire-box and circuitous path for extracting heat from the hot flue gases. The boiler was virtually identical to Cruickshank's model of 1834 and the water was distributed by siphon action previously demonstrated by Kewley in 1828. To meet the market of the emerging middle-class gardener who had a more modest greenhouse, Hitchings & Co. also patented a domestic, water-jacketed, siphonic heater, which had to be below the level of the plant chamber if the thermosiphon was to work. The run of pipes was terminated in the house with an expansion tank that could be easily topped up (50).

51   The interior of Leyden Victoria Regia House—a delicate
wrought-iron structure. A small child sits on one of the leaves.

4 *The Artificial Climate* II: *Automatic Gardens*

In his *Treatise on Improvements Recently made in Hothouses* (1805), Loudon was one of the first environmentalists to note the need for both ventilation—the changing of the air in a hot house—and air movement inside it. Ventilation in the summer was no problem as sashes could be removed or the glass skin could be made to open like venetian blinds (skilfully demonstrated in his designs in *Remarks on the Construction of Hothouses* [1817]). When the houses were sealed in the winter, however, the problem of introducing outside air into the damp stuffy plant chamber presented itself. Loudon suggested that the air from the sheds behind the plant chamber be blown in with bellows or his own box-like air pump (52).

It was, however, just the movement of air that Loudon found most needed and most difficult to reproduce in the artificial climates of the early nineteenth-century hothouses. He had observed that most hothouse plants, even though they received adequate air, heat and light, grew weak and spindly. When exposed to the breeze in the summer, they developed bushy and vigorous shoots. In his 1805 *Treatise* . . . he emphasizes man's success in imitating nature, up to a point:

In hothouses, nature has been imitated, more or less perfectly in most things. Heat is produced from the furnaces and flues. Light is admitted through the glass; rain is supplied from the syringe or watering-pot; dew is rarified by pouring water upon the flues or by steam apparatus and fresh air is admitted at pleasure. There is still something missing. What makes up the want of those refreshing and genial breezes, which fan and invigorate the real nature . . . in nature, there is no

such thing as vegetables living for three months in the year without enjoying the breeze.

Loudon adapted a common winnowing machine, hand-powered and hung from the rafters, to produce wind. He modelled one on the roasting jack, with a fan powered by descending weights, positioned in a box on wheels which could be pulled to any place in the house. The air was fanned out of a horizontal tube that was also fixed to a mechanism that caused it to revolve in all directions. His third apparatus was a proper windmill or fan, powered by a spring that needed winding by a key.

James Anderson in *Description of a Patented Hothouse* (1803), was certainly one of the first persons to describe a solar heat sink for heating and ventilation. He proposed that air chambers under or adjoining the greenhouse be filled with the 'superfluous' air, heated by the sun during the day and 'sucked' into the house at night with a winnowing machine in a cylinder.

Ventilation was being adopted in factories, hospitals and homes in the early 1800s. In 1811 Mr Strutt of Derby provided a type of natural ventilation for his house and the Derby Infirmary. He connected a funnel-mouthed tube to a wind vane, and put it underground some 100 yards from his house. The constant temperature of the ground cooled the air in summer and heated it in the winter.

Benford Deacon patented in 1812 one of the first forced warm air furnaces—which was the system used to heat the Old Bailey and a greenhouse in Streatham. A description of the patent shows it to be very similar to the air-conditioners used today. A fan fixed in a semi-cylin-

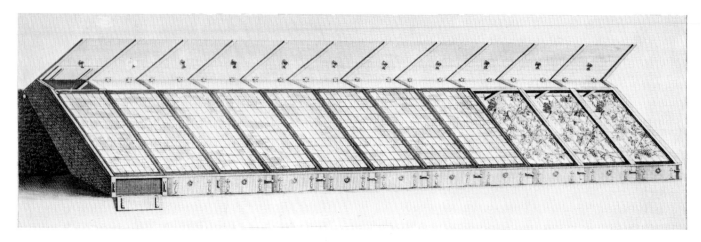

52 This Dutch eighteenth-century forcing-frame had ventilation flaps at the bottom and top of the chamber. The top hinged flap was held open by the back sun reflector, cantilevered over the glass. The glass frames could be removed to expose the vines to the sun, and for pruning and harvesting.

drical chamber in the basement draws in outside air and forces it through a tube-filled chamber. The tubes are then filled with steam or hot water in the winter. In the summer, the air is drawn from a cool cellar and the tubes filled with cold water. The fan is powered by a descending weight machine and the air distributed (as also proposed by Loudon) in canvas tubes, the way polyethylene tubes are used in greenhouses today.

Loudon thought that Deacon's hot air system combined with automatic control was all that was needed to produce a perfect artificial environment; and would be important in 'pneumatic medicine'.

'Pneumatic medicine' meant a 'sort of hothouse for invalids', which a Dr Kentish established in 1813 near Clifton. Throughout the nineteenth century, a number of similar proposals were made, including Joseph Paxton's 'Crystal Sanitarium' in 1851. It is safe to say, however, that even today the English do not like forced warm air heating, because it is too dry and ruins their antique furniture which is so attuned to the damp environment.

It was James Kewley's 'automaton gardener' that really stirred Loudon's imagination and convinced him of the feasibility of a perfect environment. Here was a thermostatic device which, when coupled with a hopper-fed steam boiler, a bell system and various types of ventilators, could control the artificial climate 'without the labour of man'. Loudon named Kewley's regulating thermometer the 'automaton gardener', for to him it was a kind of horticulturalist's robot. He was constantly suggesting the attachment of Kewley's device to his 'polyprosopic' roofs which were flat, with the glass in patterns

of ridge and furrow, or octagonal or hexagonal pyramids. The top edges of these roofs were to be hinged, creating Venetian louvres attached to rods. Chains and pulleys were actuated when the 'automaton gardener' itself reacted to temperature drops, rises, and inclement weather. The system was a precocious forerunner of today's horticultural glasshouses, which are regulated by thermostats, photo cells, celenoids and motors.

Kewley took out a patent in 1816 when he moved from Douglas, Isle of Man, to London and installed it in his apartments on the New Kent Road. The automaton was on display at W. and D. Bailey in Holborn and later Kewley applied it to a hot-house in Colvills nursery in the Kings Road, Chelsea, during the summer of 1819. The machine was shown to Sir Joseph Banks and the Horticultural Society, but the president, Thomas Knight and other members thought 'such a machine was not wanted in gardening'. Kewley's 'automaton gardener' is a fascinating, Rube Goldberg device. An alcohol and mercury-balanced thermometer tips with a change in the temperature. This is attached to a control valve that in turn regulates water from an elevated tank to a cylinder, forcing a piston which either raises the sashes or closes them. Loudon describes it more fully in his *Encyclopaedia of Gardening* (1822) [53].

Dr James Anderson's patented glasshouse contains a description of a hermetically sealed 'oblong bladder' that expanded with an increase in temperature and opened hinged sashes. Metals with a high coefficient of expansion, like brass, lead, or mercury, were connected to vertical rods, which lifted roof vents of the kind suggested by

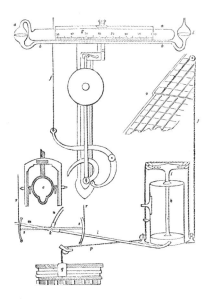

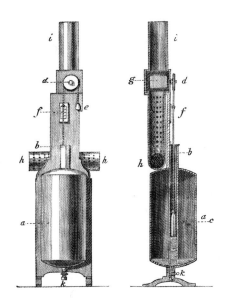

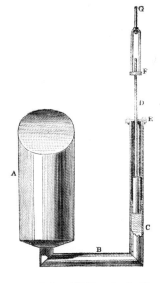

53 James Kewley's Automaton Gardener, patented in 1816.

54 George Mugliston's temperature controlled apparatus for ventilating hothouses.

55 John Williams's 'self-acting ventilator for hothouses'.

Loudon. Two papers describing similar self-acting ventilators on the expansion principle were read to the Horticultural Society on 6 April 1824. The one devised by horticulturalist, John Williams, was placed in the sun on the back wall of the hothouse. The expansion and contraction of air in a sealed tank actuated a column of water that forced a cylinder to open or close two 'registers', one high on the back wall for the escape of hot air and the other near the floor for the admission of cold air. The other self-regulator, designed by another horticulturalist, George Mugliston, from Repton in Derbyshire, was intended to protect his vinery from excessive heat during the night if the fires had been over-stoked in expectation of frost. A copper air chamber was painted black to absorb the radiant heat of the flues. A glass float (a corked bottle) was attached to a balancing weight by a cord that passed over the wheel connected to the 'air valve'. As the air expanded, the water column and bottle would rise, opening the 'air valve' in a tube connected to an air intake on the roof (54; 55).

By the 1840s at some kitchen gardens like those of Frogmore and Dalkeith, the art of ventilation was well developed. Still in tightly constructed iron and glass conservatories, like the Royal Society's Curvilinear conservatory at Chiswick, inadequate plant specimens were frequently produced because of ventilation deficiencies. The Horticultural Society's president, Thomas Knight, obviously did not have sufficient regard for ventilation. In 1822 he presented a design for an improved curvilinear hothouse, with small openings top and bottom as the only means of ventilation. However, by 1846 Dr

John Lindley, first editor of Paxton's magazine, the *Gardener's Chronicle*, wrote an article proposing solutions. He distinguished ventilation: letting external air into a forcing house, from aeration: keeping the atmosphere in motion by currents of fresh air. Realizing that the mechanical effects of motion strengthened the plants and helped the sap to rise, Lindley also hinted at the need of carbon dioxide for plant growth, and transpiration for the plant to cool itself (57).

Rain is better for plants than well water because of its good (pH) characteristics. It was therefore normal to collect rainwater from the vast roofs of the glasshouses and transfer it to huge cisterns in vaults below. The water was often piped to these cisterns through structural columns, as at The Grange conservatory in Hampshire and Paxton's Great Conservatory at Chatsworth. Constructing rain water pipes as structural columns was easy for iron founders like Boulton and Watt, who were already making pipes to convey steam and water for steam engines and structural columns for factories and markets. They only had to bolt a cast-iron structural gutter to a cast-iron column and drain water through it (56).

The Grecian style conservatory at The Grange, built in 1825 by Thomas Clark, led directly into the ladies' apartments and dining-room which had been added by C. R. Cockerell to the house originally designed by Inigo Jones. The section shows curved iron plates covering the walkways and glass pyramids spanning two planting beds. The curved covers were constructed of double-iron plates 'enclosing a body of air to prevent the escape of heat'. Iron gratings were attached to the curved top

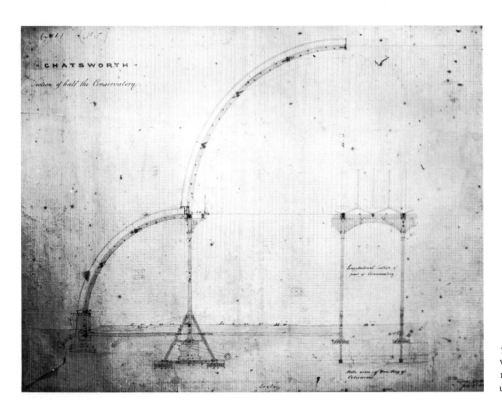

56 Section of half the Great Conservatory at Chatsworth by Joseph Paxton, 1834–8. Cast-iron columns were to be used as rain-water pipes.

58, 60 Below: section through The Grange Conservatory. Below the walk are steam pipes and ducts conveying hot air from Sylvester's furnace (k). Vaulted roof formed from two vaulted plates of rolled iron (l). Flint for drainage (m). Drain (n). Facing, below: the Grange Conservatory was erected for Alexander Baring (Lord Ashburton) by Thomas Clarke of Birmingham in 1825. The plan was 82 ft long and 49 ft wide, and 19 ft from the floor to the top of the ridges. It was roofed with cast-iron gutters supported on cast columns and rolled iron and copper sashes. (The exterior stone pilasters, columns and cornices are attributed to C. R. Cockerell.)

57 Patent self-locking sash operating apparatus. Hitchings & Co. catalogue of greenhouse heating, c. 1880.

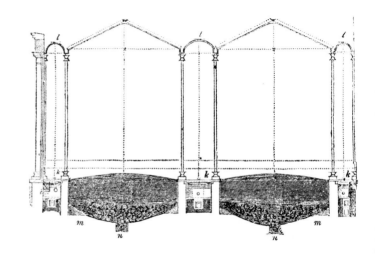

59   Interior of the Camellia House at Wollaton Hall, Nottingham,
built by Thomas Clark of Birmingham (later to become Hopes, then
Crittal-Hope). Built two years before The Grange, and with similar
components, the Camellia House can be considered a sophisticated
big sister of The Grange.

providing a maintenance walkway. The roof rainwater flowed from the cast-iron gutters down through the cast-iron columns that supported the roof into a large tank under the portico entry. The water was then brought to plants with a 'forcing pump'. The house was heated by a combination of Sylvester's hot-air stove and steam in chambers under the floor which entered the house through small plant stands in the window recesses. Charles McIntosh in *The Book of the Garden* (1853) suggested that half the columns could drain the roof water, while the other half could be pumped full with hot water for heating. The house was filled with all sorts of delicacies, including orange and lemon trees, Chinese magnolias and proteas, camellias and gardenias (58–60).

The means of transporting water have a long history because of their importance to man and his settlements, so that the science of hydraulics developed very early examples of field and well-pumps. These were adapted by gardeners in the eighteenth and nineteenth centuries. Their watering kit could include various kinds of hand-held pump-syringes and larger contraptions like the barrow watering-engine. This portable pump was invaluable to the hot house and conservatory owner, for its 40–50 ft spray watered the plants easily and helped put out any fire started by a faulty heating system. Some pumps had their own water tank as well as an attachment for a hose which could be connected to the intake side of the pump for drawing rainwater from the cisterns below.

Watering and hydroponic systems* as we know them today have their antecedents early in the nineteenth century. Hothouse steaming engines produced moisture

for the tropical exotics with a close imitation of the tropical jungle. But often the condensed moisture was injurious to the delicate plants, and the damp atmosphere produced mildew and fungus. At their commercial botanic nursery in Hackney, Conrad Loddiges and his son developed a simple rain-making system in their 60 ft Palm House, which was awarded a medal by the Horticultural Society in 1817. Water was pumped to a tank above the house and connected to half-inch lead pipes suspended below the ridge and roof at 6 to 8 ft intervals. These rain pipes, controlled by a stopcock, were pierced with fine needles every two inches, and even closer at the end of the run, to equalize the 'fine stream that, in descending is broken and falls on the plants, in a manner resembling a gentle summer shower' (Loudon). Loudon was very impressed by the Loddiges' rainmaker and enthusiastically suggested it for all artificial climates. He installed it in the experimental square dome at Bayswater House.

The giant South American water-lily, later to be named the Victoria Regia, inspired a completely new type of building, the aquatic house. There had been earlier glass houses in Britain solely for aquatic plants. One was built for the Marquess of Blandford at White Knights, near Reading by G. Tod and described in his *Hothouses, Greenhouses, and Aquaria etc.* (1807). It had a small gable roof, a hot air flue that went round the house, and two flues that heated a lead-lined tank to a proper temperature. But aquaria and aquatic houses became popular only with the excitement and challenge of nurturing blooms of the

* Feeding liquid nutrients to plants often not growing in soil.

48

61 Interior of the Victoria Regia House at Kew Gardens, built by Richard Turner in 1852. Besides the giant water lily, other varieties, together with aquatic palms, papyrus and rice plants, delighted the Victorian observer.

62 The Victoria Regia house at Chatsworth by Joseph Paxton.

63 The Victoria Regia in bloom at Chatsworth for the first time. The leaves were sufficiently strong to support the weight of a child. The small water wheel powered by running water kept the tank water in motion.

queen of the aquatics, Victoria Regia. By the early 1850s, proper pond houses could be found at Chatsworth, Syon House, the Royal Botanic Society at Regent's Park, the Veitchs' nursery at Exeter, Sheffield Botanic Garden, Dalkeith Park near Edinburgh and at Kew, built by the master of iron and glass construction, Richard Turner, and still in existence adjacent to his Great Palm House. The Victoria Regia had been known to the early botanical travellers; and in 1837 Sir Robert Schomburgk, exploring British Guiana for the Geographical Society, brought back the first specimens and drawings of the plant. It stirred the imagination of the romantic Victorian exotic collectors, and seeds were planted at Kew Gardens in 1846, but the small plants did not prosper. In 1849 Paxton set about building a heated tank in a curvilinear glass house at Chatsworth. In it, he put a small plant with leaves less than six inches in diameter, which he had procured from Sir William Hooker, Kew's director. The plant was so small that it arrived in a $13\frac{1}{2}$ inch x $13\frac{1}{2}$ inch box and was set in the soil of the 12-ft square tank on 10 August. By the end of September, the largest leaf measured 3 ft 6 in in diameter and the tank size had to be doubled. These were the Midas years for Paxton and he could do no wrong; the lily bloomed on 8 November, and a week later Paxton presented the first English bloom and a leaf to the Queen and Prince Albert at Windsor Castle. The lily tank had been, temporarily, set up in the 26 ft x 60 ft elliptical-roof glass 'stove' built on Paxton's ridge and furrow principles. The 'stove' was built in 1836 to demonstrate wood-laminated construction as a prototype of the Great Conservatory, but it was too narrow for

50

the Victoria Regia's astonishing growth habits. The construction of a new house was imminent. In the spring of 1850 the New Victoria Regia House was ready to nurture the ever expanding prize, which that year produced 112 flowers and 140 leaves (61–3).

The speed of building the new house may surprise us today. But Paxton had developed his ridge and furrow model ten years previously in a design (later abandoned) for a flat-roof conservatory on Lord Burlington's estate. Later he had a ridge and furrow glass house built on to Adam Washington's house at Darley Dale near Matlock. Paxton commanded a large force of men and had direct contact with glass manufacturers and iron founders. He had already constructed his sash-bar machine and could order pipes and boilers from the many existing companies, which were more than pleased to serve an eminence as distinguished as Joseph Paxton, a gardener as well known as his patron, the Duke of Devonshire.

Paxton's acute understanding of the lily's environmental needs were superbly realized in the Regia House. A Burbidge and Healy boiler supplied hot water to a series of cast-iron pipes around the inside of the external walls, and a Sylvester's Hot Air Furnace heated the cavities around the tanks. The pathways above were laid with boards with quarter-inch gaps between them, allowing the heat to escape into the house. In the 16 ft lower section of the tank itself were several 4-in pipes running under the earth mound, warming the roots of the plant. A cold water supply powering water wheels could be adjusted, maintaining the water temperature at $83°-85°$F, an extremely fine tolerance. Lower ventilation was drawn

through openings between the masonry piers and roof vents provided through-ventilation, keeping the temperature of the air between 80° and 90°F throughout the year.

J. C. Loudon with his incredible imagination and foresight had described, though never built, a proper aquarium for plants, which ought, he said, to resemble the natural habitat of aquatic plants, even to the turbulence of the temperate waters. Loudon's 'aquarium', presented in the *Encyclopaedia of Gardening* (1822) was circular, and contained two cisterns, one around the periphery for plants that grew in stagnant water and a central cistern for river plants. The glass was low at the edge of the tank for the short aquatics and high in the middle for taller plants. The vault below the central tank contained a furnace or a boiler and a 'wind-up-jack' descending weight machine. This machine, which needed winding twice a day, powered a turntable which kept the river plants in perpetual motion. Plants that thrived in rapid streams were to be near the edge of the large wheel, and those that required 'less agitation', towards its centre (64).

Loudon's glass design was unknowingly imitated nearly fifty years later in a Dutch house built in 1870 for the Victoria Regia in Leyden in the University's famous gardens. The house was a beautiful, delicate glass and iron construction surmounted by a cast-iron crown. First flowering at Chatsworth in 1849, then at Kew in the following year and in Amsterdam in 1859, the Victoria Regia burst forth at Leyden in 1872, where nearly thirty thousand people came to see the marvel (51; 65).

Alphonse Balat, for whom the Art Nouveau architect Victor Horta later worked in Brussels, designed a Victoria Regia House in 1854. The Royal Society of Zoology and Horticulture built it in the Jardin Zoologique de Bruxelles, later to be known as 'Parc Leopold'. The elegant curved iron trusses radiate from the corners of the octagonal plan and culminate in a large ironwork crown. The house also had a fascinating travelling history. In 1878 it was moved to the Jardin Botanique National de Belgique in Brussels, where it sheltered a Victoria Regia until the Second World War. In 1941 it was again moved, this time to the Jardin Botanique National de Belgique in Meise; where it remains today as a display house for alpine plants and ornamental flowers (67).

By the 1850s many large estates had vast horticultural glass ranges which were producing vegetables, fruits and flowers. These ranges were usually at the north end of walled-in kitchen gardens, which, in spite of their name, could be huge. Even the walls of the gardens themselves were often heated to provide agreeable microclimates for the fruit trees along them. Descriptions of these gardens show the sophistication that had been reached with heating, ventilation, and humidifying equipment installed in these great glass ranges which constituted the first integrated systems.

As late as the 1830s the British Royal table was poorly supplied in quantity and quality of fresh fruits and vegetables. The Royal gardens, nearly a dozen in number, each with various kinds of glass structures, totalled some fifty acres, but because they were many miles apart and mismanaged, the fruit and vegetables were produced at considerable expense. A Garden Inquiry Committee

65 The Victoria Regia house in Leyden, 1870. The giant lily's popularity spread throughout Europe and many houses were built for it between 1850 and 1880.

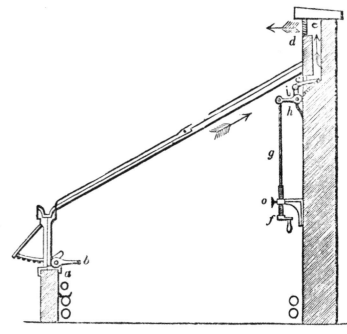

66 Typical section through the main glass range at Frogmore. Iron rafters capped with wood for insulation held the hollow copper sash bars. This roof, supplied by Thomas Clark of Birmingham, had top sashes held with chains and on rollers. These could slide over the lower sash opening half the roof. The front wall glass vent opened by turning a handle (b). This device and the back wall ventilation gear came from the engineer and hothouse builder, John B. Jones, also of Birmingham, who constructed the extensive range. At intervals in the back wall are 3 ft to 4 ft long cavities that transmit air through grilles (e). Cast-iron flaps (c) along the whole length of the range are regulated by handles at the back wall. Two 4-in heat pipes run along the front and back walls. Some of these pipes, along the front wall, have evaporating pans along their top. A $\frac{3}{4}$-inch finely perforated pipe sprays water over the pipes for extra humidity.

19 Bruxelles — Jardin Botanique de l'Etat
La Serre Victoria.

67   Alphonse Balat's Victoria Regia House of 1854, shown here in the Botanic Gardens, Brussels. Balat's glass and iron structures, along with the exotics they housed, were to make an impression on Victor Horta and Art Nouveau.

68   The Royal Kitchen Garden, Frogmore. The 840-ft glass range has the head gardener's house in the centre, with two rooms for Queen Victoria when she visited the gardens.

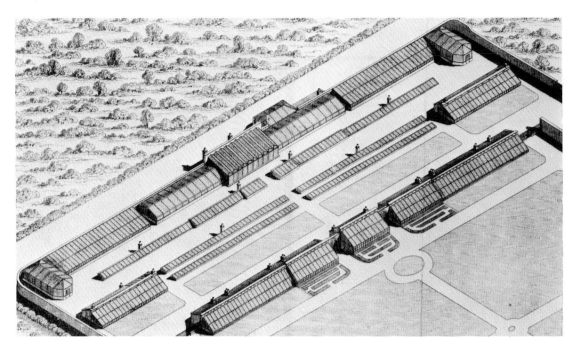

(Paxton, Lindley, Watson), appointed in 1838, recommended that the kitchen gardens at Kensington be sold, and annexed to the Royal Botanic Gardens at Kew, and to demolish the kitchen gardens at Cumberland Lodge, Cranbourne Lodge, Windsor, Buckingham Palace, Osborne and later, at Hampton Court. In 1844 a new garden was established within the brick walls surrounding a thirty-one acre site at Windsor Park where it was closer to the Royal residence. The £45,000 investment built a veritable environmental machine producing fruits, vegetables, mushrooms, decorative plants and flowers for the Queen and the Royal Family. Starting at the main East gate and porter's lodge, a visitor would first pass a 50 ft stove and greenhouse, a 52 ft pine stove, a 56 ft apricot and plum house, a 102 ft late vinery, a 56 ft peach house and a 53 ft early vinery, all connected with 7 ft glass corridors. Arriving at the gardener's house, the series then repeats symmetrically on the other side. Behind the main range were the cucumber, melon, and French bean, and pineapple pits filled with manure or compost heated with hot water, and smaller vineries. Asparagus beds in the northeast corner were forced by hot water that also heated the two fine cherry houses in the centre. Directly behind the main range were various lean-to sheds used as seed, tool and store rooms, sheds for washing vegetables and potting plants, mushroom houses and rooms for the foreman and some of the workmen.

The dwelling-house in the centre of the main range had two apartments made for the Queen's use when she visited the glasshouses. It also provided lodging for the head gardener who commanded an army of some 150 gardeners and lads. Gardening then was an extremely time-consuming art. For example, each fruit on the pear tree was tied in a separate muslin bag to keep the wasps and bees from damaging it. When the peach houses were opened to the September sun, a lad spent his days running back and forth with a swatter to keep the insects away. Cucumbers were grown in long glass jars so that they would be straight for the Royal table (66; 68).

The Book of the Garden (1853) by Charles McIntosh describes among hundreds of other examples, the Dalkeith kitchen gardens, which are a superb example of the kitchen gardens that existed throughout Scotland and England at that period, in such places as Blenheim, Syon, Bicton Gardens, Eaton Hall, Chatsworth, and Enville Hall.

At Dalkeith the twenty acres of enclosed gardens were certainly as ambitious as the Queen's at Windsor. Very little of the glass remains, but all of the sheds and walls still stand and create an image of the scene illustrated in McIntosh's book (69). The four parallel glass ranges were placed on the north side of the garden enclosed within 12 ft high and 20 in. wide hollow brick walls which were heated with 4 in hot water pipes, providing an improved micro-climate for the fruit trees, espaliered along them. From a cellar behind the back camellia house, three hot water boilers heated the entire range. Each house had its own cisterned water supply and McIntosh estimated that the 5,866 sq. yds of roof, exclusive of the pits, produced 739,116 gallons of water per annum. This was piped into a huge tank in the orchid house, individual iron cisterns

69　Four glass ranges at the north end of the Dalkeith Palace kitchen garden were designed and built by Charles McIntosh. Each glasshouse had a particular shape, depending on the requirements of the produce inside. A tropical house centred the front range—to the right, a greenhouse and peach houses: to the left, a heath house and vinery. In the sheds, behind this range were vegetable, seed, potting, and store rooms; a carpenter's, glazing, and paint shop; and sitting and sleeping rooms for the foreman and three workmen, with a kitchen in the cellar. The second range has two pineapple stoves at each end and a double row of pits; the heated back pits for asparagus and the front, cold pit for alpine plants. At the back of the pine stoves were heated sheds for rhubarb and sea kale. The third range was two heated pits for pineapples and plant propagation. The back range had a camellia house based on Paxton's ridge and furrow roof in the centre; to the right, an orchid house with a gable-roofed greenhouse behind, a fig house, and a span-roofed greenhouse; to the left were a greenhouse, a cherry, plum and apricot house, and a gable-roofed plantstove with chamfered end.

70　Section through Charles McIntosh's vinery and pine-pit at Dalkeith. The centre of this environmental machine was the coal-fired furnace (b) that heated McIntosh's own wrought-iron saddle-shaped water boiler that fed horizontal pipes extending along one end and in an open chamber along the front of the pipe pit (d). The furnace flue (e) cut diagonally through the shed to the chimneys on the back, north-facing wall. This warmed the back rooms and kept the smoke and soot as far away from the glass as possible. Rainwater was collected in the iron gutters along the back shed (o) and piped into a cast-iron cistern (k) which was kept tepid from the furnace below. The vines and pineapples were watered from this cistern which also supplied the required boiler water (t). The front sash (f) was opened in the summer as was the back top ventilation, which was similar to that at Frogmore, except that the interior shutters (i) slid vertically. Winter vent pipes (g) were introduced underground, bringing in air to the heat pipes before flowing into the house, for a direct cold blast would damage the vines.

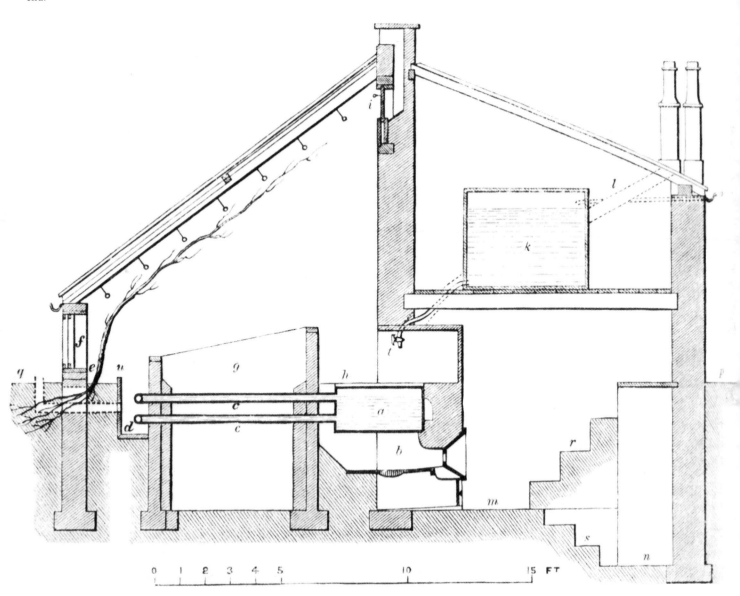

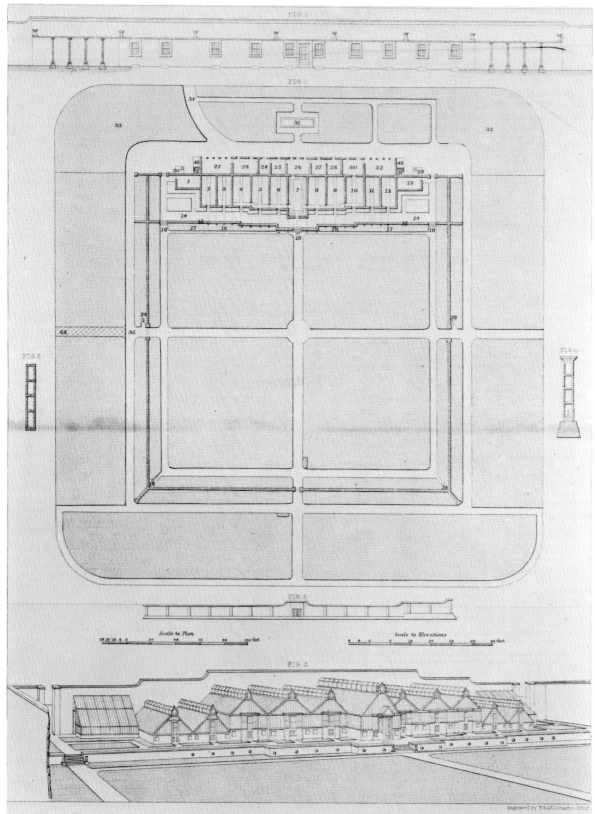

GROUND PLAN OF POLTALLOCH GARDEN, WITH ELEVATIONS.

71 The Poltalloch kitchen garden, designed by McIntosh. Fig. 1 is the plan, with the glass range at the north; Fig. 2, a perspective of the glass range showing the air intake openings along the low plateau wall; Fig. 4 is a heated brick wall which enclosed the garden.

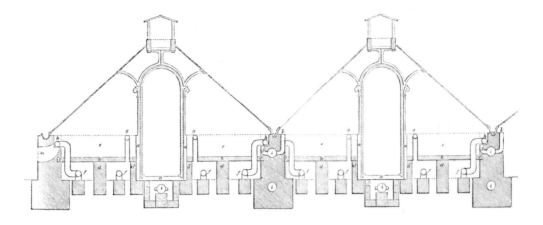

72   Section and plan of the cucumber and melon houses at Poltalloch.

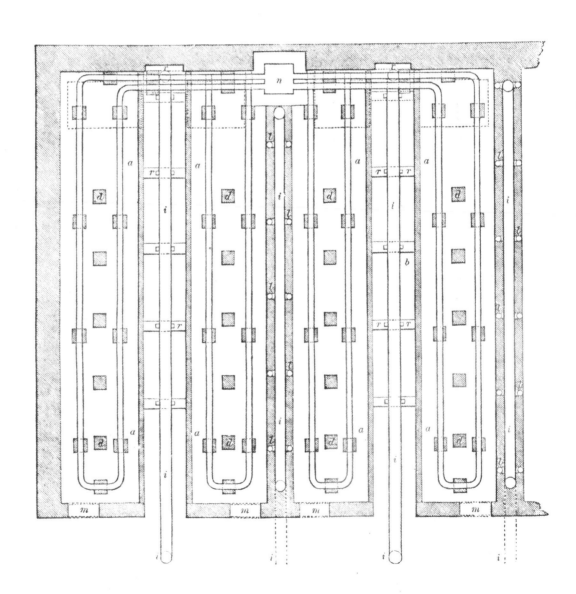

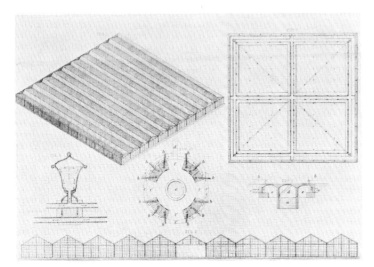

73   Design by McIntosh for a glass-covered garden at Dalkeith.

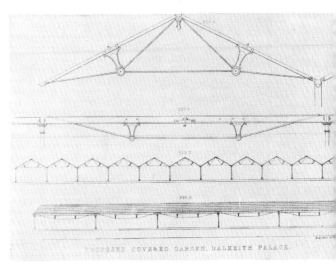

74   Vast modern ridge and furrow glasshouse near Dubbeldam, Holland which covers 7.4 acres. Its minimal supports leave ample room for machinery operation and it is possible to grow 600,000 lettuce plants, three crops per year. This is the kind of project Charles McIntosh envisaged, but never built, in 1841.

storing 1,000 cu. ft each, and the main reservoir in the front range cellar storing 2,110 cu. ft. Liquid manure was produced in a tank filled with pigeon droppings, guano, soot, and the water from the closets in the gardener's house; a forerunner of hydroponics, this fed the plants.

Charles McIntosh having visited gardens all over Scotland and England, including Frogmore, had combined all that he saw in the forcing houses at Dalkeith. Methods of water supply, heating, and ventilation meshed together, to form a highly integrated environmental package (70).

Charles McIntosh designed and built his most sophisticated glass range in a kitchen garden for Neill Malcolm at Poltalloch on the west coast of Argyllshire (71). The walls round the 300 ft by 300 ft garden were heated by hot water, as at Dalkeith. Behind the 19 ft north wall were the usual store and workrooms, apartments for the workmen and furnaces. In front of this reflecting wall were eleven gable-roof glass houses and two lean-tos providing the proper environment for pears, peaches, apricots, pineapples, grapes, melons, cucumbers and tropical plants. A section through each house would show a varying combination of water tanks and heat ventilation devices, varying with the requirements of the different species. The cucumber house [above] and the melon house [below] serve to demonstrate the degree to which McIntosh tempered the climate (72). Both houses, which are of the same construction, are also heated by one boiler [n] at the back of the wall that separates them. The pipes [f] which supply the heat below the earth beds, have vents [q] which allow the heat to pass into the house

58

when the heat becomes too great. The house is heated by a single pipe [h] running along the top of the side walls. The ventilation is the most sophisticated. Air is drawn through large grilles in the front of the house and hot air is allowed to escape through the lantern running along the ridge. During the cold Scottish winter, it is necessary to temper the outside air by drawing it through fire clay ducts [i] running underground and projecting through the wall of the plateau on which the glasshouses are constructed above the garden. As can be seen on the plan, every other air duct [i] passes under the terrace walk and rises in the cavity wall that separates each house and discharges outside air through vertical tubes [l] embedded in the wall. Air movement is caused when these small tubes pass the hot water pipes. The other alternative line of air ducts [i] runs under the entrance of the house and into a chamber below the walkway. Its end opens [r] below the hot water pipes in the back wall and other nozzles [r] allow air to pass through the iron walkway grating into the house. Thus a constant supply of outside air was brought to a desired temperature and charged with sufficient humidity before it reached the tender foliage and shoots of the plants.

McIntosh's most ingenious application of the cast-iron gutter and machined wood glazing bars was in an 1841 design to cover the kitchen garden at Dalkeith with a structure similar to commercial glasshouses today. He took as his model the new railway termini, particularly the North Midlands Trijunct railway sheds at Derby, designed by Francis Thompson and Robert Stephenson and built between 1838 and 1841 (73).

The 220 ft by 240 ft garden was enclosed with a large-scale ridge and furrow roof construction similar to that used in Paxton's Great Exhibition building some eleven years later. McIntosh believed that this type of construction could be extended over a hundred acres (74).

Some Victorian kitchen gardens were expected to produce a great variety of flowers, fruit and vegetables; grapes, figs, peaches, plums, apricots, cherries, gooseberries, currants, raspberries, strawberries, oranges, lemons, tropical fruits, peas, kidney beans, cauliflower, scarlet runners, young potatoes, salads. These all required varied artificial climate. McIntosh solved this problem with an extensive system of portable glass partitions running on iron rails. These combined with fixed partitions enclosed a variety of areas allowing varied temperatures within the structure. The wood and glass skin was to be supported by a wrought and cast-iron truss (fig. 3 and fig. 4) and a beam formed from a cast-iron gutter and an iron 'suspension rod' (figs. 5 and 6). This 20 ft by 40 ft structural module was supported on round 'architectural' cast-iron columns that transferred the gutter water to cisterns below the floor. The periphery columns at 20 ft centres rested on a stone plinth and supported a cast-iron structural gutter around the house (fig. 2). The sliding wall sashes below these gutters were on 'gunbarrel' rollers. One sash slid behind the other, or the sash could be completely removed. A ventilating lantern provided an operable gap all along the ridge for summer ventilation. Winter ventilation was drawn by ducts at 10 ft centres from the periphery wall of the platform on which the building was constructed. Each interior column was sup-

ported by a slab spanning a small reservoir of rain-water. A hose connected to a pump could draw out this water to spray the plants and fill the heating vases. The superfluous water in the reservoirs was piped to a central cistern used for the boilers.

The most interesting part of McIntosh's environmental machine was the hot water heating system. A huge circular vault was to be constructed under the very centre of the house (fig. 9 and fig. 10). The building was divided into four heating zones (fig. 7), and three boilers [a] fed hot water in pipes to each zone. Besides radiation from the pipes themselves, ornamental cast-iron vases (fig. 8) were positioned along them in each quadrant, a total of ninety-six for the building. The vases were shaped in such a way that convection currents of water rose up the middle and the cooler water descended to the return pipe. The lids were tight fitting and provided a steam-proof dry atmosphere; a humid atmosphere was created by removing the lids. In the summer, all the lids were removed and the vases were filled with pots of ornamental flowers. Under the center vault (fig. 9) stair was the boiler water reservoir [a]. The flue [c] is shown in fig. 10. It transferred the smoke and gases from the twelve boilers to the main horizontal flue [d] and to a chimney hidden in the woods. This main flue [d] paralleled a 7 ft by 7 ft service tunnel running from the vault to an outside door. Coal was to have been brought through the tunnel [f in fig. 10] and ash taken away through the same passage. Combustion air for the boilers was drawn down the tunnel by convection currents. These details are similar to the tunnel for the Great Conservatory at Chatsworth (1836–40).

75 Dutch intensive farming under glass around Naaldwijk, a centre of the glasshouse district, Westland.

5 The Industrialization of Horticulture

Solar radiation is our planet's major source of energy, accounting for 99.8 per cent of the world's total power input (the other 0.2 per cent coming from interior and gravitational tidal energy).

Photosynthesis, the chemical process of plant growth, is the planet's fundamental means of storing the sun's energy. A year's total land plant and microscopic ocean algae growth yields at least 40×10^2 watts or 110,000,000,000 tons of organic matter. All living organisms, including man, are dependent on this supply of energy for their very survival.

A plant utilizes only the solar energy in the visible and near-visible portions of the light spectrum. The food manufacturing process of photosynthesis operates after chlorophyll absorbs this light and combines carbon dioxide from the air with water and other nutrients from the soil, producing oxygen and the carbohydrate substances.

All life is dependent on this simple formula for plant growth:

$$6CO_2 + 12H_2O \xrightarrow[\text{chlorophyll}]{\text{light}} = C_6H_{12}O_6 + 6O_2 + 6H_2O$$
carbon + water chlorophyll = glucose + oxygen + water
dioxide

The carbon dioxide content of the earth's atmosphere today is between 300–350 parts per million. It is interesting to note that in past millennia, in periods of incredible plant growth, this concentration was ten to a hundred times greater than today. These prehistoric plants produced the fossil fuels, the oil, natural gas, coal, and carbonates that we are busily depleting today. It is, therefore, no wonder that controlled-environment experiments that maintain a high carbon dioxide concentration in glasshouses and phytotrons have produced exciting results.

Respiration is another important chemical process and is a characteristic of all living things, both animal and plant. Although the term was originally used to denote the breathing of animals, its use has now been extended to cover those processes, of which breathing is only a part, in which chemical energy in organic compounds is released from living organisms.

The process of respiration is in fact the reverse of photosynthesis, with the oxidation of carbohydrates yielding energy, some in form of heat, carbon dioxide and water. The complete oxidation of 180 gms of glucose, for example, releases approximately 700,000 calories.

$$C_6H_{12}O_6 + 6O_2 = 6H_2O + 6CO_2 + \text{energy}$$
glucose + oxygen = water + carbon
dioxide

This potential heat in the form of food maintains life and provides for animal and human work.

A plant also transpires. It is the means that the plant uses to cool itself by giving off water from its leaves. Vast quantities of water are lost from irrigated deserts where plants, left exposed directly to the sun, transpire to keep cool. During daylight hours, green plants are both photosynthesizing and transpiring. At night photosynthesis stops for lack of light, but respiration continues to produce carbon dioxide concentrations as high as 1,000 parts per million near the ground, a good reason for the removal of flowers from hospital rooms at night.

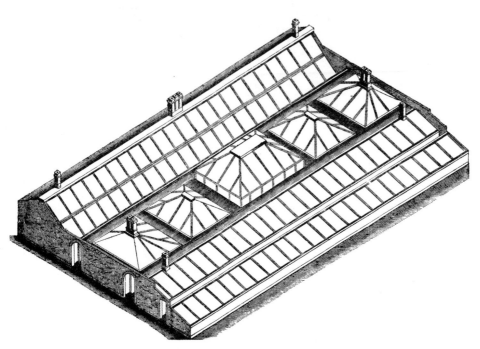

Plants require subtle combinations of light, heat, water vapour, carbon dioxide and oxygen at all stages of their development. A new field of phyto-engineering has developed to study the delicate environmental balance that maximizes growth and hardiness. Most countries have advanced research groups, like the Phyto-Engineering Laboratories for the U.S. Department of Agriculture; the Environmental Research Laboratory at the University of Arizona; the Environmental Control Division, N.I.A.E. at Silsoe, Bedford, England; Instituut voor Tuinbouwtechniek, Wageningen, Holland and the Ruthner Co., Vienna. These groups have built their phytotrons (controlled environment chambers for plant growth), artificially lighted plant growth rooms, natural light (glasshouse) cabinets and monitoring devices, just to study the results of varying environmental conditions.

Plants flourish when the two environments, air and soil, meet certain requirements. The air must have a combination of proper temperature, moisture, carbon dioxide and oxygen, while its movement helps increase carbon dioxide intake through the small stomata openings in the leaves. The soil or root environment must have a balanced and correct temperature, moisture content, nutritional value, aeration and pH (acidic content). Once these are achieved, the plant must receive the right light intensity.

Glass is transparent to most solar energy reaching the earth's surface. It allows the passage of visible and near-visible light (.3 to 3 microns), which is necessary for photosynthesis. All objects, human beings included, emit long-wave radiation. Glass is opaque to this radiation

of 3 to 30 microns, the kind given off by the soil, a masonry wall, or the plants themselves after being struck with short-wave radiation. The glasshouse effect is simple in the extreme. Solar short-wave radiation can enter the glasshouse, but the longer (infra-red) waves from the plants and soil cannot radiate out again. This raises the air and soil temperature for free, as it were. Heating pipes, braziers and the like radiate long-wave energy which is also trapped by the thin tegument. Though the glass enclosure protects plants from heat loss by direct wind and convection, heat loss does occur by conduction through the glass and infiltration through joints.

The glasshouse is therefore an environmental machine that traps solar energy by maximizing plant temperature, retains the moisture of transpiration, encloses a finite volume for carbon dioxide enrichment, and protects the plant from insects, disease and urban pollution. It is an environmental device which horticulturalists use to nurture several crops a year with little regard to the natural season, thus producing very high yields on an ever-decreasing commodity, land. In fact, as we shall see in this chapter, inert material fed with nutrient solutions can replace arable land. This new field of hydroponics in experimental glass towers built for cities and in desert areas demonstrates exciting potentialities.

An attempt is being made in this chapter to show that the spirit of horticultural experimentation in the seventeenth, eighteenth and nineteenth centuries has new dimensions today, and that the control of environment has reached a sophistication that was beyond the imagination of J. C. Loudon. It is possible for technology to have

76 This urban glasshouse, a prototype fruit and vegetable growing complex for urban plots, was designed by A. Forsyth of Isleworth, London in 1836. It looks every bit as modern as the buildings designed now by, say, James Stirling. The glasshouse supplied the house to which it was attached with fruit, flowers and vegetables in one compact unit that reduced the amount of side glass and was easier to heat. The angles of the glass roof are designed to provide the best light for the particular crop.

77–79 Top: huge boilers, thermostatically controlled day and night, are housed in a glasshouse and distribute heat to a vast area of glass. Below, left: an oil-fired portable stove for heating and enriching the atmosphere with CO_2 by using carbon fuels. Below, right: a fan-powered hot water radiator hangs from the roof of a Dutch glasshouse.

a beneficial, as well as a destructive influence on man's natural environment. The technical devices produced by a long heritage of horticultural experimentation offer a solution to the problems of feeding the world's population, by eliminating starvation with quantity, and malnutrition with quality, controlled environment food (76).

The University of Arizona's Environmental Research Laboratory units in Mexico and Abu Dhabi dramatically demonstrate how a small diesel engine can run a simple desalination plant and inflated plastic greenhouses. It produces no pollutants but can manufacture crops of tomatoes, egg-plants, peppers, and salad vegetables on arid land. Imagine a diesel engine producing peppers and you will understand what it is all about.

The idea of growing vegetables and flowers in a short period of time for pleasure and profit has been with us for a very long time. One of the most amusing accounts is in a book printed in London in 1717, which is a translation from the High Dutch of Doctor George Andreas Agricola of Ratisbon. The book's long title conveys the good doctor's excitement: *The Artificial Gardiner, being a discovery of a new invention for the sudden growth of all sorts of Trees and Plants. Whereby gardens may be stocked with Variety of plants and fruit-trees; and forests raised upon the most barren grounds in a very short time, also how to produce flowers in the midst of Winter, the whole confirmed by experiment.* The book contains an article called 'How to raise a Salad in Two Hours Time': That salad is supposedly grown thus:

... take the Ashes of Horse Litter and burnt Moss, mix them well together, and moisten them frequently with the Water of a Dunghill, drying the Mixture from time

to time in the Sun, till at length you have a Compost, or prepar'd Soil proper for the reception of the Seeds you intend to Sow.'
The mixture requires:

... Heat equal to that of the Sun in July, and Two Hours time the Seeds will sprout and put forth Leaves, if Care be taken to keep them moist with Dunghill Water during the Operation.'

Horticultural glasshouses can be found in countries throughout the world; in Europe especially in the rose-growing region along the French Riviera, or the Island of Jersey, in Russia and Scandinavia, but most especially in the compact countries of Belgium and Holland. In 1965 Holland had 15,600 acres (6,339 hectares) under glass, one quarter of the world's acreage. By 1969 the total had increased to 17,600 acres, (7,124 hectares) which amounts to an increase of 500 glass acres a year (75).

Holland, the most densely populated agro-urban country in the world, has an average population density of 355 inhabitants per square kilometre. Six to seven million Netherlanders are concentrated in the west of the country (the major glasshouse area), and the problem facing economists and urban planners is how to create living, working and recreational space for a population which yearly devours an average 7,600 acres (3,100 hectares) of agricultural land in town expansion and development.

Two remedial measures have been taken to increase food production: the reclamation of large areas of fertile land from the sea, for example the Zuyder Zee polder, and the switch from agriculture to horticulture, by truck farmers using glass to intensify their land production. In

63

1950 with the help of 5,500 acres (2,200 hectares) covered with glass, Holland produced some 500 million guilders' worth of fruits and vegetables. In 1968 with the help of over 17,000 acres of glass, the total production was some 2,000 million guilders' worth, making Holland, one of the world's smallest countries, a leading exporter of food.

Mass producing quality fruits and vegetables at a high rate in a competitive market requires extensive labour-saving devices. Inside the glasshouse, the Dutch land becomes a veritable machine. Automatic heating, ventilation, irrigation and fertilizing systems, carbon dioxide enrichment equipment, systems of cold storage, internal roads and canals, along with high-quality glasshouse manufacturing, produce quality food at low cost (77–79).

The South Holland glass district, which contains over seventy per cent of all the glass in the Netherlands, lies in a triangle formed by the Hook of Holland, Leiden and Gouda. The area is of prime importance to Holland's national economy, as seventy per cent of the South Holland produce is exported. The Westland, one of South Holland's two horticultural centres, is formed by a triangle of The Hague, Maassluis and Hook of Holland, with Naaldwijk at the centre. It is an intensive vegetable growing area, the principal glasshouse products being tomatoes, peppers, melons, cucumbers and lettuce (81).

As urbanism encroaches on the countryside, a conflict of interest can arise between the city dweller and the farmer. The townsman's desire for more open space and freedom from built form can interfere with livestock and crops. However, the future requires that people be integrated into the countryside, and the trend of building

64

in the United States, Britain and Western Europe shows a greater development in the surrounding country than centre city. Frank Lloyd Wright's Broadacre City, once scoffed at as too rural, is essentially the model of what has been experienced in the last few years. Instead of devouring land, office, factory and the farm could make a happy marriage beneficial to all. On one hand, housing enjoys open land around it for views and vistas; fields and orchards could add enormously to this sense of being in nature. On the other hand farming could also benefit from a direct recycling of human wastes back to the soil, local marketing and a readily-available labour-force at harvest times. But this takes co-operation. The Danes, whose development has been intimately connected to the farm, have built high-density housing around Copenhagen, particularly in the north and north-west suburbs. These tower-blocks and high-density, low-rise developments are situated among farmed areas. Parks are laced with a myriad of bicycle paths affording access along the edges of fields to recreation areas. The Benelux countries, by necessity, have also demonstrated that farming, including agricultural, horticultural, and animal husbandry industries, can exist side by side with other industries and urbanism (80).

Flevohof is the Netherlands' attempt to provide urban man, so accustomed to frozen vegetables and packaged meats, with an understanding of farming and the countryside. Flevohof is 350 acres of Eastern Flevoland, a polder reclaimed from the Zuyder Zee, seventy-five miles northeast of Amsterdam. Built by a foundation supported by several agricultural organizations, Flevohof has a model

80, 81   Far left: Dutch glasshouses generally have a smaller span than those in England or the U.S.A. They fit in with the scale of the agro-urban countryside. Left: Dutch lettuce crop covered by short-span wood and glass system. The pipes overhead are an automatic sprinkler system. The pulleys and cords on the columns adjust ventilation. Portable furnaces in the background provide heat and CO_2 enrichment.

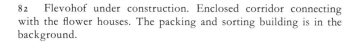

82   Flevohof under construction. Enclosed corridor connecting with the flower houses. The packing and sorting building is in the background.

pig, cattle and chicken farm; an agriculture farm where wheat, corn and potatoes are grown; a dairy where cows are milked, butter churned and cheese cured; mushroom houses; one large glasshouse in which tomatoes, cucumbers, lettuce, melons and beans are grown, and another glasshouse where roses, carnations and chrysanthemums are harvested. These areas are connected by heated corridors and interspersed with subsidiary demonstration pavilions designed to bridge the gulf between the town and the farmer. Flevohof is an agrarian microcosm portrayed realistically to demonstrate how intensively Dutch soil is cultivated and why Holland is one of the world's greatest exporters of agrarian products (82).

Before the advent of railways, nearly all commercial production of fruits and vegetables had to take place within or on the edge of towns and cities. This was the era when the horse and cart brought the produce to market and returned with a load of horse manure from the city stables. With the advent of the railways, market gardeners, with their glasshouses, moved away from the polluted air and poor light conditions of the city to areas like the Lea Valley between London and Cambridge. The railway-line put the produce within an hour's reach of the morning markets in London. Motor transportation has today allowed many English glasshouse farmers to move even further away. Though a majority of the glasshouses are still to be found in the Lea Valley between Hertfordshire, Sussex and Essex, huge areas of glass have been removed to the southern coast and the Isle of Wight, which is a little warmer and gets more sun. In 1965 there were 3,647 acres under glass in England and Wales and by 1970, 4,211 acres, an increase of 100 acres per year as compared to the Netherlands' 500 acres per year. The major crops produced under glass are tomatoes, lettuce, cucumbers, chrysanthemums, bulbs, pot-plants, carnations and roses.

The English and Dutch farmers use aluminium, galvanized steel or wood structures almost exclusively. These glasshouse structures are normally stationary, but horticulturalists also use houses on rails, moving them along to new areas after the seedlings have gained their strength. Whether mobile or stationary, these structures are normally covered with structural aluminium or steel glazing-bars that hold horticultural glass in dry (neoprene) glazing gaskets or the traditional mastic. Most glass panes are 16 to 24 in wide, and overlap one another, with a small film of condensation providing a positive seal against infiltration (83).

The Dutch house is usually low with a small span but, when put together, covers vast areas and encloses enormous volumes. The English, on the other hand, prefer larger houses spanning thirty to eighty feet. These large shiny structures look imposing in the country landscape, and their large volumes regulate rapid fluctuation in temperature (86, 87).

The English glasshouses are assembled from prefabricated parts delivered by lorry to the site—even as far away as Turkey and Russia. The parts are joined with simple connections: bolts, screws, or friction clips. Glazing-bars have slots in them to take special headed bolts that slide to eliminate tolerance problems. The building is easy to assemble: merely tip up the truss and

columns, attach the purlins, then bolt on the glazing bars and snap in the glass with aluminium or neoprene caps, or stainless-steel clips.

In North America new types of buildings using rigid or flexible plastic skins to cover wood or metal structures are becoming increasingly popular. The plastics that have been used are flexible polyethylene, polyvinyl chloride, polyvinyl fluoride and polyester, or the rigid polyvinyl chloride, fibre-glass, and acrylic.

Plastics have been around for a very long time (polyethylene sheet film for example was developed in Britain in 1938) but its use in building is relatively new. It is therefore useful to describe briefly the application of these plastics to greenhouses.

Polyethylene greenhouses are usually covered with 4 to 6 mil film on the outside and 2 to 4 mil as an inside lining to prevent heat loss. Polyethylene is the cheapest film on the market and can be purchased in widths up to forty feet, which is enough to cover small structures. It has a similar light transparency to glass, though it allows the escape of infra-red energy at night. One would imagine that this results in lower temperatures, but condensation on the inner side of the film retains the heat. Two layers of polyethylene can reduce fuel requirements as much as 40 per cent. The biggest disadvantage of polyethylene is its poor resistance to ultraviolet disintegration and consequent short life of nine or ten months in sunny climates. An ultraviolet-resistant variety costs half as much again but lasts from twelve to eighteen months. The farmer, in weighing low capital costs against high maintenance costs, should consider the skin of his houses as an

expendable item and part of the running costs. *Polyvinyl chloride* film is manufactured in four- to six-foot widths which must be electronically sealed to make an impervious membrane large enough to cover a greenhouse. Present vinyls last from twelve to twenty-four months and cost more than polyethylene, but with an added ultra-violet inhibitor, have been known to last up to four years. Many vinyls are not satisfactory for greenhouse films because they attract dirt and dust from the air and are subject to attack from fungi. *Polyvinyl fluoride* film, now being tested, has not been available for greenhouses but has been used extensively to coat lumber and aluminium siding and fibre-glass panels because of its excellent resistance to weather (up to twenty years). *Polyester* film, available in widths from 36 to 51 in, is a high strength weatherable film. Though it may last from four to five years on a greenhouse, it costs as much as double-strength glass, making its use questionable for a commercial greenhouse. *Rigid polyvinyl chloride* is manufactured in flat or structural-corrugated sheets. Its light transmission characteristics and durability have not been fully tested, but it lasts approximately five years. Sagging occurs at high temperatures and the material must be fixed properly because of its high thermal expansion coefficient. The panels will not burn but will char and melt. *Rigid fibreglass* panels, mainly corrugated, are becoming increasingly popular particularly in the American West where the light intensity is high and there are dramatic and destructive hail storms. Inexpensive grades will weather on the surface and reduce light transmission. Quality grades are often coated with polyvinyl fluoride or resin on the exterior and

83, 84   Facing, left: travelling glasshouses on steel rails are popular in England and Holland. These vast moving structures protect a crop until it is ready to be independent, then move to protect other areas. Facing, right: timber, gothic-arched, fibreglass-covered greenhouse. A ventilation fan is at the end and a polyethylene tube runs down the centre. Longwood Gardens.

85   Above: carnation house in Colorado formed with 42 ft clear spans of galvanized cold-rolled steel sections, covered with corrugated fibreglass. It is ventilated with side fans and warmed by hanging unit heaters. Ickes-Braun Glasshouses.

86   Eight wide-span glasshouses, each 428 ft long and interconnected by glass corridors, cover an area of 6·65 acres. All are heated from the boiler house on the right. The roadway loops through the centre of the houses. This horticultural factory is in Barnham, Sussex. Frampton Ferguson Ltd.

87   In contrast to the Dutch multi-span glasshouse, these galvanized steel structures span 86 ft unrestricted, enabling large machinery to work. Cambridge Glasshouse Co., England.

88 Above: greenhouse formed of four-part arches composed of steel tube. Cloth woven from polypropylene tape is stretched over the arches. This new material is claimed to have a life of 2½–3 years. Its open weave disperses heat and relieves condensation problems. Steel Tube Division of Tube Investment and Polyweave Ltd., England.

89 Right: one-acre pneumatic structure covering tomatoes near Wooster, Ohio. The polyethylene film is held down by a cable network. The polyethylene tube suspended from the cables, when inflated, carries heated or cooled air or CO_2 enrichment. Goodyear Tyre and Rubber Company.

90 Below: a vast air-supported greenhouse project by Frei Otto.

91 The United States Pavilion at Expo. '67, Montreal. The exo-skeleton supports an internal glazing system of 600 acrylic domes.

92 Acrylic covered pool at Regency Hyatt house, near O'Hare International Airport, Chicago. Architect, John Portman.

carry guarantees up to fifteen years. The panels are made from polyester resin reinforced with glass fibres, which have a high strength-to-weight ratio, but burn easily. *Acrylic sheet* is widely used in special conservatory construction. This clear, flexible plastic can be readily shaped to form domes and transparent bubbles. Though only $\frac{1}{16}$ in thicker than double-strength glass, it is ten times more impact resistant and so is used in special locations, on eaves and gutters, where ice and snow would break glass. It is easily scratched, sensitive to solvents and burns readily. The Climatron in the Missouri Shaw Botanical Gardens and the American pavilion at Montreal are covered with acrylic skin (84; 85; 88; 91; 92).

A variety of framed structures covered with plastic film or sheet are being constructed and tested by university horticulture departments and experimental extension services throughout North America. Most of the structures are made of timber. Some of these framed houses are air pressurized to support the plastic skin under snow and wind, while others have air pumped between the layers of double skin.

Strong plastic membranes and electric motors bring close to reality Loudon's dream in 1822 of covering vast tracts of land with an artificial environment. Frei Otto's early greenhouses with a skin supported by pneumatics have recently culminated in a study for a 3 km² air-supported cover, to give a temperate climate to an Arctic city (90).

The air-supported structure enjoys its popularity in horticulture for very good reason. Most traditional greenhouses are made up of two components, the supporting framework and the external cladding. To maximize light transmission to the crops, larger glass panes and larger spans have been tried. The aluminium or steel and glass structures become more sophisticated but also more expensive. In the United States, small-span timber frames supporting plastic films are inexpensive enough to compete with pneumatic structures, but in countries where wood is expensive, the air structures with no structural members to shade the crop have a future.

An example of one such horticultural air structure was inflated in 1969 near Wooster, Ohio, in a co-operative research project of the Goodyear Tyre and Rubber Company, which developed the plastic structure, and the Cleveland Greenhouse Vegetable Growers' Co-operative Association (which wanted to grow three crops a year). The greenhouse is 100 ft wide, 428 ft long and covers one acre of lettuce or tomatoes. In contrast to traditional greenhouse practice, which relies on hand labour, the obstruction-free enclosure allows common farm equipment to carry out planting, cultivating and harvesting. Modest-sized blowers maintain the pressure without blocking vehicular passageways. As in any transparent air structure, making a durable transparent plastic film is the major object of research. Once this problem is solved, the structure requires only steel or plastic cables and a blower to support large sheets of tough, flexible plastic film over trees and buildings. The created environment has its own temperate climate and filtered air for the plants (89).

Pneumatic structures are new to horticulture and with their potential, deserve a brief history and discussion of their basic design principles. For these I am indebted to

69

93   Left: using a net over the thin polyvinylchloride film takes advantage of its reasonable ageing characteristics and the strength of the net. Two counter-weighted flaps can be seen at the end of the greenhouse. Wageningen, Holland.

94a–d   Right: automatic storm switch arrangement: excessive sideways movement at the top of the structure causes the counterweight (w) to oscillate vertically, completing an electrical circuit through microswitches (s). Far right: Three methods of anchoring pneumatic horticultural structures: simple water sac, and modification, which would be less liable to water loss through accidental puncture; anchoring the film to the wall separating watercress beds. ▷

A. E. Canham.* As far back as 1911 in Britain, Dr F. W. Lanchester proposed the idea of flexible fabric buildings using air pressure as support. In his patent for the *Construction of tents in field hospitals, depots and like purposes*, balloon fabric was recommended, with an inflation pressure of one inch water gauge, increasing to two or three inches in storms. The pneumatic concept appears to have been little used until 1948 when the Cornell Aeronautical Laboratory developed air-supported 'radomes' to shelter radar equipment for navigation and defence systems. The first recorded use of pneumatics in horticulture was in a patent application for *Inflatable Greenhouse* made in Britain in 1954 by F. Micklewhite, but unfortunately it was allowed to lapse because of a lack of commercial interest. In 1958, early attempts to construct and test houses were made at Michigan State University, and then in Washington State. In Britain the first air-supported greenhouse was inflated on a Hertfordshire farm in 1960, but it had environment problems because no provision was made for ventilation. By 1965 a similar polyethylene structure, this time with ventilation control, was erected in England by the National Vegetable Research Station, and later two more were put up at the Electrical Research Station at Shinfield in England. Parallel researches were being developed by the Agricultural Research Centre for the United States Department of Agriculture.

The shape of an air-supported structure made from a rectangular sheet of film approximates a semi-cylinder, with quarter spheres at each end. In still air, the stresses which will depend on the air pressure will be primarily circumferential and longitudinal. A relatively low pressure differential is adequate to maintain the shape in the absence of disturbing forces, though this depends on the weight of the material used. In practice, the normal support pressure required is that which provides an adequate degree of rigidity under practical conditions. Most of the experimental installations have shown a pressure of 0.25 in water gauge to provide adequate rigidity under normal weather conditions but this needs to be increased to 0.35 to 1.0 w.g. in storms and gale-force winds. Disregarding the weight of the material, the circumferential stress under still air conditions will be uniform and equal to the force tending to pull the film vertically from its anchorage. For a structure of radius (r) ft, inflated to a pressure (p) lb/ft², this will be given by

$$L = p \cdot r$$

where L is the upward lift in pounds per linear foot on each side of the house. A steady wind at right angles to the structure will add to this lift, since it creates a negative pressure on the top and on the leeward side. The effect of a gust of wind will be greater still, since transient stresses will make an uplift greater than those in a steady wind. The material used for air-supported greenhouses is normally 500 gauge ultraviolet inhibited polyethylene. When new, it has a tensile strength at breaking point of 3,240 lb/in² which falls to 2,480 lb/in² after twelve months' exposure, according to manufacturers' data. It is clearly necessary to use the lower figure as the critical one for

* A. E. Canham, *Air-Supported Plastic Structures—Materials and Design Factors*. Applied Research Section, Department of Horticulture, University of Reading.

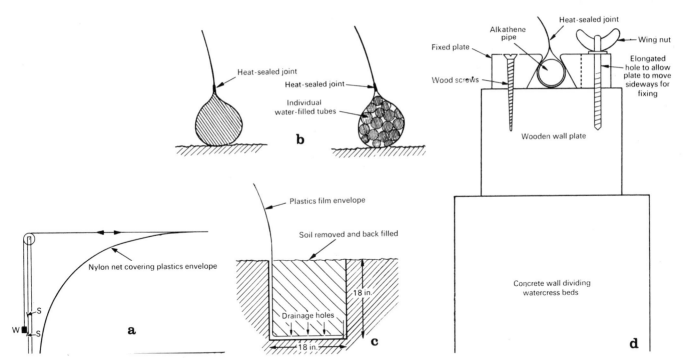

design purposes, together with a factor of safety of at least 2 and preferably 3. This limits the permitted uplift to 50 lb per linear foot, which in turn restricts the width of the structure to 20 ft at a pressure of 1.0 in w.g., or to 40 ft at a pressure of 0.5 in w.g. even without taking into account the additional lifting forces superimposed by strong wind conditions. Using the recommended American design practice for Nissen and Quonset huts, which approximates an air house pressurized to 0.75–1.00 in w.g., the weight of about 110 lb per linear foot is necessary on each side of a house 20 ft wide in order to withstand winds of 88 mph and an inflation pressure of 0.75 in w.g. This is almost three times the lifting force due to inflation pressure alone in still-air conditions. There will, of course, be a simultaneous longitudinal stress which will be about half the circumferential stress under still air-conditions, but there are also likely to be additional local stresses due to irregularities of shape, rigid fixtures, etc. Therefore, even without taking into consideration the additional forces imposed by high winds, the best way to cover a large area is with a number of narrow structures, rather than a single large one. For structures over 30 ft wide, stronger materials than polyethylene should be used.

Ventilation is an important factor in greenhouse design and air-supported structures are no exception. In order to prevent excessive heat in summer, twenty or more air changes per hour are required, depending on the height of the house. But systems can be simple; one fan can pressurize the building while another, activated on thermostatic demand, brings outside air into the house. The air inside is forced out through a counter-weighted ventilator flap that remains closed when no ventilation is required. Since the structures are dependent on the continuous operation of a fan, it is necessary to have an emergency source of supply, either battery powered d.c. fans or engine-generator power sets. There is usually enough time to switch over, because lightweight skins take a considerable time to lose their total volume, even in a wind. While an internal pressure of 0.3 in appears to be adequate under normal conditions, this allows for too much movement in stormy weather. To improve stability under such conditions the pressure should be increased to at least 0.5 in. This is easily done in pneumatic structures by switching on the ventilator fan while restricting the aperture. The experimental structures at the Instituut voor Tuinbouwtechniek, Wageningen, Netherlands, are equipped with a device that senses excessive lateral motion and operates a micro-switch for additional fan pressure (94a).

To maintain air pressure under a flexible canopy there must be an anchorage system round the base, which should be as simple, cheap and air-tight as possible. Digging a trench for the plastic film is one simple method requiring extra labour. Another system is to have a tube full of water round the periphery of the structure. A. E. Canham staked down a wood periphery curb with a short plastic film strip to seal the curb into the ground. The air-supported film was then wrapped around a batten, nailed to the curb. The experimental house in Wageningen provided anchorage by means of a tension net rather than the thin p.v.c. fabric. The net was held down by spiralled steel rods screwed into the ground (93; 94b,c,d).

Human beings can easily adapt to their physical en-

95 Access ladders to thermostatically controlled ridge ventilator motors. These vents are in constant movement in the summer, controlling the air temperature. Frampton Ferguson Ltd, Sussex.

96 The central control panel monitoring seven climatic zones in a botanical greenhouse of the Chicago Horticultural Society. Day and night temperatures are programmed for each zone. The panel controls roof and side vents, the heating and cooling equipment and the misting of two propagation areas. Below are the aspirated sensing modules which draw in air at plant level to determine its temperature. Wadsworth Electric and Ickes-Braun Glasshouses Inc.

97 Hot-air heating distributed at low level to 3·4 acres of tomato plants at Sun Ripe, Vega, Texas.

vironment. Small changes in light intensity, temperature and humidity levels are not critical to our existence, and generally speaking, few physiological changes occur when our physical environment is less than ideal. This is not true of plants. The right balance of light, air, temperature and moisture is essential to the plant's self-sustaining process, photosynthesis. Insufficient light, or the wrong temperature, for even a brief interval, can inhibit their growth to a marked degree.

Plant requirements for normal growth vary throughout the day and even throughout the plant's life. All the requirements for normal growth or any combination of factors designed to force, inhibit, or alter plant growth, can be controlled by an environment system that is designed specifically for horticultural applications. The heart of the automatic climate system is the control panel that monitors information from several sensing devices and operates fans, roof and side vents, heaters, humidifiers, and carbon dioxide enrichers according to a predetermined programme for the particular crop. *Aspirated sensing modules* are placed throughout the enclosed houses at crop level. These fan-assisted devices draw in a large air volume across solid state thermistors, which are a refinement on bi-metallic thermostats, to provide a high degree of sensitivity to air temperature. *Photoconductive cell control modules* automatically relate the greenhouse temperature to the light level. As the light intensity decreases, a switch reduces the temperature. The *wind and rain control module* is also a sensing device that by-passes the temperature control by automatically closing the ventilating sash whenever a drop of rain touches it.

An anemometer is built into this module to measure and record wind velocity and close vents automatically when a pre-set limit is reached, regardless of temperature. The control panel contains several sequential timing controls and twenty-four-hour time-clocks. These controls operate cyclic lighting, automatic watering and hydroponic systems to a predetermined programme. The *night temperature set-back module* has a time signal that reduces temperature at night to match natural conditions (95–97).

These plant factories take advantage of the natural climate and simply modulate it when it becomes undesirable. The whole system is dependent on electrical power, and so a diesel or gas engine-generator should be available in emergencies, and an alarm system connected to the farmer's house monitors all equipment.

In the past few years, plant physiologists have begun to isolate the environmental factors required for optimum plant growth. The isolation of these factors has led to the automatic control of glasshouse environment and an increasing interest in industrial techniques in plant production (98).

Industrial plant production is based on the familiar system of conveyor belts; raw materials are fed in one side and the finished product emerges at the other. The advantages derived from the industrial system of plant growth are mainly in terms of space and labour economy, extremely important in urban areas where large quantities of food are required and labour is expensive. The traditional glasshouse has paths allowing the gardener to service and harvest the crop, which require an extra volume that has to be heated or cooled. In the new system,

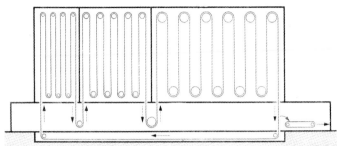

98–101 Left: the Ruthner phytocyclon. The test chamber is divided into two zones for study of sprouting and roots. Above: plant growth from seed to fruit can be divided into sequences of growth requiring different optimum environmental factors. Industrial plant production conveys plants through different environmental chambers until they are large enough to market. Right: looking up the glass-fibre tower at the School of Gardeners at Langenlois, Austria. Far right: the glass tower erected in Vienna for the 1964 International Horticultural Exhibition has over 1,000 m² of cultivation area and occupies only 63 m² of ground. Ruthner & Co., Vienna.

man-movement is replaced by plant-movement, making planting, watering, hydroponics and harvesting easier on a production line in a smaller, more controlled artificial environment. Plant growth, from the seed to the fruit, can be divided into a sequence of different physiological requirements; thus the plants are moved through a number of climatic chambers, meeting optimum environmental factors at every stage of growth. Every plant can be held in favourable light conditions, while the motion helps carbon dioxide absorption and decreases insect and disease problems (99).

It is easy to visualize horizontal industrial plant production, but the tests that have been carried out since 1958 on conveyor systems in Vienna have resulted in high-rise tower glasshouses. In 1963 Othmar Ruthner and his company, Industrianlagen für Pflanzenbau, built two prototype loop conveyor glass towers for the School of Gardeners in Langenlois, Austria. The first was a glass-covered hexagonal-based cylinder 10.57 m high, the second, a corrugated polyester glass-fibre cylinder 22.65 m high. The potted plants, resting on free swinging supports, rise and descend on a continuous conveyor within the cylinder. A water tank at the bottom immerses the base of the pots in water or nutrients (101).

Ventilators at the top and bottom of the towers produce a chimney effect that is very effective in the summer. Hot air recirculates in the oil-fired hot air system. Circulation provided by the movement of the conveyor, gives an even temperature to the whole tower. Heating and labour costs were found to be lower than in the traditional glasshouses at the School in Langenlois

and so following this success, another tower glasshouse was erected in the exhibition grounds at Vienna for the 1964 International Horticultural Exhibition. It is still in use for commercial growing. The tower follows the general design of the two earlier structures, with corrugated polyester fibre-glass attached to the steel structure. The unit is especially impressive when one considers that it has over 1,000 m² under cultivation and covers only 63 m² of land. The tower is 41 m high by 9 m diameter and the conveyor, which is 240 m long, runs in three loops with six columns of plants, each 38 m high. The 282 plant supports have a capacity of 35,000 pot plants. When, however, seedling plants are being raised, these are in containers which hold at least 80 plants and a total capacity of over 200,000 plants. The conveyor, driven by a 5.5 h.p. motor, provides normal speeds of 0.60 to 2.8 m per minute with circuit times ranging from nine hours to two hours per revolution. The top speed provides one complete revolution in 80 minutes, which facilitates the selection of plants for marketing (100).

Horticulturalists, plant physiologists and engineers meet in Vienna for a yearly symposium on industrialized plant production. Their current work gives all the indications for developing automatic plant factories (102).

Population increases in the twentieth century have generated a great deal of research into making habitable hitherto barren parts of the world, such as the cold Arctic and hot wind-swept deserts, although the equipment necessary to support human and plant life is often complex. One of the most exciting 'real' projects has come from the Environmental Research Laboratory at

the University of Arizona in Tucson. The project, called *Controlled Environment Agriculture for Coastal Desert Areas,* is another example of horticulture using sophisticated environmental equipment. Desert irrigation has been in operation in California and Arizona for a considerable time. The increasing demand for water, however, has already upset ecological systems in the West and, with the proposal to have pipe lines tap the rich water source of the Canadian Rockies, the ecological consequences could be disastrous. Desert irrigation is expensive and absurd. Millions of gallons of water are pumped into open troughs only to evaporate or be wasted by the plants which, in a desert, transpire 95 per cent of the water they absorb, just to keep cool. The challenge then was to surround the plant with an economical environment that would keep it cool and provide a water vapour gradient (high humidity) at the leaves to reduce transpiration. Since plants and vegetables are mainly water anyway, the ideal would be to have a closed system, in which most of the water introduced would leave in the form of consumable vegetation. The best enclosure was found to be an inflated polyethylene air structure.

Since the earth has 20,000 miles of desert on the edge of sea water, desalination could provide the key to making the desert bloom. With the help of a Rockefeller Foundation grant, a simple system was developed at Puerto Peñasco, on the Gulf of California in north-west Mexico and later installed in the Shaikhdom of Abu Dhabi, five hundred miles south of Kuwait. The heart of the system is a simple diesel engine which powers an electric generator, since most coastal areas are not connected to any grid for electric power. The generator powers the pumps and fans and furnishes lighting for the research station. The engine of this diesel-electric set is conventional, except that it is fitted with waste heat recovery equipment, for with most internal combustion engines two-thirds of the input fuel energy is wasted in cooling the engine and producing hot gases. In this engine, however, there is no radiator and both the hot jacket water and the exhaust gases are fed into a waste heat exchanger which heats a sea-water stream to 160°F—for pumping into the desalting plant. The hot sea-water goes into an evaporation chamber where air is forced in and saturated by the sea-water, which is then distilled in a condenser cooled by fresh sea-water at temperatures normally between 76°F and 81°F. The water being distilled actually comes from pits dug near the sea where marine debris is filtered and the temperature is constant, winter and summer. Ninety per cent of the waste water, used in distillation but not itself distilled, has a temperature of 90°F at the end of the process. It can be used to heat the controlled environment chamber on extremely cold days or at night. Normally it is pumped back into the sea, though it could be used to heat or cool an agricultural-industrial town. At Puerto Peñasco, 2,400 gallons of distilled water are produced daily (103; 104; 106; 107).

The plant chambers are made of inflated polyethylene. Depending on the weather, their temperature can be raised with the 90°F waste water, or cooled with fresh sea-water. The operation takes place in a packed column heat-exchanger, as the air within the chambers is con-

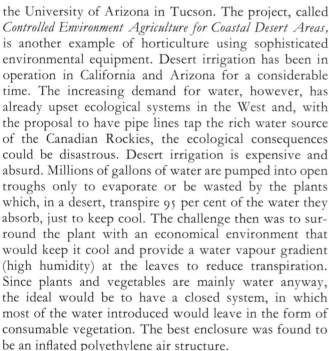

tinually circulating in a closed loop through the exchanger's spray. The packed column is not an evaporative cooler, but a direct contact heat exchanger. It is filled with corrugated asbestos which disperses the water and increases the heat transfer area. Sea-water at 76°F to 81°F flows in at 120 gallons per minute, and on hot days at 140 gallons per minute, thus keeping the interior close to the sea-water temperature. Winter and summer, damp tropical conditions prevail within the greenhouses, which are sheltered from the hot winds and sand storms of the surrounding desert. The air is very near 100 per cent saturated, which prevents the plants from transpiring. Only 5 per cent of the water that plants would require in the open desert is needed in the closed environment. Desert countries can, therefore, afford to desalinate the water required by the plants. In the winter, the closed environmental chamber acts as a condenser itself. Water from the sea-water spray condenses on the cold plastic membrane. As much as 1,500 gallons a day forms in this way, which allows the distilled water from the desalination plant to be stored for use in the summer months. The greenhouse is made of two 23 ft x 100 ft inflated plastic structures. These polyethylene structures are connected at both ends by short underground tunnels which allow for circular air movement. The tunnel at one end has a ramp to each inflated house and an air lock to the outside. The air lock contains the electronic control panel, which monitors outside wind speed and regulates the internal pressure accordingly, while it also monitors inside humidity, temperature and amounts of water and nutrients fed to plants. The other tunnel contains the two

inflation blowers, the two air circulation fans and the asbestos-packed column heat exchanger. The two $\frac{3}{4}$ h.p. circulation blowers can inflate the two chambers in less than two minutes. Once the structures are up a primary $\frac{1}{6}$ h.p. centrifugal inflation blower maintains a positive pressure of .01 to .02 psi. When storm winds begin to blow, the pressure inside the house must be increased for structural stability. This is done with a 1 h.p. blower which switches on automatically. The two $\frac{3}{4}$ h.p. circulation blowers (used in the initial inflation operation) circulate the air in the two chambers in a two-minute counter clockwise cycle. This air, forced against the spray in the heat exchanger, picks up the sea moisture and temperature that maintains the house to the desirable degree. Travelling at 100 ft per minute, the air creates a turbulence which helps the leaf absorb carbon dioxide.

The 12 mil. light-stablized polyethylene covers are fastened into redwood sills on concrete curbing around the periphery. Starting from the polyethylene film in its packing box, it takes four men $2\frac{1}{2}$ hours to fabricate and erect both chambers of the greenhouse. The houses are 23 ft wide because the 10–14 mil. polyethylene is manufactured only in 32 ft widths. Though the material is light-stabilized and has a yield strength of 1,400 psi., the intense ultra-violet radiation in the desert gives it an expected life of twelve to fourteen months, which at its moderate cost of $85 per chamber (in 1971) makes it an operational expense, like the diesel fuel.

The whole integrated system that provides power, water and food in the desert does not pollute the outside air. The plants' photosynthesis in the closed environment

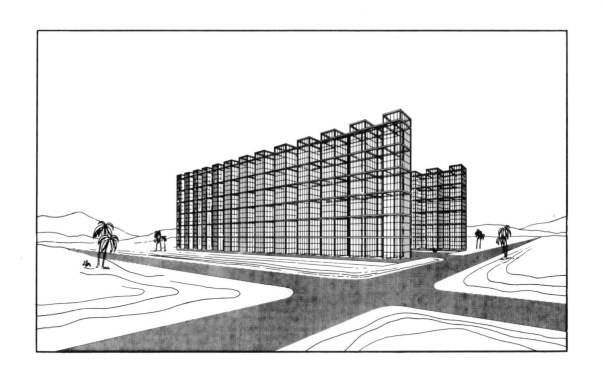

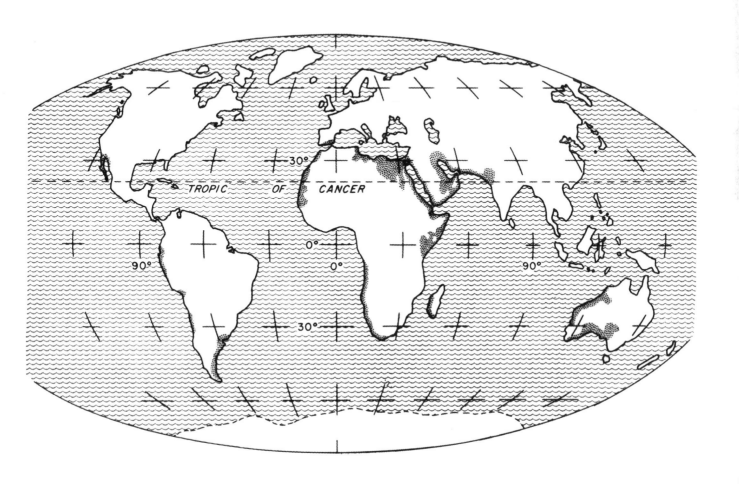

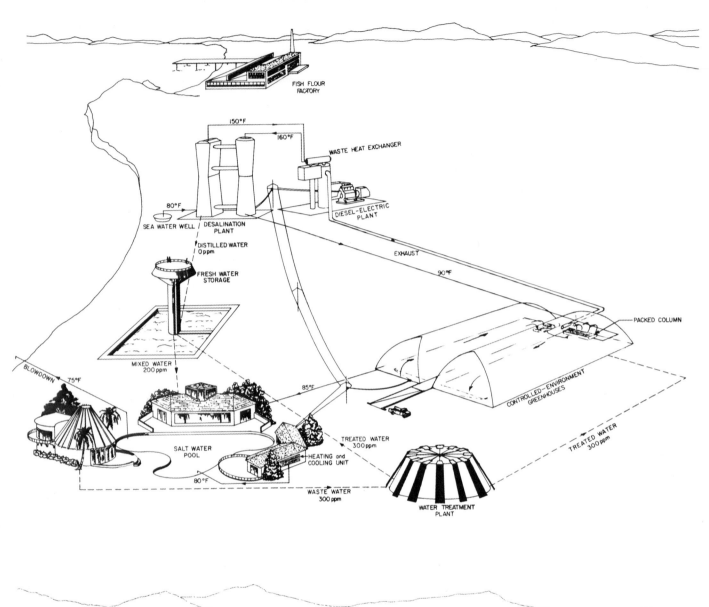

FISH FLOUR FACTORY

150°F

160°F

WASTE HEAT EXCHANGER

DIESEL-ELECTRIC PLANT

80°F

SEA WATER WELL / DESALINATION PLANT

DISTILLED WATER 0 ppm

FRESH WATER STORAGE

EXHAUST

90°F

PACKED COLUMN

MIXED WATER 200 ppm

BLOWDOWN 75°F

85°F

CONTROLLED-ENVIRONMENT GREENHOUSES

TREATED WATER 300 ppm

SALT WATER POOL

HEATING and COOLING UNIT

TREATED WATER 300 ppm

80°F

WASTE WATER 300 ppm

WATER TREATMENT PLANT

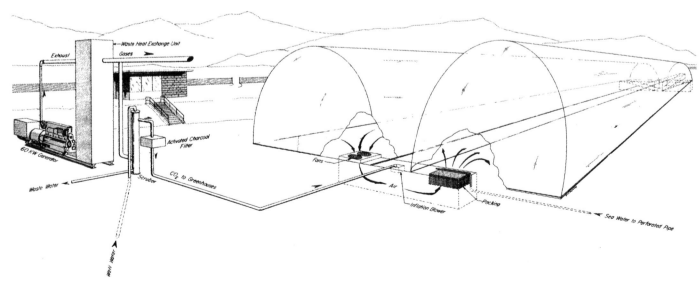

Exhaust

Waste Heat Exchange Unit

Gases

60 KW Generator

Activated Charcoal Filter

Waste Water

Scrubber

CO₂ to Greenhouses

Fans

Air

Inflation Blower

Packing

Sea Water to Perforated Pipe

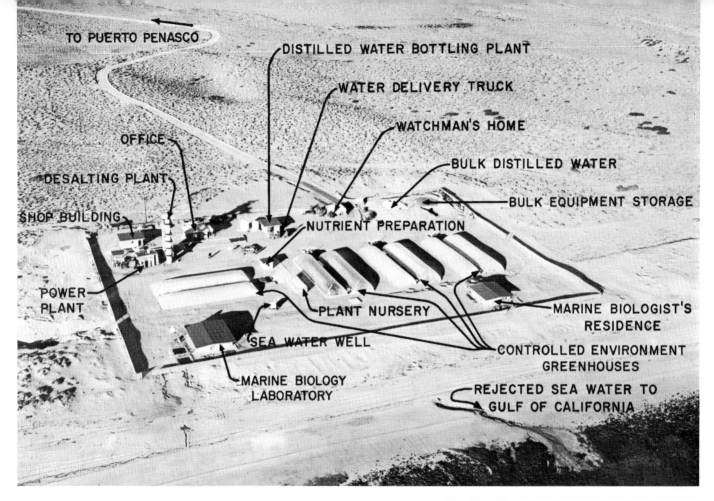

TO PUERTO PENASCO

DISTILLED WATER BOTTLING PLANT

WATER DELIVERY TRUCK

WATCHMAN'S HOME

OFFICE

BULK DISTILLED WATER

DESALTING PLANT

BULK EQUIPMENT STORAGE

SHOP BUILDING

NUTRIENT PREPARATION

POWER PLANT

PLANT NURSERY

MARINE BIOLOGIST'S RESIDENCE

SEA WATER WELL

CONTROLLED ENVIRONMENT GREENHOUSES

MARINE BIOLOGY LABORATORY

REJECTED SEA WATER TO GULF OF CALIFORNIA

104, 105, 107   Facing, above: diagram of Total Flow system for a viable living unit. Facing, below: diagram of environmental control system showing diesel engine–generator combination, waste heat exchange, the exhaust scrubber and filter with CO_2 entering the controlled environment plant chambers. Below: design of controlled environment plant chambers. Environmental Research Laboratory, University of Arizona.

106   Puerto Peñasco, Mexico, experimental unit. Environmental Research Laboratory, University of Arizona.

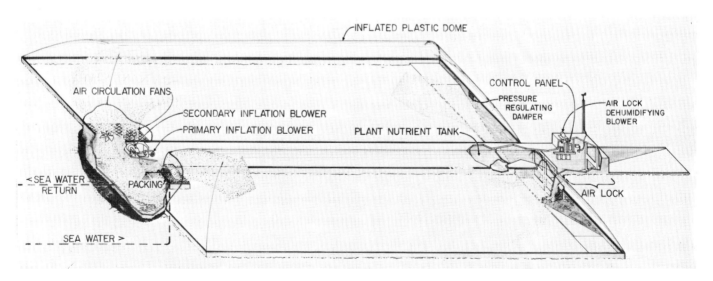

INFLATED PLASTIC DOME

AIR CIRCULATION FANS

CONTROL PANEL
PRESSURE REGULATING DAMPER

AIR LOCK DEHUMIDIFYING BLOWER

SECONDARY INFLATION BLOWER

PRIMARY INFLATION BLOWER

PLANT NUTRIENT TANK

SEA WATER RETURN

PACKING

AIR LOCK

SEA WATER

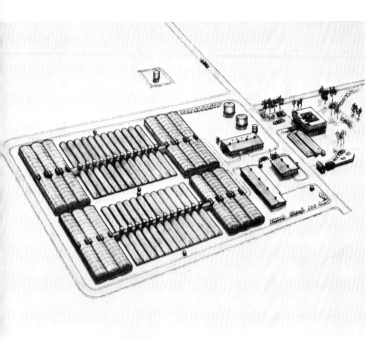

108   Left: Arid Lands Research Centre, the Abu Dhabi power/water/ food system. The greenhouse complex is composed of $2\frac{1}{2}$ acres of curved, rigid frames covered with polyethylene and 48 air-supported bubbles, covering a further $2\frac{1}{2}$ acres. Environmental Research Laboratory, University of Arizona.

109   Above: egg-plant and pepper crop in the controlled environment greenhouse at the Puerto Peñasco unit.

quickly exhausts the supply of carbon dioxide, and so it is important to supply additional carbon dioxide from the exhaust of the diesel engine, which is turbocharged to provide excess oxygen and minimize carbon monoxide. The exhaust, cleaned in a sea water scrubber and filtered through activated charcoal, raises the level of carbon dioxide within the chamber to far above the 300 parts per million found in the air outside. As the other parameters for plant growth (light, temperature, moisture, nutrients) are maintained near the optimum, raising the carbon dioxide gradient has caused significant increases in the production of crops (105).

Vegetables are either directly seeded in the sand (radishes, spinach, beets, onions and carrots) or transplanted (tomatoes, egg-plant and peppers). Plastic irrigation systems either spray the growing area from aboveground sprinklers or release small droplets at soil level. Liquid-feed solution supplies the nutrients. The heat and intense light mature the crop more rapidly than crops grown outside. Bibb lettuce in the inflated chambers matures in thirty-five to forty days, compared to fifty-eight to sixty days in the open fields. This allows more crops to be harvested (109).

The Environmental Research Laboratory in Arizona was given a grant from Shaikh Zaid Bin Sultan Al-Nahyah in 1969 to design and inaugurate a power/water/food package for Abu Dhabi (108). The projected economics are promising, for, if two million pounds of vegetables can be harvested each year in Abu Dhabi from the ten-acre unit, the cost per pound of the produce should be very low.* The Shaikhdom grows only a few seasonal vegetables at an

inland oasis, and has to air-freight the bulk of high-quality vegetables from the Lebanon, putting the price as high as $1.50 per pound.

The Abu Dhabi experience should enormously enrich the data available on controlled environment horticulture. The potential is enormous, considering that adjacent to coastal deserts and a hundred feet or less above sea level, there are 2.6 million square miles of barren land in the world.**

We have therefore a man-made environment situated in the uninhabitable desert, which can provide a tropical climate for plants to grow, perhaps during a sand storm or in the heat of the mid-day sun. We are entering an age of machine-produced foodstuffs made possible by the internal combustion engine, generator, electric motors, and non-corrosive plastics which horticulturalists can now take for granted as their new bricks and mortar. Certainly there is much for architects and engineers to learn here.

* So far, yields have been high, 102 tons of cucumbers and 70 tons of tomatoes being harvested per acre. Compare U.S.A. 12 tons (cucumbers), 30 tons (tomatoes) per acre. By the end of 1971, vegetable production for the five covered acres was in the region of 3,000 pounds per day.

** This description is based on reports and papers by Carl N. Hodges and Carl O. Hodge of the Environmental Research Laboratory, University of Arizona, Tucson.

6 *The Private Conservatory*

During Queen Victoria's reign, when industrial cities belched smoke and absorbed human labour at a prodigious rate, the private conservatory, as J. C. Loudon had already said in the 1820s, was 'not indeed one of the first necessities, but one which is felt to be appropriate and highly desirable and which mankind recognizes as a mark of elegance and refined enjoyment'.

From the distance of a century, Walter Benjamin, the twentieth-century German intellectual, looked back on a Europe of which Victorian England was very much a part. In *Paris, Capital of the Nineteenth Century*, he wrote:

> For the private citizen, for the first time the living-space became distinguished from the place of work. . . . From this sprang the phatasmagorias of the interior. . . . The collector dreamed that he was in a world which was not only far off in distance and in time. From this epoch spring the arcades and the interiors, the exhibition halls and the dioramas. They are residues of a dream world.

On the Continent of Europe winter gardens were part of the society of dignified men and elegant ladies who could parade around these great architectural structures in Schoenbrunn, Brussels, Vienna, Berlin, Karlsruhe and St Petersburg. In England, the small private conservatory evolved from the exotic and romantic botanist's hot house. It became a place of retreat and recreation, which enjoyed great popularity throughout the nineteenth century and, in North America, well into the twentieth.

The late seventeenth and the early eighteenth centuries had also seen the garden as the setting for the banqueting hall and summer supper-house. The hall gave the garden more accessibility, while the garden gave the hall isolation from the mundane world. The hall doubled as a winter storage place for the exotic plants and so changed roles with the seasons (110).

Thomas Langford noted this in his work *On Fruit Trees* (1696):

> Greenhouses are of late built as ornaments to gardens, as summer and banqueting houses were formerly, as well as for a conservatory for tender plants, and when the curiosities in the summer time are dispersed in their proper places in the garden, the house being accommodated for that purpose, may serve for an entertaining room.

Christopher Wren, with the help of Nicholas Hawksmoor* and John Vanbrugh built a beautiful orangery at Kensington Palace for Queen Anne in 1704 that was also intended as a winter promenade and summer supper-house. The orangery in Kew Gardens, now used as a museum, was built for Augusta, the Dowager Princess of Wales, in 1761, in the same tradition.

Orangeries can be found at Chatsworth, built for the First Duke of Devonshire in about 1700; Durham Park, Gloucestershire; Brickling Hall, Norfolk; Ickworth, Suffolk; and the 327 ft long orangery at Margam Abbey, Glamorgan was the largest in Britain, built in the late eighteenth century.

Garden orangeries were often turned into glasshouses just by replacing the slate or tile roof with glass. These were early architectural conservatories, so called because their pilasters, cornices and friezes followed formalist

* See Kerry Downes, *Hawksmoor*, p. 64.

110, 111 Left: the eighteenth-century Architectural Orangery at Wye House, Mills River Neck, Maryland. Above: the large domed architectural conservatory at Alton Towers by Robert Abraham, still extant.

styles and attitudes of the day. Architectural styles were generally opposed by the botanists and gardeners who wanted these conservatories to cater more directly for the plants and their environment.

In 1718 Richard Bradley, Professor of Botany at the University of Cambridge, presented an early design for a decorative greenhouse that conformed to the 'Rules of Architecture', and at the same time considered the welfare of the plants. Bradley measured the success of such a house by the health of the plants in winter and the usefulness of the room for entertaining in summer (112).

A compromise between the architect and the gardener is illustrated in a structure erected at the villa of M. Caters de Wolfe near Antwerp by the London firm of W. & D. Bailey, in the 1820s. Two hothouses, curved to maximize the sun's impact, frame the architect's conservatory. Architectural conservatories can still be found throughout England and Europe as at Belton House, Grantham, where a beautiful architectural orangery designed by Jeffry Wyatville in 1820 sits above the garden.

In 1814, the Fifteenth Earl of Shrewsbury started building Alton Towers, his estate in Staffordshire. He employed hundreds of artisans and labourers to build a house and a vast garden in a valley, which was to contain a pagoda, Greek temple, caves, waterfalls, 'a cottage for a blind harper', moss-houses, an imitation of Stonehenge, Indian temples and conservatories. Shrewsbury was just one of the many nineteenth-century eccentrics seeking the elusive Garden of Eden with his vast fortune. One of the architects that he employed toward the end of his life was Robert Abraham, who built a small Greek-styled archi-

tectural conservatory with a glass roof and another huge one with seven gilded glass domes. This conservatory, still standing today, was built on the same large scale as the conservatory designed by the architect, Charles Fowler, at Syon House, a magnificent 280-ft structure with domes in the Italian style (111).

Another architectural conservatory familiar to Londoners is in Kew Gardens, but was originally built adjoining Buckingham Palace. In fact, three identical conservatories were built at the palace from the designs of Sir Jeffry Wyatville (1776–1840), one was converted into a chapel (now a gallery), one remained as a conservatory, and the third was transported in 1836 to Kew where it was fitted with a new Perkins's high-pressure water boiler. The conservatory, though seemingly of masonry construction, has a cast-iron truss on cast-iron columns supporting the glass roof [114] (see *Artificial Climate* 1).

The Scottish architect, William Burn (1789–1870), designed a highly decorative white sandstone conservatory for the Duchess of Buccleuch at Dalkeith Park, south of Edinburgh. The conservatory was built before the arrival at Dalkeith in 1840 of the industrious writer-gardener, Charles McIntosh. Huge trusses from a central chimney supported the glass and wood frame roof of the conservatory. These over-sized trusses kept out the light, but were in keeping with the aesthetics of the building. The raised platform of polished pavement housed two hot water boilers which were considered the first used in Scotland. With the smoke pouring out of the centre chimney, no doubt staining the glass below, the conservatory must have been an impressive sight (113).

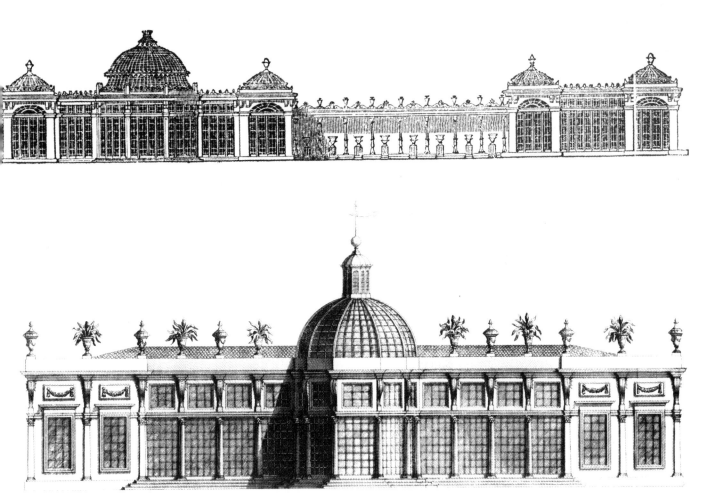

112   Architectural Conservatory by Richard Bradley, Professor of Botany at Cambridge. A glass dome was proposed directly over the most tender plants 'to receive more of the sun's warmth'. The Corinthian columns were as thin as possible to maximize insolation. The walls were covered with white Dutch tiles reflecting the light to the orange, lemon and myrtle trees inside.

113, 114   Below, left: circular conservatory at Dalkeith Palace, near Edinburgh, by William Burn. Right: the architectural conservatory at Kew Gardens was moved there from Buckingham Palace in 1836. Sir Jeffry Wyatville.

115   Fern house at Ashridge (1864) by Matthew Digby Wyatt.

I. K. Brunel, the brilliant railway and iron steamship engineer, designed, in collaboration with the architect Matthew Digby Wyatt, Paddington Station in London as we know it today. Wyatt contributed the station's decoration which is inventive and sympathetic to the spirit of new transportation and to Brunel's structural details. It was designed between 1853 and 1854 (Wyatt had been on the Building Committee of the 1851 Crystal Palace). Much later, even after the great conservatories at Chatsworth, Kew and Regent's Park had been built, he was to resort to masonry, producing a neo-Greek architectural fern-house for the Earl of Brownlow and, even later, an architectural conservatory at Castle Ashby, Northamptonshire, right at the height of the glass and iron mania. But even Paxton, in his role of architect, used masonry and tried nearly every style imaginable (115).*

Mrs Beaumont's all glass and iron conservatory at Bretton Hall was, in 1827, one of the first curvilinear houses to stand as a transparent object in the garden (see *Liberal and Improving Age*). In contrast to the architectural conservatory, this environmental chamber developed from a horticulturalist's search for light and new construction materials, iron and glass (116).

The rise in popularity of the conservatory had indeed been rapid as demonstrated in the writings of Humphry Repton, the noted landscape designer at the turn of the century. In 1803 in his *Observations on the Theory and Practice of Landscape Gardening,* he proposed that the greenhouse resemble a nurseryman's stove, which would make it suitable for the flower garden, but not be near the main house. By 1816, however, Repton, being a man of the

fashion, was humming a different tune, for in his new book *Fragments on the Theory and Practice of Landscape Gardening,* he advocated connecting the house to a conservatory to alleviate the 'parlour's formal gloom'. He illustrated this with a delightful pair of before-and-after drawings, a graphic technique used throughout his beautiful books. After all, even the poet William Cowper wrote 'who loves a garden loves a greenhouse too' (117).

Repton had given advice at Sezincote, Gloucestershire, on Indianizing the gardens and new villa designed by Samuel Pepys Cockerell for his brother-in-law Sir Charles Cockerell, a retired Indian nabob. The house was finished in 1806 and its attached Oriental conservatory (118) was one of two important examples of the Indian style, the other being the Royal Stables and Riding House with its glass roof designed by William Porden for the Prince of Wales at Brighton. Repton was then summoned to Brighton to give his opinion on the style of architecture for the Pavilion that the Prince Regent wanted to remodel. He found the stables in the garden 'a stupendous and magnificent building', and proposed Indian-styled alterations to the Pavilion, which were to influence the actual remodelling by John Nash. Repton produced the beautifully illustrated *Designs for the Pavillon at Brighton* (1808), commissioned by the Prince, in which he presented a new idea in garden architecture, aspiring to make the garden 'enriched with productions of every clime' that would not be affected by seasonal change. He proposed to surround

* George F. Chadwick, *The Works of Sir Joseph Paxton,* chapter on 'Paxton the Architect'.

84

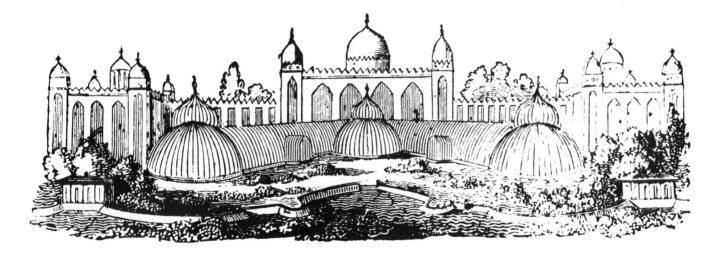

116 The Indian style, made popular by the Prince of Wales at Brighton and by Humphry Repton's work at Sezincote, was easily adapted to iron and glass conservatories. This one is proposed by Loudon as a necessary extension to any gentleman's house.

117 Above: 'parlour's formal gloom'. Below: the delights that come from an attached conservatory (Humphry Repton).

118   The Indian Villa at Sezincote, near Moreton-in-the-Marsh, Gloucestershire. Designed by Samuel Pepys Cockerell with the influence of Humphry Repton, it was finished in 1806. The conservatory is on the left.

119   The 'flower passage' proposed by Humphry Repton to enclose the Prince of Wales's garden at Brighton, forming a perpetual garden connected to the new Pavilion.

120   Facing: an attached conservatory and billiard room at Theydon Grove, Epping. Both built by Weeks & Co., Horticultural Engineers. ▷

it with a glazed corridor or 'flower passage', a continuous conservatory linking the main Pavilion with the stables, a greenhouse, hothouses, an aviary, pheasantry, and an orangery that, with its glazed panels removed, could be transformed into a summer kiosk (119).

Even for the ordinary citizen, an attached conservatory became almost a necessity. Usually adjacent to the drawing-room, it was first considered mainly for feminine use as at the Grange, Hampshire, where it was put opposite the lady's chambers by C. R. Cockerell. The Papworth collection at the Royal Institute of British Architects has many drawings of attached conservatories, most of which have a small aviary between the conservatory and drawing-room. I. B. Papworth designed conservatories for London *clientèle* who wished to display their taste in the new gardening art even in the city. Throughout London's Belgravia, the remnants of these city conservatories still exist, though lead has now replaced the glass roofs.

A detailed example of this kind of city conservatory is presented in McIntosh's *Book of the Garden* 1853. The conservatory, designed by MacKenzie and Matthews, is an addition to a house in Scotland. Besides providing a plant environment and fountain off the drawing room, the boiler below heated a bathroom and the bath water, and so upgraded the gentleman's amenities, as a sort of nineteenth-century 'service module'. Two sliding doors, one of glass and the other of wood, separated the conservatory from the house. The owner could look out at the verdant world through the glass, close the view off completely when servants were watering the plants, or open it to let in the 'odoriferous aroma . . . which could

incite even a valetudinarian to quit his couch and take a stroll amongst them', as McIntosh observed. In order not to see the servant watering the plants, McIntosh suggested that a flower stage with a trap door and stair replace the fountain for the stealthful entrance and egress of those 'little' men.

By 1864, Robert Kerr's *The English Gentleman's House* takes for granted the necessity of a conservatory. No longer is it seen as a simple extension to the dwelling, but as an integral part of the way of life. One of the illustrations in the book is the plan of Somerleyton Hall, Suffolk. Its 100 ft by 100 ft winter garden nurtured a rare collection of plants interspersed with sculpture, rockwork, shellwork, fountains and pillars in masses of creepers and runners. This garden was no doubt the largest and most entertaining room of the house. Centred on the conservatory, Victorian house plans read more like recreation centres than our mundane houses of today (121–123).

The *Floral World* was one of many new periodicals on the art of horticulture available to the new middle-class conservatory owner in the later nineteenth century. In the magazine the editor, Shirley Hibberd, described the use of conservatories for civilized Victorian living.

Conservatories were obvious places to hold parties, but many parties were held just to show off the conservatory. At Wollaton Hall, gooseberries were a speciality served with great ceremony. At some dinners a fruit tree stood behind every chair so a guest could pick his own dessert, or, where there was one bountiful tree, the dinner table was arranged so that the hostess could sit in front of it and distribute the fruit for dessert. In a bad year, fruit

121 'He felt somewhat as if he were walking in an enchanted ground as he followed her into the large room, the windows opening into the conservatory, the whole air fragrant with flowers . . . the door into the conservatory was opened, and Meta cut sprays of beautiful geranium, delicious heliotrope, fragrant calycanthus, deep blue tree violet, and exquisite hot house fern; perfect wonders to Norman. . . . Margaret, I would give something for you to see the beautiful conservatory. It is a real bower for a maiden of romance, with its rich green fragrance in the midst of winter. It is like a picture in a dream. One could imagine it a fairy land, where no care, or grief, or weariness could come; as choice beauty and sweetness waiting on the creature within. I can hardly believe that it is a real place and that I have seen it.' Charlotte M. Yonge, *The Daisy Chain*. Drawing: Conservatory at Lessness by Messenger & Co.

122 'I built the conservatory, to be sure. Henrietta could not live without a conservatory', answered Mr Temple. 'Miss Temple is quite right,' pronounced Ferdinand, 'it is impossible to live without a conservatory'. Benjamin Disraeli, *Henrietta Temple*. (The drawing is of the Conservatory at Cherkley Court.)

123 '. . . Well, you shall see my conservatory, Captain Armine', said Miss Temple. So saying, she entered the conservatory, and Ferdinand followed her. 'Do you admire my fountain and my birds?' she continued after a short pause. '. . . Ducie [the Temple Estate] is Paradise', said Ferdinand. 'I should like to pass my life in this conservatory'. Benjamin Disraeli, *Henrietta Temple*. (Illustrated: the Winter Garden at Willaston, Harrogate.)

124 The Glass Wall at Chatsworth, 1848, built by Joseph Paxton.

might be bought and tied to the tree; for underlying the gaiety of this new recreation was a social rivalry in successful growing and unique exotic acquisition (129).

It was William Cobbett, the nineteenth-century writer concerned with industrialization, who noticed the unique moral contribution of conservatories in a changing society, which he describes in *The English Gardener* (1829):

It is the moral effects naturally attending a green house that I set most value upon. There must be amusement in every family. Children observe and follow their parents in almost everything. How much better during the long and dreary winter for daughters and even sons to assist their mother in a green house than to be seated with her at cards or in the blubberings over a stupid novel or at any other amusement than can possibly be conceived!

However, by the 1870s and 80s, the attached conservatory was often combined with a games room, smoking balcony, or music room to provide more than resting among the plants. An example is the attached conservatory and billiard room constructed by Weeks and Co. at Theydon Grove, Epping. The billiard table rested on brass rails embedded in the floor so that it could be pushed away for dancing and concerts. At one end of the billiard room was the smoking gallery fitted with an organ, the whole overlooking the conservatory and its fountain through large plate glass windows (120).

As the popularity of the conservatory grew, so did the demand for greater environmental control and size, which only intensified the debate between gardener and architect. The gardener's complaint was simple: too much

effort was put on the architecture to the detriment of proper environment for the plants. Robert Marnock (1800–89), Curator of the Royal Botanic Gardens at Regent's Park, succinctly put the position of the gardener in an article in the *Gardeners' Journal:*

. . . instead of spending £5,000 or £10,000 [$25,000] to cover a few square yards of ground with a mass of expensive but useless masonry, we would say, spend it in a manner adapted only to the growth of plants; and on this principle £10,000 would cover an acre of ground, or any quantity in the same proportion.

Marnock must have been pleased with Joseph Paxton's great conservatory at Chatsworth, built between 1836 and 1840. Though it cost some £33,000, its 123 ft width and 277 ft length enclosed three-quarters of an acre and had a 67 ft high roof. The conservatory was just a part of the enormous spectacle of waterworks, landscape, and exotics which Paxton's patron, the Sixth Duke of Devonshire, had built with some of his enormous wealth. The total landscape design transcended horticultural considerations. Visitors to Chatsworth passed the stepped waterfall, through the rhododendrons, bamboo, and artificial rockworks onto a platform overlooking the great glass structure. Inside the immense double doors, everything was subordinated to the spectators' escape into fantasy. The eight hot-water boilers that fed the seven miles of four-inch pipe were discreetly hidden below in vaults. A tunnel was ingeniously laid and fitted with a tramway to supply coal to the furnaces and remove the ash. The smoke passed through a tunnel and a chimney into the surrounding woods. At the height of the Great

125–27 Facing: the Great Conservatory, Chatsworth (1836–1920). Above: the figure in the centre dramatizes the size of the vast structure. Ventilation was provided through the arches in the foundations. Below, left: the central path, slicing through a profusion of palms, tree-ferns and bananas. Below, right: in 1920, with maintenance bills mounting after the First World War, the Great Conservatory was demolished. It withstood five attempts, but finally succumbed to dynamite.

128   Right: interior of Capesthorne Conservatory, Cheshire. The conservatory was 150 ft long and 40 ft wide. It formed a corridor connecting the library to the chapel. It was unfortunately pulled down around 1920, like its great contemporary at Chatsworth.

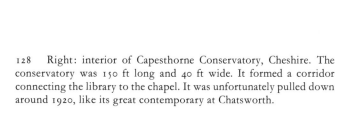

Conservatory's fame, it was filled with the most glorious plants from the Duke's vast collection, tropical birds flew among the branches of the palms, gold and silver fish swam in the pools below, and there were displays of large crystals and rock ores. The centre aisle was designed to allow visitors to glide though in an open coach and pair, as did the Queen, her Consort and the Royal Entourage in December 1843, when the conservatory was illuminated by twelve thousand lamps along the ribs. No expense was spared for the Royal visit and the response was rapturous.

The immense conservatory was made of wood except for the cast-iron columns that supported the laminated wood arches and doubled as rainwater pipes (see section in *Artificial Climate* 11). The roof was a curvilinear ridge and furrow. Paxton had previously experimented with the ridge and furrow skin on a pine house in 1833 and on a greenhouse against a brick wall in 1834. This prototype, and another 26 ft by 60 ft elliptical ridge and furrow hot-house gave Paxton enough confidence to use it on the Great Conservatory and, eventually, on the 1851 Crystal Palace (125, 126).

Paxton saved thousands of hours of work with his sash cutting machine which put grooves in the forty miles of glazing bar that enclosed the Chatsworth Conservatory. It is not clear how he managed to paint and glaze this glass mound, but he undoubtedly used a block and tackle, a less sophisticated form of the glazing platform in operation at the Crystal Palace. A cast-iron gallery, running around the periphery of the main space, enabled visitors to see all the exotics from above and gave the gardeners a perfect watering platform (127).

Before the Great Conservatory was finished, Paxton was working on a large conservatory for Edward Davies Davenport at Capesthorne Hall (Cheshire [128]). According to Professor G. F. Chadwick in his excellent book *The Works of Sir Joseph Paxton,* the building must have been designed before Paxton went on the Grand Tour with the Duke in October 1838. This conservatory, which formed an addition to the mansion was, however, not curvilinear like the Great Conservatory at Chatsworth. The framework of laminated wood arches that formed the main nave and two side aisles was curved like those of the Great Conservatory and the ridge and furrow skin was slightly pitched giving the appearance of being rectangular. He was later to draw a blotting-paper sketch of the Crystal Palace which recalled this form of construction (see *The Crystal Palace and after* below, especially ill. 206).

Paxton built other conservatories with the ridge and furrow skin before and after the Great Exhibition building of 1851. One that he built before was a small ridge and furrow flat-roof conservatory attached to Darley House, Darley Dale, not far from Chatsworth. Critics claimed that the ridge and furrow on the Crystal Palace would fall and cause vast damage to the exhibition below. In his own defence, Paxton requested and received a testimonial letter from Adam Washington, who was living at Darley House, and read it to the Society of Arts in November 1850, while the exhibition building was under construction. The cunning Paxton certainly had a way of rebutting his critics. This, combined with exuberance and ability, resulted in a fantastic and productive career, which

developed from garden apprentice to knighthood; with, of course, the help of one of the richest men in England, the Sixth Duke of Devonshire.

The conservatory wall was not an invention of Paxton's and could be found in many walled gardens in one form or another. But the conservatory wall that Paxton built at Chatsworth in 1848 is, as most of his building, very large and dramatic, being some 330 ft long. The original roof construction was, of course, ridge and furrow and similar to the extant glass wall at Burton Closes, near Bakewell, which was built around the same time (124).

The conservatory was not exclusively for the country, however: roofs in congested urban areas have always attracted the eye of the visionary. As land is scarce and expensive, it provides the ideal location for a sun garden. In London, several roof-top conservatories were built or suggested in the nineteenth century. This was rather courageous, since pollution from coal heating was infamous and glass was certainly difficult to maintain and clean. The recent London clean-air acts have, however, created an environment in which the roof garden should be reconsidered. If we use conservatory principles of the nineteenth century combined with the insulative plastics and heating devices of the twentieth, the roof-top, especially in a low-rise city like London, Paris or Amsterdam, could have a micro-climate surpassing any in the streets below.

Some of the first roof-top conservatories were on the upper terrace of the new market for Covent Garden, London, designed by Charles Fowler in 1827* for the Sixth Duke of Bedford. On the terrace above the east (Russell Street) entrance colonnade, the Duke had two conservatories built with four staircases leading to the street. Between the conservatories was a highly polished Devonshire marble fountain fed by tanks in the market roof that took water from an artesian well (130).

W. Bridges Adams, a major proponent of iron and glass construction and an urban visionary of the nineteenth century, proposed stripping off the existing roofs of London terraces and replacing them with roof gardens (132).

. . Gardens of this kind would be as in the East, the resort of the family in fine weather and in bad weather a warm greenhouse on the roof would be a more pleasant thing than a dark parlour. Scarcely anything could be conceived more beautiful than the enormous expanse of London roofs covered with shrubs and flowers. And it would be a perfectly practicable thing so to construct the greenhouses that they might be opened or closed at pleasure.

He appeals straightforwardly to fashion and snobbery: Every housekeeper might possess his own bit of Crystal Palace, his own fountains, his own flower-baskets, watered not by hand, but by art without labour, so that the lady of the house, by a process as easy as ringing a bell would effect this object. Think too of the wine parties, supper parties and open air dinners

* Charles Fowler was also the architect of the huge conservatory built for the Duke of Northumberland at Syon House in 1827 and the designer of Hungerford Market, erected in 1835.

129 The Saracenic and Gothic conservatory at Enville Hall, Staffordshire, built for the Earl of Stamford and Warrington around 1854. The 70 × 150 ft structure was designed and put up by horticultural builders Gray and Ormson of Danvers Street, Chelsea. The design was a decorative reaction to the unadorned conservatories at Kew, Chatsworth and Regent's Park.

130 The roof-top conservatories built for Covent Garden Market by the Duke of Bedford, its owner.

that might take place with the upper crust of London restored to its proprietors.*

The editor of *Cassell's Popular Gardening*, D. T. Fish, proselytized for the house-top conservatories for all:

Glass, through being so long and so heavily taxed, is still by many of the working classes considered a luxury beyond their reach. On the contrary, it is now among the cheapest of all roofing materials, taking into account its durability; being virtually indestructible, unless in the case of accidents.

He was not deterred by obstacles:

From the almost universal prevalency of sloping opaque roof, of course such structures have hitherto been rare. But they exist in sufficient numbers to prove the practicability of growing plants, flowers and even fruit, to perfection in crowded cities.**

The premises of Barr and Sugden, plant sellers in Kings Street, Covent Garden, were designed in 1875 by the

* From an article by W. Bridges Adams in *The Gardeners' Chronicle and Agriculture Gazette*, 14 June 1860.

** *Cassell's Popular Gardening*, vol. III, p. 46.

† Barr and Sugden's roof-top conservatory was not the first to be erected in London. The horticultural builder W. H. Lascelles had also built one above his offices at Bunhill Row, Finsbury.

‡ H. Noël Humphreys (1810–79), author, artist, contributed to Loudon's magazine as a young man and later to William Robinson's *The Gardener*.

§ Edouard André, a French writer on gardens, also contributed to magazines like William Robinson's *The Gardener*.

architects Spalding and Knight. The whole facade was a show-case for plants. In order to comply with the Duke of Bedford's lease, a flat lead roof was built under the floor of the roof-top conservatory (131).†

At Penllergare in Wales, a conservatory designed for Dillwyn Llewellyn was one of the first 'planted in admirable disorder' like a tropical forest. The idea was suggested by the explorer Schomburgk's description of the Berbice and Essequibo Falls in Guyana. An artificial fall of heated water splashed over the rockwork and into an aquarium in the middle of the conservatory, with an island of rockwork covered with ferns, orchids, and lycopodia. Tropical species floated on blocks of wood or hung in baskets suspended from the roof, all growing in wild profusion, imitating their native world.

The Natural or Picturesque Style became popular in the Sixties and Seventies, with such proponents as the writers H. Noël Humphreys‡ and Edouard André§ who turned away from Victorian geometry and individual specimen planting. Every effort was made to hide the iron structure and the enclosing glass roof and walls in order to recreate the natural exotic habitat of tropical Brazil, Africa, or India. The path leading to a typical enclosed 'tropical forest' would wind its way through the 'valleys of rocks' covered with Yuccas and other exotic plants which could withstand the English climate. A curved rock-work tunnel hid the conservatory door in its darkness. Once mysteriously inside, the visitor found the ground irregularly banked against the enclosing walls. Larger thickly branched trees, ferns, and climbing vines stood as a macabre backdrop to this verdant stage set.

131–32 Left: the roof-top conservatory of the nurserymen and florists Barr & Sugden at King Street, Covent Garden in 1875. Above: W. Bridges Adams proposed roof gardens for London. St Paul's is in the background of this drawing.

Some of the props were dead tree-trunks held with iron stakes just above the ground to prevent them from decomposing in the moist and dripping atmosphere; or rockeries, bubbling with tepid water and robed in moss and ferns which formed around the pools filled with bright tropical fish. Streams flowed between fragments of rock and boulders; above the fine gravel path and natural stone benches, the giant ferns, palms, and climbing Passiflora covered the roof with their dense foliage. Imported chrysalids matured into exotic butterflies that fluttered about the tropical flora.

The grand conservatory and its associated glasshouses could have only come about with the great affluence of the few in the nineteenth century. The conservatory's delight, as we have seen, was brought on with the efforts of gardeners, butlers, maids and labourers attached to each estate and city dwelling. This dependence on armies of labour, of course, contributed to the decline of the era of the private conservatory. As the glass began to crack and paint flaked from the sashes, which then rotted, and boilers burnt out their fire-boxes, decisions were made to do away with many great conservatories. Industry lured gardeners with higher wages, and fuel rationing in the First World War killed many of England's vast botanic collections. The Second World War was the *coup de grâce,* for survival was at stake and art, whether painting or horticulture, fell by the wayside. The twentieth century had brought with it other forms of entertainment, and transportation drew families away from their isolated islands of recreation. The conservatory seemed a little dull and mundane compared to picture magazines, the cinema, the automobile, and the airplane, which made trips possible even to the origins of the exotics.

The increased availability of foreign produce, especially with the introduction of refrigerated ships and rolling stock, brought a marked price reduction in foods once reserved for the rich. Market gardens of vast proportion began to grow under glass in the Lea Valley north of London and in other areas away from smoke and pollution. Glasshouse nurserymen* responded to the demands of the city's Victorian middle class who had money to buy produce but no land. By the turn of the century, the major cities were ringed by these large market nurseries, which reduced the need for private glass, resulting in its dismantling and destruction.

Tastes, moreover, were changing. William Robinson wrote an important book, *The English Flower Garden,* in 1883. In it he argued for a return to nature instead of the artificiality of the conservatory. His ideal was the English cottage flower garden. Robinson had caught the new mood against the conservatory, for the book sold out eight editions and had six reprints by 1903. There is no doubt that Robinson had a great deal of influence on the changing gardening scene, and was instrumental in closing the Paxton era with remarks such as these from *The English Flower Garden* demonstrate:

A few years ago, before the true flower garden began to get a place in men's minds, many of the young gardeners refused to work in places where there was no

* The nursery houses of Rochford, Larsen, Stevens, Shoults, Cobley, Pollard and Hamilton.

133 This conservatory and swimming pool in Los Angeles, built in 1913 by Lord & Burnham, recreated the Garden of Eden in the 1920s.

glass. A horrid race this pot and kettle idea of a garden would have led to; men to get chills if their gloves were not aired. I met the difficulty myself by abolishing glass altogether. . . . To bloom the rose and carnation in midwinter, to ripen fruits that will not mature in our climate, to enable us to see many fair flowers of the tropics—for these purposes glass houses are a precious gain; but for a beautiful flower garden they are almost needless and numerous glasshouses in our gardens may be turned to better use.

The United States was quick to make the conservatory stylish after the Civil War. The American industrialists, thriving in a time of peace and influenced by Victorian taste, demanded this symbol of perpetual spring in the quiet suburbs around Philadelphia, Pittsburgh, New York and Boston, or on their estate-retreats in Connecticut, upstate New York, and the Hudson Valley. Client references in the catalogues of two major conservatory manufacturers, Lord and Burnham of Irvington, New York, and Hitchings and Co. of Jersey City, read like a social register: names included Warren Delano, Jr, Helen Gould, John D. Rockefeller, John A. Roosevelt, W. K. Vanderbilt and J. P. Morgan, to list but a few. Later generations of glass house enthusiasts included John Jacob Astor, Jr, William Buckley, Jascha Heifetz, Mrs Thomas A. Edison, Dr W. J. Mayo, E. H. Maytag, H. S. Firestone, W. E. Boeing (133).

The American conservatory was not a shuttle-cock in the game of style as it was in England at the end of the nineteenth century. The structural simplicity represented at Chatsworth, Kew and Hyde Park, which was soon abandoned in England, remained an ideal in America. The mail-order conservatories in the American catalogues, limited in style, flourished all along the East coast and later to the suburbs of Chicago, San Francisco and Seattle.

The prominent architect, Alexander Jackson Davis, designed a significant Gothic Revival house for the ex-mayor of New York, General William Paulding, in 1838. The house, near Tarrytown, New York, was purchased later by a wealthy New York merchant, George Merritt, who named the estate Lyndhurst. Merritt hired Davis to build a tower and other additions to the house and also the so-called Merritt's Folly, the largest conservatory then in the United States. This great greenhouse, in a modified Saracenic and easy-to-construct Gothic style, was one of the few to be built using a decorative theme. Its dimensions were enormous for a private conservatory even by comparison with English models, for it was nearly 380 ft long, with two wings on either side of a central portion. This central hall was 80 ft long and 95 ft wide. On the north side were a carpenter's shop, bedrooms and games rooms for billiards, a gymnasium and a bowling alley. In the cellar were the boiler rooms, coal storage, mushroom cellar, water tanks and various potting implements and materials. But most spectacular was Merritt's 100 ft tower which rose behind the central hall. It was topped with a glass cupola, affording an elevated view of the surrounding estates. Merritt was said to have invested $100,000 in his horticultural ventures, which included a series of 250 ft long forcing pits built to the north of the conservatory and his collection of exotics and grapes. When he died in 1873, the plants were disposed of and the

134–6 Left: interior of the vinery in the Lyndhurst greenhouse, rebuilt by Lord & Burnham. Below: the central portion of the greenhouse, *c.* 1870. Facing, The National Trust for Historic Preservation has taken over Lyndhurst, and with the help of the Historic American Building Survey, is laying plans to restore the conservatory, here devoid of glass and of many wood glazing bars. Filled with the appropriate exotics, it will serve as a splendid memorial of a bygone age.

estate offered for sale. It then lay derelict until it was purchased in 1880 by Jay Gould, the railroad magnate, who re-fitted and re-stocked the glass structures. Soon after, on 11 December 1880, the great greenhouse caught fire from beams built into the chimney and was ruined. Undaunted, Gould hired Lord & Burnham to build a new structure on the existing foundations. These curvilinear structures are the first steel-framed greenhouses ever built in the United States. Ironically, Lord and Burnham's horticultural factory burned to the ground while the new Gould conservatory was being prefabricated. Gould offered them a loan to rebuild the factory and gave additional time to complete the contract (134–136).

The most regal and extensive private conservatories are found at Laeken Palace in north Brussels, built by the arch-imperialist and lover of plants, Leopold II, King of the Belgians. In 1865, Leopold II succeeded his father to the throne and enthusiastically created the Laeken park which grew from its original area of 70 hectares to 200 hectares during his reign (1865–1909). The extent of the conservatories and the flower-lined glass corridors totalling a mile is extraordinary. They enclose nearly 5 acres of varied climates under 10 acres of glass surface. On Leopold's accession there existed a beautiful orangery but few glass buildings. Behind the orangery he constructed a large glass corridor (camellia house) that led to the great rotunda winter garden eventually constructed in 1876 and designed by the architect and professor of the *Académie,* Alphonse Balat (1818–95). Balat's glass rotunda is today the most grandiose in Europe. Its diameter is nearly 60 m and its height to the top of the cupola crown nearly 30 m.

Tuscan-styled marble columns, 18 m high, support an exo-skeleton of thirty-six ornamental curved iron ribs that pierce the glass skin and structure the upper dome. The external structure is reminiscent of Balat's earlier Victoria Regia House for the Jardin Zoologique de Bruxelles some twenty years before (see *Artificial Climate* 11). An extensive heating plant was built next to the rotunda with its chimney disguised as an oriental minaret, and pipes were laid under grates around the periphery of the winter garden. In the central room formed by the columns, the floor was handsomely tiled to be used as a ballroom with fountains on each side and the great plants all around. Today visitors are reaping the legacy of those early plantings for the palms are great indeed. One is 25 m high, nearly through the roof. During the ensuing years Leopold built an extensive array of glass environments along the connecting corridors. The large Congo House, enclosing palms and tropicals, was built to commemorate Leopold's newly acquired lands in west central Africa. He had a yellow star mounted at the top in celebration of the event. Next to this another house was constructed which makes a transition to the underground gallery that was dug and covered with glass so that the walk could pass below a service road. The glass corridor then climbs the hill to another group of conservatories culminated by another Balat palm house built in 1892. The king's extravagance did not end with this palm house, for further on and also connected to the corridor system, Leopold designed and built a glass and iron church that was used regularly for services. Constructed in 1894, the round church is approximately 140 ft in diameter and 100 ft

138　Plan of the Greenhouses, Laeken:
1. Loggia and entrance house
2. Palm house
3. Junction of Palm house and Chapel
4. Sacristy
5. Glasshouse-Chapel
6. Smaller Palm house
7. Junction of (6) and Azalea house
8. Round house
9. Azalea house
10. Glasshouse and building for making up bouquets
11. Gallery between the House of Diana and the Azalea house
12. House of Diana and the Pavilion of Narcissus
13. Gallery linking the old Pavilion of Narcissus and the Diana House
14. Old Pavilion of Narcissus
15. Subterranean gallery
16. White staircase and landing-stage
17. Congo house
18. Corridor for palms
19. Winter garden
20. Fern corridor
21. Orangery
22. Orangery Annex
23. Glasshouse theatre
24. Glasshouse Dining room
25. Camellia house
26. Maquet house
27. New orangery
28. Gallery linking new orangery and old Pavilion of Narcissus
29. Rhododendron house
30. Flower houses
31. Group of palm houses
32. Linking gallery
33–5. Orchid houses
36. Forcing house

137　Above: the Congo house, palm corridor and winter garden (17, 18, 19, on plan) at Laeken.

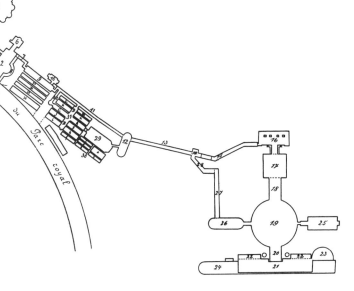

139　Above: the iron and glass conservatory-cum-chapel (5, on plan).

140　Left: Palm House, attributed to Alphonse Balat, in the huge complex of greenhouses at Laeken. This is (2) on the plan above.

141   Above: palms growing up into the dome of the winter garden.

142   The former Pavilion of Narcissus (foreground) is linked to the present one by a climbing corridor (13).

143   Right: a remarkable underground greenhouse corridor (15) leads to the landing-stage. The Congo house is on the right.

144 Conservatory on the garden façade of the Hôtel Max Hallet, 344 avenue Louise, Brussels. Victor Horta, 1903.

high. Ten pairs of polished red granite columns support the main dome. A 20 ft walk was designed around the periphery, and on its outer side, glass niches were planted with palms and the walk lined with flowering shrubs replaced on each occasion. Between the circle of columns, an altar, an organ, and centre aisle seating generated the religious ceremony among the palms. Without them, an observer at the time described the church as a great conservatory. Heating pipes were laid under cast-iron gratings in all the corridors and under the walkway around the church. By 1894 all the glass buildings, including this crystal chapel, were lighted with electricity (137–143).

Leopold was a fanatic about gardens, flowers, and exotic plants. He is perhaps the best example of the nineteenth-century imperialist whose infamous Congo policies taints the history of that time, but whose exploitations were no doubt forgotten in the glazed dream world he created for himself at Laeken. Ironically, in 1909, he died in his glasshouses—in the small palm pavilion near the palmhouse on the hill.

Alphonse Balat, as professor was Victor Horta's master at the *Académie des Beaux Arts,* where Horta did well and later worked for him. It is difficult to trace the exact origins of Horta's Art Nouveau work, for example as seen in the Maison Tassel he designed in 1892, the year he became professor of the Académie. Horta was

fascinated by plants and their structure, for in his library were found botanical books, including a book describing the Laeken conservatories. According to Marcus Binney* Horta, as secretary to the Society of Architects, described a visit to the Laeken houses. He enthuses about the tropical plants and the curvilinear metal frames that structured the winter garden. He praised Balat for not using iron in forms 'only governed by the slide rule' but forms with 'artistic character' and with 'ornament which is perfectly appropriate to the purpose of the building, and which despite its richness does not detract from the simplicity of the whole (144). Horta, like the painter Henri Rousseau at the Jardin des Plantes, had been impressed by the beauty of the tropical world under glass.

* See Marcus Binney, 'The Mystery of the "Style Jules Verne",' *Country Life Annual,* 1970.

7 Industrialization and Mass-Marketing

For the Crimean War, Joseph Paxton developed a folding frame, which made a portable tent. In 1858 he adapted it into a patent for *Improvement in the manufacture of Horticulture Buildings or Glazed Structures for Horticulture and other purposes*. The patent consisted of a series of hinged wood and glass frames, which could be shipped flat and unfolded to suit any horticultural purpose. They were inexpensive, practical and perfect for the new Victorian middle-class which was creating suburbs around major English cities. The mass-produced glass-frame afforded this new suburbanite the opportunity to own a glasshouse, a luxury previously confined to the wealthy. The possibility of folding the glass modules appealed particularly to persons having temporary or limited tenures. According to law, plant houses fixed in the soil were the property of the freeholder. Tenants could pack up and move when their lease ran out (149).

The sole agents for manufacturing and marketing Paxton's patent were Hereman and Morton of 7 Pall Mall East, London. Hereman produced a do-it-yourself *Handbook of Vine and Fruit tree Cultivation under Glass, with a Description of Sir Joseph Paxton's Hot Houses* with instructions for the new glass gardeners, whom he obviously expected in profusion, from his optimistic advertisement: 'Hot Houses for the Million'. Railway transport had obviously made hothouse mail-order feasible, while the new middle-class journals provided the communication medium, all of which Paxton understood and exploited.

Paxton's was just one of a host of prefabricated glass structures produced for the middle-class. Companies manufacturing horticultural buildings began to flourish in the 1860s, 1870s and 1880s.* Some of these, like Weeks & Co. and Ormson & Co., were located in the Kings Road, Chelsea, which had a long tradition of glasshouses, not only at the Chelsea Apothecaries' Garden but also several nurseries, including the huge Veitch establishment. Most of the manufacturers provided prefabricated buildings to meet various needs and tastes. They also provided, as we have seen previously, boilers usually made under their own patent (145–8).

Weeks & Co., Horticultural Engineers, were typical of these manufacturers. They built a display winter garden next to their works in the Kings Road and provided the complete conservatory package—iron and wood glazed structures, heating and ventilating equipment, and even the plants. Horticultural magazines of the 1870s and 1880s are filled with Weeks's designs, including, for example, the glass at Hampton Court and the Folkstone winter garden, erected for South-Eastern Railway at their Royal Pavilion Hotel in 1885 (151).

By the 1880s the packaged conservatory was well established. Designs presented in brochures, pamphlets and catalogues were printed and distributed throughout England. Messenger & Co., Horticultural Builders from Loughborough, hired the architect, Edward William Godwin, and his assistant Maurice B. Adams to make a series of designs to be included in a booklet called *Artistic Conservatories* (1880). The booklet was obviously made to demonstrate the 'packaged' conservatories that could be

* Weeks & Co.; H. Ormson & Co.; W. H. Lascelles & Co.; Messenger & Co.; Boulton & Paul; Halliday & Co.

145–8 The 'A' frame design met various horticultural needs with different sized panels and varied angles of inclination, as borne out by the advertisements in the 1860s and 1870s. Here are: top left, a Paxtonian plant-house: top right, a span-roof vinery for summer and autumn; centre a tree-filled conservatory and below, an orchard house cum aviary complete with fountain.

112   THE GARDENERS' CHRONICLE AND AGRICULTURAL GAZETTE.   [FEBRUARY 4, 1

HOTHOUSES FOR THE MILLION.

SAMUEL HEREMAN

BEGS TO INFORM THE PUBLIC THAT HE HAS BEEN APPOINTED SOLE AGENT FOR THE MANUFACTURE AND SALE OF

THE NEW PORTABLE AND ECONOMICAL HOTHOUSE

INVENTED AND PATENTED BY

SIR JOSEPH PAXTON, M.P.

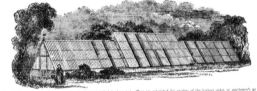

HEATING APPARATUS of the best description can be supplied and adapted if required.

Letters prepaid addressed to S. HEREMAN, 7, Pall Mall East, S.W., will receive immediate attention.

150 Right: Ewing's Patent Glass Walls in the garden of the Horticultural Society, Chiswick. The glass side panels, 9 ft high, could be removed in summer. McIntosh praised these narrow glasshouses as a substitute for inelegant and expensive brick and stone walls, but he questioned whether they had the heat retention capacity of massive walls. He suggested that the walls be sloped to improve insolation along the lines of Spencer's walls, a similar fruit protection system also marketed in the 1850s.

151 Weeks' advertisement in *The Gardener's Chronicle*, February, 1860.

149 Facing, below: Sir Joseph Paxton's Patent Hothouses for the Million. This 1876 advertisement indicates the successful marketing methods of Hereman and Morton, Paxton's agents since the 1860s.

ELEVATION OF CONSERVATORY
NOW BEING CONSTRUCTED FOR A NOBLEMAN,

BY

JOHN WEEKS & COMPANY,

HORTICULTURAL BUILDERS AND HOT-WATER APPARATUS MANUFACTURERS, ENGINEERS, AND IRON FOUNDERS,

KING'S ROAD, CHELSEA, S.W.

PLAN

WINTER · GARDEN · IN · THE · ANGLO · JAPANESE · STYLE — CONSTRUCTED · ON · THE · PATENT · SYSTEM · OF · MESSENGER · & COMPANY · HORTICULTURAL · BUILDERS · LOUGHBOROUGH · 1880 — FROM SKETCHES BY E.W.GODWIN, F.S.A.

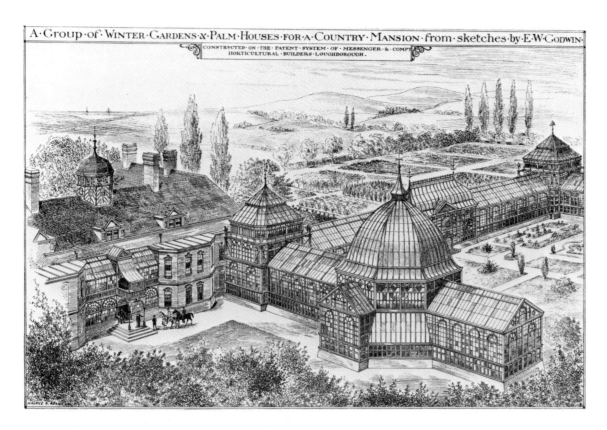

A · Group · of · WINTER · GARDENS · & · PALM · HOUSES · FOR · A · COUNTRY · MANSION · from · sketches · by · E.W.GODWIN · CONSTRUCTED · ON · THE · PATENT · SYSTEM · OF · MESSENGER · & · COMP.Y HORTICULTURAL · BUILDERS · LOUGHBOROUGH ·

152   E. W. Godwin's Anglo-Japanese style Conservatory, made by Messenger & Co.

153   The *pièce de résistance* of Godwin's country mansion was this large winter garden, with a two-storey glass porch on the house.

154   Cranston's Patent Building for Horticulture was another late nineteenth-century system for glass buildings. In this case the glass overlaps a wooden strip, perforated for ventilation. A surviving example of Cranston's Patented Construction can be found in the grounds of a Victorian castle near Devizes.

made up from their patented construction system, mainly in the newly popular Anglo-Japanese or Anglo-Italian style (152–4).

To the worker who spent most of his time in the offices, factories or mines, the glasshouse had to be as maintenance free as possible. Such a house was patented and manufactured by a Mr Beard at Bury St Edmunds, Norfolk. Beard's prefabricated house was a forerunner of the standard dry-glazed buildings that suburbanites purchase today. The erection of the house was simple and rapid. The wrought-iron dry glazing bar was the unique feature of the house, for small conservatories had relied on putty and wood glazing bars. The glass was sandwiched between thick asphalt strips and held in place with a white metal bar. The house was again, as was Paxton's, popular with the tenant who could dis-assemble and transport it to another garden. The iron bars were covered with baked enamel, reducing maintenance.

With the repeal of the glass tax in the late forties, novel applications of now inexpensive glass were being discovered. One of these was Ewing's Patent Glass Walls. Masonry walls, every gardener knew, trapped sun and protected fruit trees. According to Ewing, the grey skies and 'variableness of the British climate', however, often dampened the gardener's hopes and his crop. Ewing's cast-iron and glass walls, with fruit and vines inside, were linear showcases with sliding or casement glass sides. The quality of evening light refracted through them onto the trees must have been an added delight (150).

One of the earliest prefabricators and builders of metal hothouses was Thomas Clark who founded his business in the autumn of 1818 in Lionel Street, Birmingham. The firm's name was originally Jones and Clark and it provided the components for the Camellia House at Wollaton Hall in Nottinghamshire, built in 1823 and for the Grange in Hampshire (1825). The firm's first order book from 1818, which is still intact, shows on the first page two lean-to forcing houses, one for the Duke of Newcastle, at Clumber Park, Nottinghamshire. The subsequent order books are filled with sales to nobility, including in 1844 the glass sashes for Queen Victoria's Frogmore, the glass range near Windsor. The first order for abroad was in 1839 for 'two ranges of hot water apparatus for heating a pine house for His Majesty the King of Württemberg, Stuttgart'. Before the publication of their *Book of Designs of Horticulture Buildings* (1875), an elaborate conservatory had been manufactured and shipped to Buenos Aires. This order marked the beginning of their export business, which was to expand to prefabricated buildings and windows for Japan, New Zealand, Australia, Africa, Holland and America. By this time the firm's name was Henry Hope, with the letterhead 'late Clark and Hope, formerly Clark'. Hope's metal windows are still known throughout the world (156, 157).

It was not only small glass buildings that were being prefabricated and assembled throughout England. The 1860s saw many iron foundries producing large conservatories and winter gardens. One of these foundries, Andrew Handyside and Co., built the cast-iron conservatory in the gardens of the Royal Horticultural Society, which had returned from Chiswick to South Kensington to prepare for the 1862 exhibition. Another of Handy-

155   Above: the Grecian Camellia House, 1823, built at Wollaton Hall by Clark and Jones, metallic hothouse builders of Birmingham.

156   Below: iron conservatory in the garden of the Royal Horticultural Society at South Kensington by Andrew Handyside & Co. In the foreground is the Albert Hall, under construction.

157 The roof of the Camellia House, Woollaton. Double-skinned iron vaults cover the pathways, while glass skylights cover the flower beds. Rain drains into the cast-iron gutter beams at the edge of the skylights and into the columns.

158 'Moorish' iron structure with tile and glass infill erected in the Royal Horticultural Society's Garden at South Kensington in 1867, to be marketed throughout the world, by R. M. Ordish and Owen Jones.

side's many buildings was an 1868 addition to Henry Bessemer's mansion at Denmark Hill, Camberwell. Designed by the architects Robert Banks and Charles Barry (son of the architect of the Houses of Parliament, Westminster), seventy tons of wrought and cast iron were used to produce the ornate structure. While demonstrating the use of remarkably complicated casting, architects began to exhibit a taste that obscured the simple functional expression of Kew and the Crystal Palace. What appeals to us today and appealed to earlier Victorians, was obviously not to the taste of the mid and late Victorians (155).

Engineer R. M. Ordish was involved with several iron constructions, including the Albert Suspension Bridge over the Thames. He worked with Owen Jones on an iron structure to be marketed and transported throughout the Empire, and with the architect, Alfred G. Jones, and the engineer, Le Feuvre, built the Exhibition Palace and Winter Garden in Dublin (1865). Another winter garden for the Infirmary at Leeds designed by Sir George Gilbert Scott was also engineered by Ordish and built by Handyside & Co. in 1866 (158).

Throughout the nineteenth century, cast-iron had developed into a sophisticated building material.* Its relative high ratio of strength to weight allowed delicate casting to be produced, packed and transported throughout the Empire. The art of casting intricate shapes enabled the designers of the components to pursue a 'Battle of Styles' while under this decorative foliage lay the pure structural shapes of the columns, brackets, and

* See Richard Sheppard, *Cast-Iron in Building*.

beams. The cast-iron component, be it a truss, rainwater gutter, or column, was cast with a sophisticated connection joint which minimized the assembly time on the building site. Charles Fox's 'snap-on' joint between the cast girder and column connectors, used on the 1850–51 Crystal Palace, was secured by only an iron wedge.

By the 1880s, hundreds of foundries employing thousands of men were casting the integrated components as a 'kit of parts' that built the bridges, railway stations and factories still used today. One of these companies, Walter MacFarlane's Saracen Foundry in Glasgow and later London, started before the 1850s, casting rainwater goods, kiosks, street urinals, park benches and sewage equipment. An inspection of their early catalogues shows their understanding of component integration, and by their sixth edition in 1880, they had entered the large iron and glass building market. Sales in the Empire were particularly successful as the desire for the sophisticated styles of European and British buildings could only be satisfied by mail order. The MacFarlane company consequently produced beautiful catalogues of components and designs which whetted the appetites of the established colonists in Johannesburg, Singapore, Cairo and Calcutta. The MacFarlanes' castings were often used as facings to existing buildings in the same way that in the United States tin façades were shipped from St Louis and Chicago to the hardware stores of the mid and far West. The completely-packaged, mail-order building that could be easily assembled in tropical climates hinted at a potential that has never been as successfully exploited as it was then. Structural components formed the structure with

159, 160 Page from Walter MacFarlane's Casting Book; compare with (left) the Barton Arcade, Manchester, assembled from Walter MacFarlane's Books by architects Corbett, Raby and Sawyer in the early 1870s.

161 An attached conservatory in Glasgow, *c.* 1870–80, assembled from Walter MacFarlane's Casting Book.

162   The Metropolitan Meat Market at Smithfield designed by Sir Horace Jones (1819–87) is 631 ft long and 246 ft wide, covering 3½ acres. The central hall of this large building is a modest span. Begun in 1867, it was opened in November 1868.

the help of a few bolts; crestings, terminals and frieze rails could be added for instant style. Clear, translucent or decorated flat glass was infilled in the iron lattice enclosing smoking rooms, arcades, aquariums, pavilions, conservatories and winter gardens, all found in the illustrated catalogue. Exported, cast-iron and glass used with galvanized tin were excellent materials for the tropical or sub-tropical climates, as glass kept out the tropical rain and cast-iron had good resistance to corrosion (159–61).

There is an important building lesson to be learned from the great conservatories of the past, including the Crystal Palace, the Winter Garden at Regent's Park, the Palm House at Kew, and the numerous buildings of MacFarlane. However large, they were made from components limited in size by the manufacturing process and transportation facilities. Their major spans were relatively modest and were often enhanced with smaller spans that, altogether, made a building of vast size. For Victorian engineers used the column to great advantage to overcome the span limitations of cast-iron. Recurring components gave a human scale to even vast buildings, harmonizing the whole with a family of parts. Our recent

building components have been too large, and too difficult to market. The Crystal Palace was built essentially from one component—a truss 3 ft by 23 ft 3 in, weighing 900 lbs and easily manoeuvred with a jib crane, block and tackle. A single firm usually designed, prefabricated and built a structure, and efficiency was always in mind (162). The 18-acre Crystal Palace took only six months to build.

Today each new building requires its own standardized parts and is always more expensive than anticipated. Most architects design and detail a building with no awareness of available components and little interest in improving the building process. The component manufacturer, for his part, produces, for instance, a standard 8 by 4 ft sheet material with no concern for where or how it can be used. He adds a substantial safety margin and use-limitation to protect himself. The builder ends up with plans that he knows are somewhat impractical, but he is only a middle-man, who hires subcontractors who in turn do only their specialized work. Compared to nineteenth-century glasshouse construction, we have reverted to elementary practices without the skills that those specialists had.

163   Queen Victoria and Prince Albert at the Royal Surrey Zoological
Gardens on Tuesday, 27 June 1848, viewing the tigress and spaniel in
the same cage.

8 Glass in the Public Garden

In 1831, J. C. Loudon prepared designs for the Birmingham Horticultural Society's Botanical Garden on a sixteen-acre site situated at Edgbaston, then two miles from the centre of the city. Much to Loudon's disappointment the design was never carried out, though it would certainly have been one of the finest gardens and far ahead of its time, since Loudon's plans included functional glass domes of great beauty that pre-dated the large conservatories at Chatsworth and Kew. Their size, the heating, ventilating, and rain-making apparatus, along with a unique construction sequence, can be attributed to the confidence, and justified confidence, of this inventor, gardener, encyclopaedist and editor of the first gardening periodicals.

The Horticultural Society wanted a scientific ornamental garden, combined with a nursery for selling plants to help defray their expenses. The plan could only be executed by degrees as funds were low. The garden would be open to the public at a charge, for this was before the advent of free gardens, prevalent later in the century.

Loudon developed two glasshouse designs in detail. Both had circular plans calculated to look well from all sides when placed on the highest corner of the garden site. The first design was a circular glass corridor that surrounded a central tower. The steam boilers were placed in the tower's basement, along with the coal which was brought in an underground passageway. Besides the main boiler a second boiler stood by in case of an emergency. Above was a potting and tool shed and a water tank that supplied the glasshouse and fountains in the garden. Water descended to a pond at the lowest area of the garden and was recirculated by steam pumps. The glasshouse had an inner and outer ring of glass-covered pits for smaller plants. Inside trees were to be planted directly in the ground and other plants set around in pots. Cast-iron cisterns under the pathways were to collect rain-water from the roof. Heated by steam, it flowed through pipes pierced with holes and would imitate a shower of rain like that at the Loddige's tropical house at Hackney. A walkway at the ridge of the glasshouse was designed to store mats that could be rolled down over the glass during cold weather (165, 166, 167).

As an alternative building Loudon proposed what he admitted was a design 'if expense were not an object'. It covered nearly an acre with its 200 ft diameter conical roof, which was 100 ft high. The ground level was laid out in concentric beds and walks with four radiating partitions which separated four artificial climates (168).

At the centre, in a glass chamber 30 ft in diameter, the most rapidly growing and tallest tropical trees, 'their trunks and branches clothed with epiphytes and climbers', would be planted and the ground covered with ferns. Surrounding this tropical cyclinder a spiral ramp, its railings draped with creepers, would connect the various plant galleries. As in the more modest design, the conical roof had walkways for the gardeners to put out matting or oil cloth to cover the glass on winter nights. Immediately under the glass were pipes heated by steam, while over the glass there was even a system of conducting rods for 'guarding against the effects of electricity'. The glass was in separate panels supported by rafters and could be removed during the two to four months of summer, for

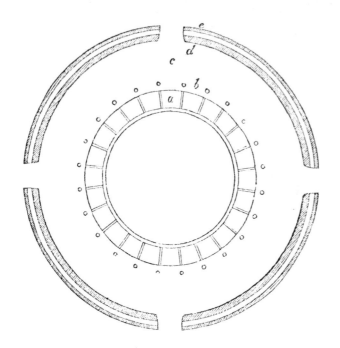

164, 165   The glass menagerie built at the Surrey Zoological Gardens in 1830–31. 'In the plan of this building the animals (. . .) are kept in separate cages or compartments (a) towards the centre; exterior to them is a colonnade (b) supporting the glazed roof, and also for cages of birds; within this colonnade will be placed hot water pipes for heating the whole, and beyond it is an open paved area for spectators (c). Next, there is a channel for a stream of water, intended for gold, silver and other exotic fishes (d) and beyond, a border under the front wall, for climbing plants (e) to be trained on wires under the roof.'

as Loudon correctly believed, this strengthened the vegetation. This glazing design followed the method invented by John Jones of Birmingham, who Loudon considered the best hothouse builder in Britain.

Loudon's ambitious proposal was substantially larger than the St Louis Climatron built in 1959, which is 175 ft in diameter and 70 ft high. Still, he told the Birmingham Society that 'there would be no difficulty in erecting such a building', and it would be easier to heat than his less expensive design. In the same discussion of the Birmingham project, Loudon also predicted the possibility of public gardens:

> When towns and their suburbs are legislated for and governed as a whole, and not, as they are now, in petty detail, by corporations and vestries; and when the recreation and enjoyment of the whole society are cared for by their representatives; public gardens, with hot-houses of this sort, or even of far greater magnificence, will be erected, for the general enjoyment, at the general expense.

Loudon was never to see the realization of his prediction in the Crystal Palace or the Palm Stove at Kew, for he died in 1843, the year Queen Victoria drove through the Chatsworth conservatory in her carriage.

According to an 1840 guide book of London, a three-penny omnibus ride from Charing Cross toward Camberwell would deliver a visitor at the Royal Surrey Zoological Gardens. With its varied attractions the garden was one of the most popular in the 1830s, 1840s and 1850s. On an average day eight thousand visitors promenaded around the grounds, and on special occasions

this figure was doubled. The caged and roaming animals were the main attractions but there were also concerts, balloon ascents and a five-acre model of Rome. Edward Cross, the founder, had previously kept his huge menagerie at Exeter Exchange, a three-storey building that jutted out into the Strand. Its widening forced Cross to move his animals temporarily to Kings Mews (site of Trafalgar Square) in 1830 while the new zoological gardens were under construction on the eighteen-acre site of Walworth Manor House. Henry Phillips (1779–1840), schoolmaster turned horticulturalist, author of *Sylva Florifera* and other plant histories, laid out the garden which was opened in 1831. Phillips was later to instigate the ill-fated Antheum at Hove, near Brighton. He arranged to be built for Mr Cross what was regarded as the largest glass conservatory in England, though few people knew of Mrs Beaumont's similar construction at Bretton Hall, Yorkshire (1827). The 'conservatory' as it was called, was actually a menagerie for Cross's 'wild beasts' (163, 164). The greatest attraction was the cage shared by an Indian tigress and an English spaniel, a curiosity viewed by Victoria and Albert. The Surrey menagerie lasted beyond Cross's retirement in 1844. The animals were sold in 1855 and the structure torn down in 1856 to provide the site for the Royal Surrey Music Hall, an ugly Victorian edifice designed by Sir Horace Jones, also the architect for the cast-iron and glass Smithfield Market.*

* Horace Jones's music hall unfortunately suffered a fire in which several people were killed in a panic. It was rebuilt and used as the temporary St Thomas's Hospital. The Surrey Zoological Garden is now completely built over.

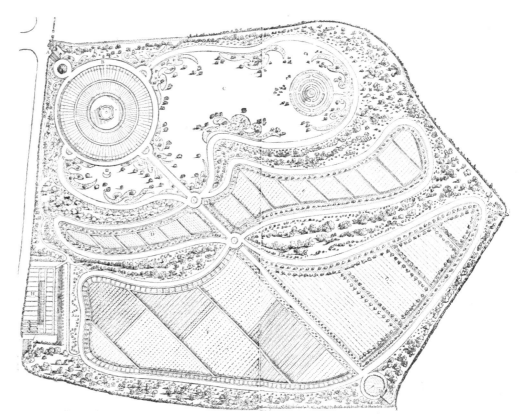

166–8   Above: the plan of the Birmingham Botanical Horticultural Garden, 1831. Loudon's huge glasshouse is at the upper left. This original conception put Loudon far ahead of his time. Centre: the first circular glasshouse proposed by Loudon for the Birmingham Horticultural Garden, 1831. Below, the second design proposed by Loudon 'if expense were not an object'.

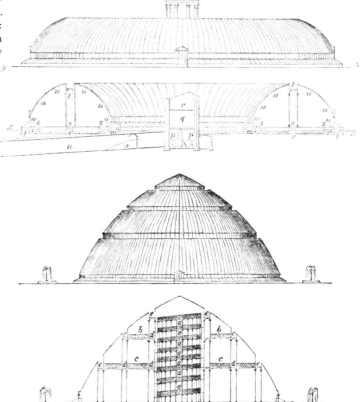

169–71 Left: greenhouses of the Jardin des Plantes, Paris, begun in 1833 by Rohault de Fleury. Right: the glasshouses in the Botanic Garden of Liège and those of another garden, as illustrated by Rohault in an article on glasshouses designed by other architects. Far right: the eighteenth-century glasshouses removed to make way for Rohault's construction in the Jardin des Plantes.

Before laying out the Surrey Zoological Gardens and proposing its glass and iron menagerie in 1830, Henry Phillips had designed, in 1825, an oriental garden near his home in Brighton. The garden centred on a large glass conservatory, the Athenaeum, which was large enough to house palms in its steam-heated tropical section. It also had a literary institute comprising a library, museum, reading room, and school of science where Phillips proposed to lecture. A start was made on the building but abandoned in June 1827 for lack of funds.

In 1832 the oriental garden project was revived at Hove near Brighton. A domed conservatory, now called the Antheum, was planned to excell anything of its kind, enclosing full-size trees with birds, a lake with fish, a hill of rocks, and an amphitheatre for eight hundred people. By July 1833 Joseph Paxton, on a visit to the Duke of Devonshire's house in Brighton, was able to inspect the nearly completed structure. The dimensions of the structure were formidable. The 60 ft high glass dome was constructed from twenty cast-iron ribs forming ten elliptical arches spanning nearly 170 ft. Each cast iron rib was 3 ft deep at its base and 2 ft deep at the top. These ribs were in turn assembled from six castings held together with bolts and flanges. A 7 ft diameter circular casting held the ribs together at the top and their lower part was encased in a 12 ft high brick pier, a part of a brick circular wall. Light cast-iron purlins spanned between the ribs forming a series of concentric circles at various elevations. An immense wood scaffolding was built to hold all the structural members in position until the whole building had been bolted together. An oversight in the design was

unfortunately the lack of diagonal braces between the ribs, according to the supervising architect Anson Henry Wilds. As no provision had been made in the ribs to receive this bracing, and to make it would have resulted in considerable expense, the contractor refused to provide it. The scaffolding was afterwards removed and immediately the weight of the glass and iron caused the unbraced ribs to swerve in serpentine lines, cracking some of the purlins. J. C. Loudon made a visit to inspect the great glass bubble on 12 September 1833 and found that the whole centre had collapsed, 'breaking with a report like the running fire of light artillery, giving out sparks, as to produce the effect of a powerful flash of lightning', to quote an observing architect, Charles Busby, in the *Brighton Herald*. The shock of the collapse sent poor Phillips blind and he died seven years later. However, half the iron work and all the brickwork remained intact and the Brighton architect, Charles Augustus Busby, who was often a collaborator of Wilds, undertook to rebuild the Antheum, but nothing came of the scheme. The wreckage remained until the mid fifties when Baron Goldschmid had the ground cleared to lay out Palmeira Square.

In 1833 construction was started on the glass house in the Botanical gardens of Paris, the Jardin des Plantes. In 1834 while the glasshouses were still unfinished because of operational difficulties of the steam heat, Rohault de Fleury, the architect, made a visit to England to study construction and heating in new buildings including the glasshouses of the Loddiges brothers in Hackney, the Colosseum, Kew, the Horticultural Society, Covent

Garden Market, the Baileys, and Loudon's glasshouses in Bayswater (169–171).

Sigfried Giedion in *Space, Time and Architecture* (1940) describes the Rohault glasshouse as 'the prototype of all large iron-framed conservatories', 'the first large structure consisting mainly of iron and glass'. Though there is no doubt that these public conservatories did influence other architects in Europe, it is hard to believe that in England, where many fantastic schemes were being devised and built on grander scales, any notice was paid to Rohault's houses,* though Paxton visited them in the year of construction while on a grand tour with Devonshire.**

In Europe, however, Rohault's glass houses did make a strong impact on at least two botanic gardens, Liège and Ghent in Belgium. On return from a study trip to those two towns in 1849, Rohault showed how similar the glasshouses there were to his own, publishing plans of the two Belgian buildings in the *Revue de l'Architecture et des Travaux Publics*. The Jardin Botanique, Liège, and the Jardin Botanique, Ghent, are directly inspired by Rohault's prototype—in fact nearly copies. At the conclusion of his article in the *Revue* he expressed his desire to go again to England to see the many new and wonderful constructions (e.g. Chatsworth, Kew). Perhaps this was in anticipation of the ambitious building plans outlined by a contemporary, Gottfried Semper—a scheme for completely covering the Jardin des Plantes with an immense portable glass roof which could be removed in the summer (172).

London's Royal Horticultural Society leased a 31-acre plot behind Chiswick house from the Duke of Devonshire in 1821. The Society's small garden at Kensington was given up in 1823, and a more substantial establishment with new roads, paths, walls, glasshouses, and offices containing a council room, was constructed at Chiswick. By 1824 a national school for the propagation of horticultural knowledge was established, Joseph Paxton's name being one of the earliest entries in its log book. Paxton was soon upgraded from labourer to under-gardener in the arboretum where his work apparently attracted the eye of the Duke, a frequent visitor. In 1826 he lured Paxton away to Chatsworth, where that famous gardener's remarkable career began.

The 1830s saw the Chiswick gardens as a popular place for horticultural exhibitions, competitions and a fashionable promenade. The horticultural competitions for which the gold Knightion and gold Banksian medals were awarded became so popular that twelve thousand tickets could be sold for a single show.

The Society had been almost exclusively interested in indigenous plants but exotics were being brought back to the gardens, mainly through the efforts of the Society's collector, Theodore Hartwick. A controversy began about collecting them, but the beautiful orchids that required new glass were their own best argument.

In 1838 Thomas Knight, who had become famous as the Society's president, died. He was succeeded by William Cavendish, Duke of Devonshire, whose interest

* Two main glass pavilions and only one lean-to arm were built in 1833.

** See George F. Chadwick, *The Works of Sir Joseph Paxton*, p. 93.

172–74   Left: Rohault's design for an extensive range of glasshouses at the Jardin des Plantes, Paris, in 1854. The design, made after his second trip to England, is a derivative of the Chatsworth Conservatory and Kew Palm House. Right: the curved wrought-iron ladder on wheels used for harvesting and pruning in the converted vinery at Chiswick. Far right: the wing of the imposing conservatory built by D. & E. Bailey for the Royal Horticultural Society at Chiswick.

in glass building had already resulted in the conservatory at Chatsworth and was to emerge again in plans for a large conservatory at Chiswick. The conservatory was to have a central dome 120 ft in diameter and four wings 185 ft long and 30 ft wide. Only one wing was constructed at Chiswick, by D. & E. Bailey in 1840, owing to the exorbitant cost of glass duty (174).

In 1857, the conservatory which had housed many of the exotics was turned into a vinery, and it so remained into the twentieth century. In a good season it produced 4,500 pounds of some 83 varieties of grapes, ranging from Black Hamburg to Buckland Sweetwater to Muscat of Alexandria. Such a bountiful harvest required machinery, and a wrought-iron ladder on wheels and curved to the shape of the glass skin was built to support the workmen. A continuous ridge ventilator, with an aperture and butterfly shutters, provided ventilation similar to the Bicton Palm House in Devon, which is still extant (173).

Paris had two winter gardens in quick succession on the same site, between the Rond Point and the Avenue Marbœuf on the Champs Elysées. The first and ill-fated glass garden was erected in 1846, built along with eight fountains in a scheme to decorate the alleys of the Champs Elysées. The building had a reading-room at one end and the Salles des Bouquets and office at the other. In between was the gable-roofed winter garden, 120 ft long and 30 ft wide and only 18 ft high.* To the Parisians the garden was not grand enough for a winter promenade and social meeting-place. The low roof produced a 'heavy' effect. The house was pulled down six months after its erection and another was started on the site. That this new

house was a real success, is perhaps best conveyed by the Englishman, W. Bridges Adam, who was writing in 1850, about the kind of winter garden the Crystal Palace ought to be.

Something of the kind has recently been established at Paris as a private speculation and has become one of the most popular places of resort in that city. Public dinners, balls and concerts, are continually held in the Jardin d'Hiver of the Champs Elysées, and with frost out of doors, and the snow covering the ground, visitors there find themselves in another and more genial climate, surrounded by tropical trees, flowering shrubs and plants, interspersed with statues and fountains.**

The new Jardin d'Hiver in Paris was a magnificent building, with its ballroom, Jardin Anglais, promenades, fountains, reading-room, café and *pâtisserie*; the perfect rendez-vous on a winter's day. Designed by Hector Horeau† it was opened to the public in January 1848. The entrance led through a ballroom, sky-lighted and hung with pictures and works of art for sale. The covered garden was a grand 300 ft long and 180 ft wide at the crossing. A raised promenade around its periphery afforded views of the other promenaders and those relaxing, reading and writing at the tables below. Four ornamental fountains framed the major space and on one side bou-

* According to the *Encyclopaedia of Gardening*, 1850, p. 94 (edited by Mrs Loudon).

** *Westminster and Quarterly Review*, April 1850.

† H. R. Hitchcock, *Architecture in the 19th and 20th Century*, pp. 177–8.

EXHIBITION OF THE HORTICULTURAL SOCIETY OF LONDON, CHISWICK GARDENS, ON SATURDAY LAST. [FOR DESCRIPTION, SEE PAGE 104.]

quets, coffee and pastry were sold. The whole was filled with camellias, ericas, azaleas and orange trees. Down the nave, the Jardin Anglais had a lawn, interspersed with large shrubs and trees and the 50-ft *araucaria excelsa** brought from the Jardin des Plantes. The Jardin Anglais ended in a dramatic fountain playing near the roof and cascading on the rockwork below. The delicate iron and glass arched roof hovered 60 ft above and was supported on rows of double and quadruple iron columns that also supported a narrow gallery filled with rhododendrons and dwarf palms. The curved walls of the cross and both ends of the building were entirely covered with mirrors set in filigree. Along the promenades were basins of gold fish and aviaries full of ornamental and song birds; the whole immense building was steam-heated to a minimum 56°F on the coldest winter day (175–177).

The Jardin d'Hiver was an inspiration to Paxton and was most probably the reason for his wish that the Crystal Palace be turned into a winter garden (he visited the Paris garden in its opening year).**

At the time his Jardin d'Hiver was under construction, Hector Horeau was also erecting a Jardin d'Hiver in Lyons on the left bank of the Rhone. The work started in May and the glass structure was formally opened to the public seven months later, on 20 December, in time for Christmas 1847. The central hall was filled with flowers, shrubs, trees, fountains, and kiosks for selling *bon-bons*,

birds and curiosities. Around it was the raised promenade, as in Paris. On the north side, overlooking the Rhone were a restaurant and café and the covered principal entrance. To the south were two higher-temperature conservatories facing the Summer Garden. The west wall housed a glass-enclosed rockwork covered with tropical shrubs and flowers, with a stream of tepid water issuing and cascading down its top and flowing into and irrigating the winter garden (178).

Working with the new materials, iron and glass, created an unusual relationship between the architect and engineer in the nineteenth century, for the architect was inordinately dependent on the engineer's design and fabricating skills. This close collaboration has led to the questioning of authorship of iron buildings wholly credited to architects. Two major nineteenth-century glass gardens, in Kew and Regent's Park, are popularly attributed to the architect Decimus Burton and little is said of Richard Turner and his Hammersmith Works, Dublin. Yet Turner engineered, fabricated and to a considerable extent designed these two structures, the finest glass and iron conservatories ever built in Britain. For though Joseph Paxton is rightfully acclaimed for his marvellous crystal palaces, it must be remembered that they were clad with glass and timber while Turner, on the other hand, built structures totally of cast iron and spanned them elegantly with curved wrought-iron arches or trusses made with iron circles. The resulting glass forms, unsurpassed even today, were manipulated by an engineer who understood the constructional potential of iron.

* The Norfolk Island Pine is found in New Zealand and is similar to the Monkey-Puzzle, popular in Victorian England.

** See George F. Chadwick, *The Works of Sir Joseph Paxton.*

175–7   Above, left: the first Jardin d'Hiver on the
Champs Elysées. Disliked by the Parisians, it was pulled
down six months after erection in 1846. It was replaced
by the structure on the right, opened in January 1848.
Centre: plan of the 1848 Jardin d'Hiver, Paris, designed
by Hector Horeau.

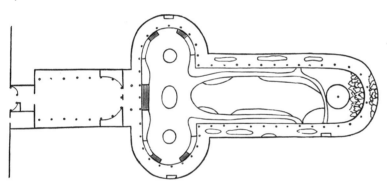

178   Below: section of the Jardin d'Hiver, Lyons,
planned by Hector Horeau and opened in December
1847.

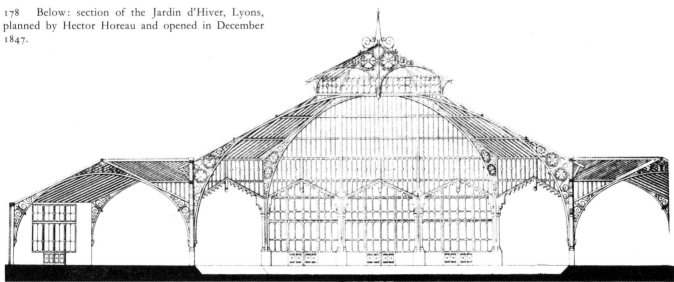

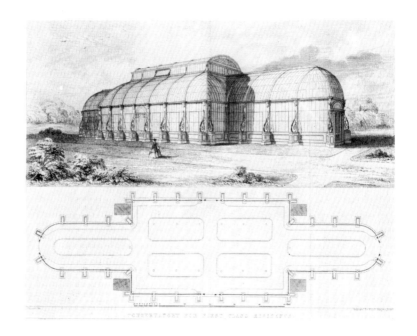

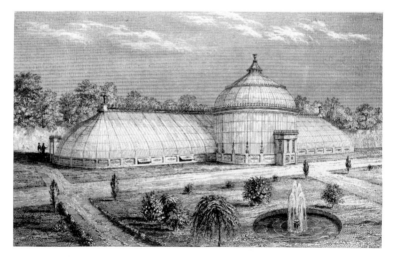

179–81 Right, top: Richard Turner's 'Conservatory for a First Class Residence' was cast in an Ionic style like that at Kew. The high central space with two curvilinear wings allows the gardener to partition the house into three separate climates for 'tropical, extra tropical or temperate plants according to his taste'. Centre: Turner's Conservatory and Fruit House for Colonel White at Killikee, near Dublin. Bottom: in Turner's dome, the main ribs connect to a four foot diameter ring at the top. Pulling down on a chain below would cause the four-foot lid to rise for ventilation. The split pilaster was used at the winter garden in Regent's Park, at Glasnevin and in a small conservatory added to Ballyfin House, Portlaoise in about 1850.

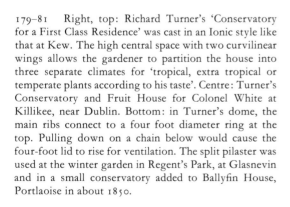

182, 183   The curvilinear range at Dublin's
Botanic Garden, Glasnevin, 1842. Apart
from the east wing, the original construction
and the 1869 enlargement are the work of
Richard Turner. Below, the west wing of the
curvilinear range at Glasnevin. The sliding
glass ventilating sashes were used extensively
on Turner's winter gardens.

184   Belfast Palm House. Richard Turner supplied the iron work for
design by Charles Lanyon in 1839. The dome was added before 1853.

According to Eileen McCracken, Turner's first known work is the construction of the Botanic Gardens Palm House in Belfast (184). This was begun in 1839 and by the next year two wings were completed. The design, however, was not by Turner but by the Antrim county surveyor, Charles Lanyon. When Young & Co. of Edinburgh constructed the central building years later in 1853, it differed considerably from Lanyon's original design and showed the influence of Turner's Palm House at Kew, completed five years before.

The Belfast Palm House was followed by the Palm House and curvilinear range at Glasnevin near Dublin, built by Turner for the Royal Dublin Society in 1843 and enlarged in 1869 (182, 183). This was the prototype for many details found in his extant Kew Palm House and his demolished, and therefore little known, Winter Garden in Regent's Park (185).

The Botanic Society of London was incorporated by Royal Charter in 1839, and in the following year it acquired the 18-acre 'Inner Circle' of Regent's Park previously owned by Jenkin's Nursery. It then commissioned Decimus Burton to design a winter garden.

* Drawing in Westminster Library, Marylebone Road, signed by Burton, dated 1842.

** Burton had previously been associated with Joseph Paxton on the Great Conservatory at Chatsworth; his office had prepared the working drawings. No doubt this led Burton to suggest the ridge and furrow for Regent's Park.

† Documented in Westminster Reference Library, London.

Burton suggested a huge 315 ft by 165 ft wood and glass construction* made with five spans of ridge and furrow roofing,** the centre span with a curvilinear dome. A model was made, but nothing was done until Burton submitted a revised plan in April 1845, which had an iron ridge and furrow roof. The dome had been removed and a curvilinear apse replaced it in the middle of the front facade. Bids were submitted for the central portion of the large enclosed garden, one from Cubitt and Co. for £5,500, partly made of wood, and the other from Richard Turner which cost less and was made entirely of iron and glass. This he outlined in his bid to Burton on 16 April 1845 disproving the latter's advice that wood was cheaper.† The Society made some modifications to the design, replacing the end wall with curvilinear lean-tos for strength and appearance. This was acceptable to the co-operative Turner.

Opened to the public on 20 May 1846, the Winter Garden covered an area of 19,000 sq ft and was truly a garden, for the floor was earth, covered with gravel and topped with 'pounded' sea-shell. Access into the light and elegant structure was through rows of outward hinged french doors that afforded views in all directions and also provided ventilation (186). Turner's split pilasters on the walls infilled with red and blue ground glass must have delighted the Victorian visitors. The curvilinear ridge roofs were all supported on 14 ft cast-iron columns that transferred water to the cisterns below. The internal planting arrangement was a departure from the formal style generally followed at that time, for plants were grouped in clumps growing through the white sea-shell and

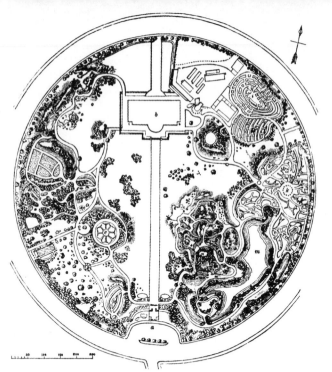

185 Left: plan of the Winter Garden of the Royal Botanic Society in Regent's Park.

186–88 Facing, above: an evening fête at the Winter Garden in Regent's Park, painted by M. M. Runciman in 1876. Below: the interior was planted informally and its ingenious ventilation system was Turner's own invention. A rod extended the length of each ridge and metal sashes opened by their own weight as the rod turned.

valuable specimens were allowed to stand on their own. Small iron tables were filled with hyacinths and narcissi, and flowers of all description formed what Knight's *Cyclopaedia of London* (1851) called 'a veritable fairy land'. To create this climate, temperature was regulated by two Burbidge and Healy ribbed boilers feeding water into nearly a mile of 4-in pipe. Six hot-water pipes ran round the periphery in a 3 ft deep channel and four pipes ran down the middle. The warmed air that rose into shafts placed at intervals throughout the entire area was controlled by iron grilles. The boiler house and chimney were some distance away and the main pipes were led through an outside covered channel. A portion of the glass garden was partitioned off and heated to a higher temperature for the tropical exotics. In addition to the heating pipes, a water-filled tank also went round the wall just below the glass. It was covered over and fitted at intervals with operable grilles to control humidity (187).

Queen Victoria was the first patroness and took great interest in the Garden. Ladies were encouraged to become members and besides lectures and meetings, large flower shows and evening fêtes were held in the summer. In 1871 Turner's Works added an east wing with apse and connecting corridor to the building, then a west wing and apse in 1876 to complete the 210 ft symmetrical façade with its three half domes. The original lease came to an end in the late 1920s, and increasing financial difficulties forced the Society to sell its rare plants at auction in September 1931. Despite the efforts of Queen Mary, who was particularly interested in saving the Winter Garden, the Society disbanded in 1932. The grounds were taken over by the

Royal Parks Department, but the Winter Garden was eventually demolished (188).

Today a controversy surrounds the relative contribution of Burton and Turner. The final building had the curvilinear ridge roofs proposed by Turner instead of Burton's ridge and furrow, and an apse instead of a dome to save money. The open pilasters filled with glass, the iron casement window detail and the sliding iron ridge vents were all Turner trademarks. Burton seems to have ended up as the go-between for the society and Turner. J. de C. Sowerby, the Botanic Society's secretary at the time, wrote 'this building, constructed of iron, was designed and built by Turner, of Dublin.' But, as at Kew, Decimus Burton did influence the overall form of the building, which was based upon his early designs.

A year after Queen Victoria's visit to the Great conservatory at Chatsworth in 1843, the Palm House was planned for the Royal Botanic Gardens at Kew, at that time under the direction of Sir William Jackson Hooker. It was to be one of the first clad in tax-free glass. The gardens, only recently made public, became increasingly popular. Nearly 64,000 people visited them in 1847, and 327,000 in 1851, the year of the Great Exhibition (189, 192).*

The 2 September 1848 and the 7 August 1852 issues of the *Illustrated London News* attribute the building to the design of Decimus Burton, and the iron-work to Richard Turner—as does the 15 January 1848 *Builder*. However, Henry-Russell Hitchcock began to sow a seed of doubt

* *Illustrated London News,* 7 Aug. 1852.

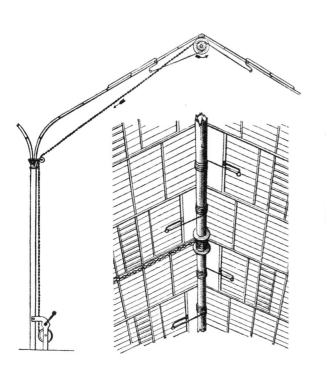

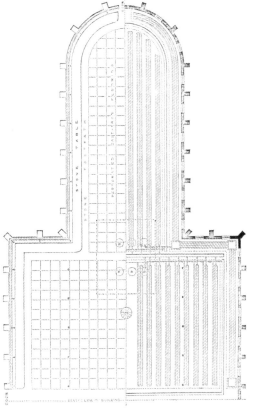

189–91   Above: the Palm House at Kew, constructed by Richard Turner, 1845–8. Left: a half-plan of the house shows half the boilers (B) in one of the vaults. Five and a half miles of four-inch pipe, arranged by Turner, were laid around the periphery and under the floor. Below, design for the Kew Palm House, signed by Burton in March, 1844, altering Turner's earlier scheme to make it similar to the Chatsworth Conservatory.

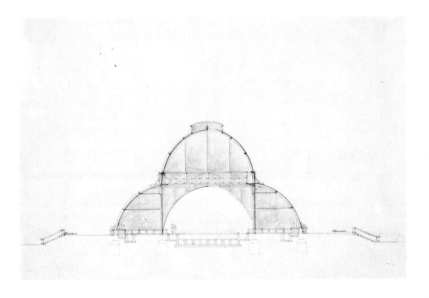

192   The Great Palm House at Kew is still the most beautiful glass-house in the world. In the background among the trees is the companile designed to draw the smoke from a tunnel connected to the boiler rooms below the palm house. In the foreground is the Victoria Regia House, built by Turner in 1852.

193   Interior of the Palm House under construction, around 1847. The tubular purlins between the main ribs contain iron rods which were post-tensioned after assembly.

194   The interior of the Great Palm House from the *Illustrated London News*.

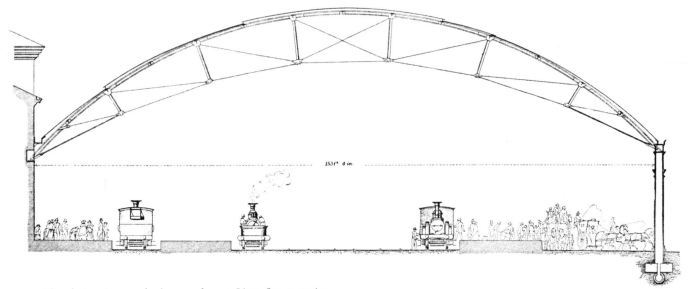

195 The daring iron and glass roof over Lime Street station, Liverpool by Richard Turner. Designed in 1847, it was completed after ten months' work in 1850.

when he questioned 'whether the ornamental restraint, combined with a real degree of expression should be credited to Turner or to Burton'.* Dr Chadwick also questioned Burton's contribution to the Great Conservatory at Chatsworth, seeing him as a supervisor and as providing working drawings for Paxton's main idea.** (Burton's office also produced drawings for the Kew Palm House.) An article in *Architectural Review* by Peter Ferriday† seems to re-establish Richard Turner in his position as designer, prefabricator, and builder at Kew. However, the former librarian and archivist of Kew, R. Desmond, credits Burton with the overall form of the Palm House in a well researched article 'Who Designed the Palm House in Kew Gardens?'§ Desmond reveals the following events based on pertinent quotes from the Kew Archives.

In 1844 Decimus Burton prepared sketch designs for the new Palm House, but Kew's director, William Hooker, and the curator, John Smith, rejected them because of the number of columns. Burton set about preparing an alternative design. About this time Turner arrived from Dublin and showed Hooker and his Commissioners a scale model with a central house and two wings. His design package, complete with estimates, was approved and it was agreed that he should make full drawings. Turner also was shown Burton's design which he confirmed as extravagant and 'encumbered with immense trussed arched columns'.

Burton had similar criticisms for Turner's plans, though he approved of the general scheme of central space and wings. He criticized Turner's inner row of columns and objected to the proportions and Turner's

126

'Ecclesiastical or Gothic style'. He forwarded a second design of his own and altered the centre section of Turner's scheme so it was similar to the Chatsworth conservatory, and added a lantern roof while suggesting a 'conventional horticultural style' (191). Turner, now with the contract for the iron work in his hand and working in collaboration with Burton, was able to write to Hooker, 'I am glad to inform you that Mr Burton is determined to make a most magnificent and beautiful range for you'. In short, Turner had suggested the overall layout of the building while Burton was responsible for the proportions of the central section as we see it today. Moreover, these great conservatories (particularly Kew) were sophisticated engineering feats requiring detailing, structural prefabrication and construction techniques natural to an engineer like Turner. After the initial form (and style) of an iron building had been decided, the architects' task appears to have been over. A similar situation occurred with Paxton's Crystal Palace, which could not have been built without the admirable skill of Charles Fox, whose firm, Fox and Henderson, were the contractors.

The dimensions of the Palm House are most impressive. The length is 362 ft 6 in; the central space 137 ft 6 in long, 100 ft wide, and 63 ft high, exclusive of the 6 ft lantern. Concrete foundations, by Grissel and Peto,

* H. R. Hitchcock, *Early Victorian Architecture in Britain,* p. 515.

** George F. Chadwick, *The Works of Sir Joseph Paxton,* p. 78.

† *Architectural Review,* Feb., 1957.

§ *Kew Bulletin,* vol. 26, 3.

196   Richard Turner's 'special mention' submission for the Great
Exhibition competition of 1850.

supported large granite blocks which had cast-iron soc-
kets for the 9-in main ribs of the framework. Turner's
wrought-iron ribs were made from lengths about 12 ft
long and welded together, then brought to the required
curve. The top part of the lower ribs is supported by cast-
iron columns and brackets which in turn support the
upper ribs and the balcony round the centre division of
the house. These ribs are braced together with wrought-
iron tie-rods inside cast-iron tubes, acting as purlins (193).
The wrought-iron rods were drawn taut after the building
was assembled. This put the unique hollow purlins in
compression, knitting the whole post-tensioned structure
together, a novel solution which formed part of a patent
granted to Turner in December 1846. The upper roof of
the centre space is supported on tubular cast-iron columns
that carry down the rain water collected in the gutter of
the upper roof into tanks formed round the whole of the
interior of the building. The water from the lower lean-to
roof is received into a gutter forming the upper part of
the plinth and is carried into the same tanks.

The Palm House created an artificial climate for the
exotic plants collected from all over the world (194). The
heating maintained an internal temperature of 80°F when
the external air was at 20°F with twelve boilers which fed
nearly $5\frac{1}{2}$ miles of pipe around the periphery and in

loops under the perforated cast-iron floor. The Victorians
went to great lengths to hide their mechanical services.
Turner's Burbidge and Healy boilers were placed in two
vaults beneath the house. Each boiler had its own set of
pipes to heat, so that, according to the temperature
required, one or more boilers could be fired. The boiler-
rooms were linked to the coal-yard and chimney campa-
nile by a 550-ft tunnel which, besides containing the smoke
flues, housed a railway, with iron wagons to carry coal
and to remove the ashes (190).

Turner designed and built the original roof of the
Broadstone Station, Dublin (1847), and the second train
shed at Lime Street Station, Liverpool (1849–1851) (195)
which has been demolished.

Richard Turner received international recognition in
the competition for the Great Exhibition Building in
Hyde Park (1850). His entry and Hector Horeau's*
received the only two 'special mention' awards among
the 245 submissions (196, 197). It is not surprising that
these two winning entries were in cast iron, wrought iron
and glass, for the Building Committee** of the Royal
Commission had a sympathetic eye for the new fireproof
materials, and hoped that prefabricated construction
could produce the largest building in the world in a year's
time.

Following the committee's guideline, Turner's entry
provided for one uninterrupted space about 1940 ft long
and 408 ft wide. Semicircular wrought-iron supporting
ribs made three avenues, the centre one 200 ft wide and
127 ft high and the side 104 ft wide and 77 ft high—impressive dimensions for the time. A transept cut across the

* Hector Horeau also received a runner-up prize in the Paris Halles
competition and was designer of the Lyons and Paris Winter Gardens.

** The Committee comprised the Duke of Buccleuch, who had many
glasshouses at Dalkeith Palace; the Earl of Ellesmere; the engineers
Robert Stephenson, I. K. Brunel and William Cubbitt and architects
C. R. Cockerell, Charles Barry and Professor T. L. Donaldson.

197 Hector Horeau's glass and iron competition entry for the 1850 Exhibition Building in Hyde Park was a simple shed roof basilica section, with four side-aisles and a transept. The nave ended in a domed, semi-circular apse.

centre of the building and a huge glass dome was proposed at the crossing of the main avenue. The ends of the building, as well as those of the transept, were filled in with tracery in the upper part and a colonnade below to protect the entrances. Galleries could be placed in the side avenues. The construction of the building was to have been principally of wrought-iron of a visual delicacy that would have delighted a Victorian visitor. The use of large quantities of wrought-iron was the scheme's downfall, for the difficulties of producing and assembling such an enormous amount in such a short period was considered impossible by the Building Committee.

In conjunction with his son, Turner had previously designed and constructed a model of an exhibition building and submitted it to the Royal Commission as early as its third meeting on 24 January 1850 (the meeting at which the Building Committee was appointed). It was obviously Turner's hope that the Commission would be favourably impressed, and appoint him as designer-builder. But the newly formed Building Committee very properly thought that the acceptance and adoption of any one person's design without competition was not in accordance with the spirit and nature of the whole undertaking,* which was, after all, an 'Exhibition of the Works of Industry of All Nations'. Turner's original model was even bigger than his commended submission. It was a huge rectangular glass conservatory 1,440 ft by 1,060 ft, with five domes rising out of the roof, the central dome 200 ft high and the others, 150 ft. Within the structure, a miniature railway was proposed to carry the public among the exhibits. The estimated cost was £300,000—

unfortunately far more than the Commission had collected from subscription.

The rules of the competition stated that the Committee did not have to build any of the entries, but could assemble ideas from them. In fact they rejected them all and a Committee design with an iron dome by I. K. Brunel was drawn up under the supervision of Matthew Digby Wyatt, Owen Jones and Charles Wild. It was published in the *Illustrated London News* of 22 June 1850 and created a great stir.

Behind the scenes Joseph Paxton with his contractors, Fox and Henderson, were manoeuvering to secure the contract** without competition, which they did on an agreed price to the Royal Commission of £79,800. Turner was furious, claiming that his 'special mention' design would have cost £69,000, or £10,800 less than Paxton's glass palace.†

Even with his defeats in the building competition, Turner had a big show at the Exhibition. Along with models of several iron-roofed buildings, including two to house a man-of-war, he displayed scale models of the Lime Street Station, the Kew Palm House, the Regent's Park Winter Garden, both of his designs for the Great Exhibition building, a range of glass conservatories

* *Minutes and Proceedings of the Institution of Civil Engineers*, 1849–50, p. 166.

** See George F. Chadwick, *The Works of Sir Joseph Paxton*.

† *Minutes and Proceedings of the Institution of Civil Engineers*, 1850–51 vol. 10, p. 167.

198   Above: in 1859 £10,000 was granted for new glasshouses at Kew. Decimus Burton prepared the plans for the five buildings and Cubitt & Co. carried them out. The whole range is 628 ft long and covers 1⅔ acres making it one of the largest groups on the world. The masonry façade afforded Burton the opportunity to introduce more 'style', resulting in a conservatory much less attractive to us today.

199   Right: in 1855 Professor John Hutton Balfour persuaded Parliament to vote £6,000 for the erection of a new Temperate Palm House, built in 1858 for the Royal Botanic Garden, Edinburgh.

(including a round one), and a ½-acre winter garden model in brass designed for the King of Prussia in Berlin.*

In 1851 Turner had another disappointment when he received only third prize for the Great Industrial Exhibition of 1853, in Dublin. It was won by John Benson of Cork, who was later knighted, as Paxton had been. There was some compensation, however, for Turner and the Hammersmith works were given the contract for the iron girders used in the construction of the mainly timber building.**

Charles McIntosh in *The Book of the Garden* refers to Richard Turner as 'one of the first hothouse architects of the day' (179–181). An exuberant and enthusiastic proponent of wrought-iron and glass, he produced drawings that show potential uses for the material that went beyond his own prolific building career. He was a visionary but also an enterprising businessman, who made full use of his engineering background, his manufacturing works and his team of Irish workmen to build a 'package deal' answering the customer's demands. Unlike today's glasshouse manufacturers who build limited designs, he distributed catalogues containing a wide variety of 'off the peg' houses and structures, for wrought and particularly, cast iron allowed a versatility in form and styles enjoyed by the Victorian consumer. Research on Richard

Turner's life and work is not complete, and a full study should be made of the designer and fabricator of the most beautiful glasshouses in the world.

Another remarkably versatile inventor was John Kibble, the son of a wealthy Glasgow merchant who described himself as an engineer, and whose talents included astronomer, photographer, botanist and glasshouse builder. He introduced a new method of propelling vessels on the Clyde by fitting the steamer, 'Queen of Beauty' with chain paddle floats. He made a large glass plate camera, which was said to be horse-drawn and to produce photographs with a degree of perfection never before attained. His sun pictures gained him a gold medal at the International Exhibition in London in 1851. His significant architectural ventures began on his retirement from Glasgow business when he moved to Coulport House, on the shores of Loch Long, around 1865. At Coulport he built his private iron-and-glass conservatory that was later to become the extraordinary Crystal Art Palace in Queen's Park, Glasgow (202).†

The Conservatory was much smaller in its original form than the one found in Glasgow today. The overall shape was similar, but the two side arms were originally only short compartments, and the large dome was supported on fewer columns. A few years after its construction, John Kibble proposed to give the structure, with enlargements, to Glasgow Corporation. With good business sense he suggested terms profitable to himself for a period of twenty years. Kibble would agree to move the building from Coulport and re-erect it in Queen's Park, and increase the size of the structure at his own expense. At the

* Great Exhibition of 1851, official illustrated catalogue.

** *The Builder,* vol. x, 1852, p. 589.

† A more detailed description of the Palace and its history can be found in a dissertation, 'The Kibble Palace' by Graham T. Smith (1971), University of Strathclyde, Glasgow.

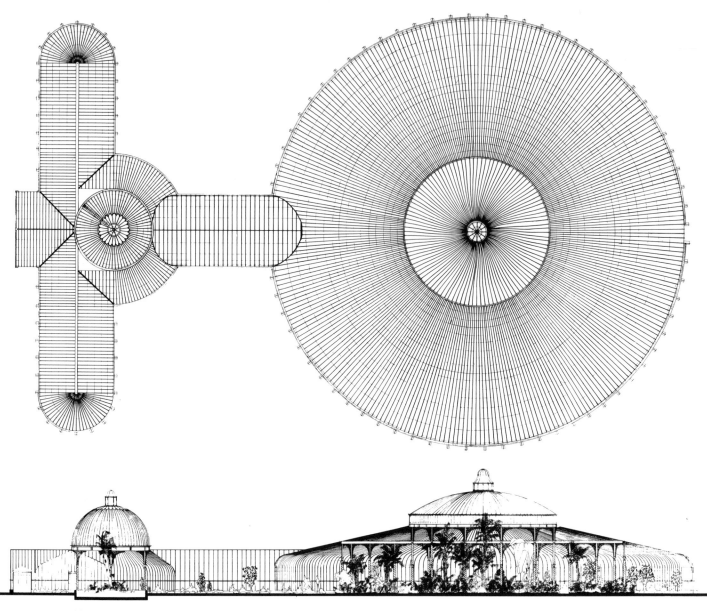

200–203   Above, the Crystal Art Palace, plan and elevation; below, as it stands today in the Queen's Park, Glasgow. Facing, left: caricature of John Kibble and right, the interior of the main hall of his Palace.

end of twenty years, he would hand the building over to the Corporation to be the property of the citizens forever. During the twenty-year period he would have the right to manage concerts and other entertainments and charge an entrance fee. In May 1872, the conservatory was dismantled and put on a raft to be towed by a Clyde 'Puffer' up the River Kelvin. As Kibble had promised the Corporation, he increased the diameter of the main dome to 146 ft, the link corridor to 36 ft and the two side arms to an imposing front elevation of 150 ft. As at Coulport, there was a rocky island, shrubs and statues, fountains, and rare plants, but now on a much grander scale. With exaggerated enthusiasm, Kibble described his Crystal Art Palace as a magnificent concert hall capable of containing 6,000 people. It was in fact a mighty attraction, at least to the middle class Glaswegians who lived in the West Side around Queen's Park, though it could have been a 'People's Paradise' and not just a 'West-end Pleasurance', had it been built, as originally intended, in the South Side Park where it would have been 'Seen of men', according to a crusading newspaper. In 1905, a glass People's Palace was in fact built for that purpose.

Kibble proposed a light and sound show with a 'powerful view-dissolving lantern' which would cover a 40 ft diameter disc. He had some hundred slides of exquisitely prepared natural objects and a 'oxyhydrogen microscope', which would show microscopic animalculæ enlarged to 3 ft. In the centre of the main dome was a large pond, under which he wanted an orchestra chamber, as 'music would form a melodious mystery to strangers', he said. The chamber was so constructed that the sounds could be admitted or shut out of the dome at will to create diminuendo and crescendo effects from the invisible performers. When this device was not in use, a fairy fountain in the middle threw forty jets to the height of 35 ft in the air, while coloured lights played on the rising and falling spray. The pond could be drained in one hour and boarded over to accommodate eight hundred people for concerts. Underneath the cast-iron fretwork floor were timber sleepers and three miles of 3-in copper heating tube. Six hundred gas jets provided light for the large glass dome which must have made a magnificent spectacle at night, both inside and out. The Kibble Crystal Art Palace Royal Botanic Gardens was officially opened with a capacity house promenade concert on 20 June 1873, just one year and a month after the glass and iron structure had been dismantled and towed from Loch Long. In the following years many shows and meetings were held in the Palace. In November 1873, the year of its opening, Disraeli made his inaugural address there as Lord Rector of the University to an audience of 4,000, as did Gladstone in December 1879 (200; 201, 203).

An extensive public glass construction was proposed for Hyde Park in 1877, this time to cover the Albert Memorial and protect it from London's putrid and damaging atmosphere (204). The project was suggested to Queen Victoria by John Wills, with the help of the architect of the Westminster Aquarium. Wills was nurseryman, florist, and bouquetist to the Queen and had several nurseries dotted throughout London with his main headquarters, The Royal Exotic Nursery, in South Kensington. He was extensively engaged in arranging and

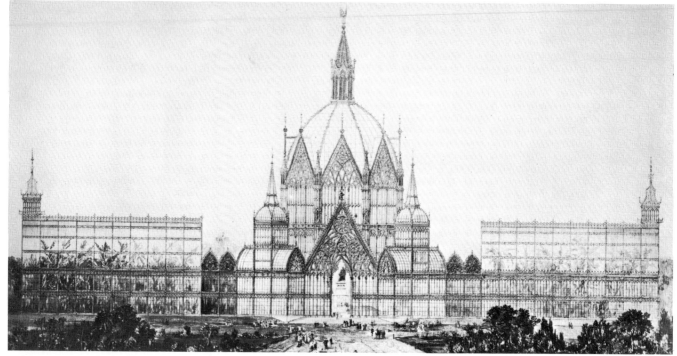

204, 205   Above: the Albert Memorial Conservatory, proposed by
John Wills in 1877. Below: Bournemouth Winter Garden by Fletcher
Lowndes & Co., 1876.

planting conservatories and constructing waterfalls and rockeries all over England and the Continent. King Leopold of Belgium summoned him to his palace at Laeken to lay out and decorate his newly-constructed palm house, orangery, and glass corridors in 1876. The huge iron, copper and glass dome, raised on the intersection of a cross 200 ft wide and surmounted by a lantern spire 350 ft high, was designed to cover the statue. Two wings were placed on each side of the central building both devoted to the illustration of vegetation from various regions of the Empire, particularly plants that served mankind by supplying food, medicine, clothing, or building materials.

The Prince Consort's idea of diffusing knowledge, and of binding different nationalities into one league by the bonds of peace and reciprocal interest, would thus be fittingly illustrated, while Horticulture, as the sister of Art, the handmaid of Science, and of ever-increasing commercial importance, would appropriately play its part.*

* *The Gardener's Chronicle*, 7 Apr. 1877.

9 The Crystal Palace and after

The Building Committee of the Royal Commission for the Great Exhibition decided in April 1850 to reject the competition designs of Hector Horeau and Richard Turner on the grounds of cost and a justified fear that they could not be built in time. The Committee's job was to produce the largest building the Victorian world had ever seen. They had no workable design, and it was just thirteen months before the Exhibition building was to open its doors to thousands of visitors on 1 May 1851. The Committee then delegated Matthew Digby Wyatt, Owen Jones and Charles Wild to design a new building based on the ideas from the competition. They designed a huge brick structure, with a vast iron dome by I. K. Brunel, which did not meet any of the competition criteria since it would take a long time to build, be difficult to dismantle, cost a great deal, and most probably collect moisture in the massive brick walls that had to be laid during the cold, damp English winter. Nevertheless, the Building Committee's design was presented to the public in the *Illustrated London News* on 22 June and sent to various contractors for bids on erecting and later removing it. This was a disappointing result for so grandoise a project, a Great Exhibition of the Industry of all Nations, initiated by Prince Albert at his Peace Congress, 'to proclaim to all foreigners that England should no longer be misunderstood', as the writer W. Bridges Adam described its purpose.

Paxton's influence in the House of Commons* and the Committee's own lack of confidence led to a clause in the specifications that allowed other bidders to submit alternative designs and costs. Paxton himself had an alternative to present, although time was short. He had already developed his construction techniques with the conservatories at Chatsworth, the Great Conservatory, and the Victoria Regia House, and had valuable communication with manufacturers and builders in the Midlands.

Sentiment had been favouring the dry method of construction (using no mortar or cement) proposed by Paxton, and rumours were rife that the Committee's massive design was seriously defective. As early as April 1850, while the Building Committee were preparing their designs, W. Bridges Adam in his *Westminster and Foreign Quarterly Review* described the criteria that the Committee should adopt for the building and what its future use could be. Adam's rational statements on the Industrial Exhibition represent him as a man of prophetic wisdom and, in proposing glass construction, a man ahead of his time.

> The design of the building should be as original as its object. It should not be suggestive of the ideas of a pyramid, a temple, or a palace; for it will not be a tomb, a place of public worship, nor a mansion of royalty. The object should determine the design. That is to say, the design should be altogether subordinate to the uses of the building, and should be of the kind that would express them, or at least harmonize with them.

Adam then enumerates the requirements of the building; that, for instance, it be fireproof, allow 'an abundance of

---

* See George F. Chadwick, *The Works of Sir Joseph Paxton,* chapter on the Great Exhibition, for an excellent detailed account.

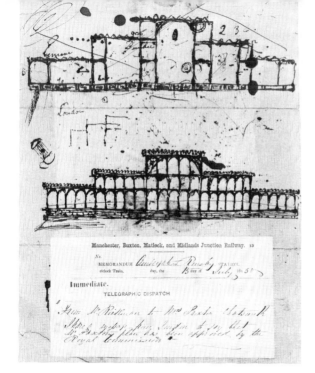

206 Joseph Paxton's first sketch of the Crystal Palace on blotting paper, 11 June 1850 together with the telegram to his wife disclosing the approval of his tender by the Royal Commission a month later. An incredible amount of work had been achieved in that month.

207 The Crystal Palace, viewed from Hyde Park, was sited near Prince's Gate, north of Kensington Road and south of the park drive called Rotten Row. In the immediate background is South Kensington and Belgravia, with the Thames far in the distance. The house in the foreground provided power to work the various steam-driven machines on display.

light', be transportable, or at least useful past the duration of the Great Exhibition. Obviously influenced by the winning designs of Turner and Horeau, Adam continues his recommendations, specifying iron and glass, 'open towards the south, . . . a system of flues' and 'ventilation for preserving an equitable temperature'. His suggestions fitted well into Paxton's plans. Assured that new designs would be considered, Paxton visited the Hyde Park site the first week of June, and on 7 June left London to visit Robert Stephenson's Menai railway bridge, which he saw on 10 June. On his return to Derby on 11 June he made his famous blotting-paper sketch (206) showing a section through a three-tiered structure with ridge and furrow roofing and a central nave with a laminated arch reminiscent of the Capesthorne conservatory. Between 12 June and 20 June, Paxton with his staff at Chatsworth and the help of the Midland Railway engineer, Henry Barlow, worked fastidiously to complete the drawings. On 22 June, he had finished designs to show to Lord Granville of the Finance Committee and on 24 June, had a long interview with Prince Albert, only two days after the Building Committee had published their design in the *Illustrated London News*. The Commission discussed both plans several times and a stormy debate developed in the House of Commons on 2 July. Paxton, full of confidence and impatient to get on with the work, appealed to the public by having his design published with a long article in the 6 July *Illustrated London News*. The article discussed the structure in great detail, explaining the ventilation 'by filling in every third upright compartment with lufferboard', using canvas on the roof and

south wall as a shield from the sun and avoiding any 'interior division-walls' with 'the whole structure supported on cast-iron columns'. Paxton had already worked out precise and appealing details for the building.

A construction of some 18 acres in size with a time schedule so tight could only come about with a maximum of team effort and familiarity with construction materials and methods. Dr G. F. Chadwick has confirmed Paxton's contribution to the overall idea and many of the major roofing and glazing details. On 22 June, Paxton showed his drawings to Charles Fox of the contractors, Fox and Henderson and to Robert Lucas Chance, the Birmingham glass manufacturer who had previously developed the blown cylinder method for producing the 10 in by 48 in sheets for the Great Conservatory at Chatsworth. They agreed to put in a joint bid, which gave them eighteen days until the final submission date of 10 July.

Fox and Henderson & Co. were a large engineering and construction firm with plants in London, Smethwick and Renfrew, which at that time mainly supplied railway stock throughout the world. After their work on the exhibition, they were involved in the construction of the roofs of the railway stations at Paddington and Waterloo in London, New Street in Birmingham, and in Oxford.* However, when they tendered on the exhibition building, they had had no experience with Paxton's ridge and furrow. On 29 June, formal agreement was signed between

* A construction similar to the Crystal Palace was built at Oxford station. The Science Museum, London, has one of the Oxford bays which it is planned to re-assemble.

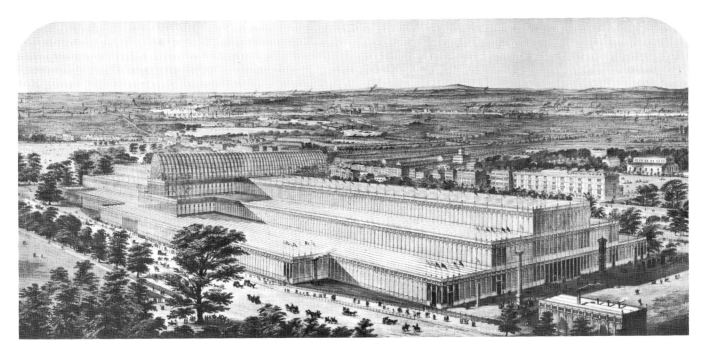

the three parties, Fox and Henderson & Co., Chance Brothers & Co. and Paxton. They then had a frantic ten days to settle the important details of the bid.

The Building Committee had assumed a bay spacing for the exhibitors of 24 ft; Paxton's proposal unfortunately assumed a building module of 20 ft. This was adjusted, and a joint bid was offered of £150,000 if the building stayed in the hands of the Commission, but, as an alternative, only £79,800 if all the materials remained the property of Fox and Henderson. This bid was much lower than those for the Building Committee's design, and Joseph Paxton had previously demonstrated that his type of construction could meet such a deadline. One difficulty remained: the group of elms that ran across the middle of the proposed site. A public outcry to save the trees made the Committee request Fox and Henderson to build over the trees without extra cost. This they were prepared to do, and as Henderson had already proposed a transept to enhance the beauty of the building, the Committee suggested that it cover the trees in question. But their transept was lower than the elms, so Paxton proposed an arched roof, on the lines of his conservatory at Chatsworth. On 15 July, the Building Committee advised the Commission to accept, which they did on 26 July.

An incredible amount of work was accomplished in the month between Paxton's inkblotter sketch on 11 June and the final submission on 10 July. Still more incredible were the events to follow immediately after the acceptance of the proposal; they certainly represent the courage of the mid-Victorian industrialists. Charles Fox with his railway engineering background immediately began working night and day to realize Paxton's ideas. He and his subcontractors had to design and manufacture all the components and build a structure in under a year. Without a signed contract for the building, Henderson had subcontracted Cochrane & Co. and Jobson, both from Dudley, to supply the cast-iron columns and girders; and Mr Birch of the Phoenix Sawmills, Cumberland Market, Regent's Park, to fabricate the wood components. Fox and Henderson themselves supplied the wrought-iron work. Chance had to increase the output of his factory to make approximately 900,000 sq.ft of 16 oz glass. The official contract was signed on 31 October, though the first column had risen on the site some five weeks before.

Charles Fox submitted his detailed designs and calculations to the engineer, William Cubitt, the Chairman of the Building Committee, who had been selected to represent the Royal Commission in supervising Fox and Henderson's construction. For his important task he was assisted by Charles Heard Wild and later knighted along with Paxton and Fox, though there is some question as to what, if any, duties Sir William had performed.

There was no question at all about the task Fox and Henderson played in constructing the 1,848 ft long by 456 ft wide structure with its 772,784 sq. ft of ground floor area, 217,100 sq. ft of gallery space, 372 roof trusses, 24 miles of Paxton gutter, 205 miles of sash bar and 600,000 cubic feet of timber. Charles Fox, besides designing and integrating all the components, later supervised the construction. The contract in which Fox functioned as an architect and builder was no different from the 'package deal' of today. Representing the Com-

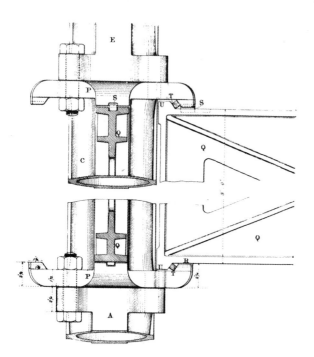

208 The 'key' detail that saved weeks of construction time: a wrought-iron wedge (T) secured the cast-iron girders to the connection collar.

209 The workman in the foreground is painting the junction between the 3 ft short column and the cast-iron truss. This special connection required no bolts, being fixed with only a wrought-iron pin. Below him the floor boards are being nailed to the sleepers. Above him some of the steeple-jacks are assembling the framed structure. In the nave, the wrought-iron trusses are being assembled. They will be positioned to take the force of the arched transept as it crosses the nave. The laminated wood arches that span the elm trees are also being fabricated, using the bottom arch as a template for the others.

mission, Cubitt was to keep his eyes on the accounts and the quality of construction, though no doubt fully aware that if Fox and Henderson were not given a free rein, the completion date would certainly not be met. The actual detailing and construction with these new materials most certainly had to be left in the hands of the engineer-builders. Architects had little to contribute to the construction as had also been Richard Turner's experience with the architect Decimus Burton, at Kew and Regent's Park. Fox and Turner organized, fabricated, delivered and erected their structures with materials that were not familiar to the architects of the day. Charles Dickens, in *Household Words,* stared in wonder, as most of the people must have done:

> Two parties in London, relying on the accuracy and good faith of certain iron-masters, glassworkers in the provinces, and of one master-carpenter in London, bound themselves for a certain sum, and in the course of four months, to cover 18 acres of ground, with a building upwards of a third of a mile long.

The manufacturing techniques and the various systems in the building represent the sophistication that the mid-century Victorian engineers and builders had attained since the first cast-iron frame construction by Boulton and Watt in Manchester in 1801. Using today's building jargon, the Exhibition building was the product of mechanization, mass production, prefabrication, standardization, modular construction, systems-integration, critical path, rapid site assembly, dismantling and . . . ingenuity, a commodity they had in abundant supply.

The Exhibition building was built with standardized

prefabricated components based on a 24 ft module. This module conformed to the Exhibition use requirements and the smallest standardized element, the glass. Paxton's ridge and furrow roof glazing system required a 49 in length of sheet glass so that it could span 8 ft furrow to furrow, or three ridges per 24 ft bay. The main ground floor of the 3-tiered building was basically 1,848 ft by 408 ft. A 72 ft timber-arched transept crossed the lengthy nave in the middle. The level above the ground contained a gallery in a 264 ft wide by 1,848 ft space, and the top roof was a strip of ridge and furrow 120 ft wide. All these dimensions, along with the subsequently added ground floor north extension (48 ft by 936 ft), are based upon the 4 ft, 8 ft, and 24 ft module. Ten double staircases 8 ft wide gave access to the $1\frac{3}{4}$ mile long gallery level that added another 5 acres of floor area to the near 18 acres at ground level (207).

The cast-iron columns arrived on the site with their ends turned on a lathe which ensured an accurate length and a sealed joint, which when bolted together, allowed the passage of rainwater. A canvas gasket dipped in white lead was fitted at the joints. At each floor and roof level, a 3 ft connection collar with its cast-iron connecting-lip was bolted on top of the longer columns. This enabled the cast-iron girders with their specially cast projections to slide into the grooves and be secured with a wrought-iron key. All the columns had the same outer diameter, so all the girders were a standardized length. The wall thickness of the column, however, varied according to the weight it had to support within the system. One can imagine the detailed system Fox had to devise to ensure

that a column arrived at its correct position on the $\frac{1}{3}$ of a mile building site. The depth of all the spanning girders was 3 ft, except where the transept crossed the nave; there it was increased to 6 ft. The basic spanning girder was of cast-iron, nominally 24 ft long. It was used to support the gallery and its upper roof. The 72 ft roof span across the nave, and the other 48 ft roof spans were carried with wrought-iron trusses, possessing better tensile strength than would those of cast-iron. Wood trusses 24 ft long were used to support the roof above the one storey ground floor area, probably for economic reasons and the light structural requirements. Across the transept, springing from a height of 63 ft, a series of wood laminated arches spanned 72 ft, creating a Chatsworth Great Conservatory in the sky, complete with the ridge and furrow glass skin (208; 209; 211).

Paxton's structural wood and iron rainwater gutter was the basic element that spanned the 24 ft between the structural girders. With its rainwater channel and its condensation grooves milled from a 5 in by 6 in timber, it rested on main water gutters supported by the girders. The large amount of wood used in Paxton's glazing system clearly belies any conception that the Crystal Palace either at Hyde Park or later at Sydenham was a complete essay in glass and iron. Dimensional stability required that sash bars and gutters used in this way should only be made of well-seasoned timber (deal). Fox and Henderson, unable to secure enough, had to use green timber in some of the areas, which resulted in leaks and some public criticism (210, 214).

Paxton's original design used a patented screw pile to dig into the ground, which pleased the committee, concerned as it was to disturb the site as little as possible. This was however abandoned. The centre line of each row of columns was set out with a theodolite, and the centre-to-centre of the columns were measured with a wood rod exactly 24 ft in length. A stake was driven to position the centre of the column, and when it came time to dig the concrete footings, two stakes were driven into the ground at a distance of 6 ft from the column stake. A right-angled triangular wood template was then used to position the 2 ft by 1 ft cast-iron base plate on the concrete footing. The footing was usually 2 ft by 3 ft, varying in dimension with the load and in depths varying from 1 ft to 4 ft according to the soil conditions. Fortunately there was a gravel stratum just below the surface, resulting in very few foundation problems. The site had a slight fall from west to east, so the whole building was constructed on an inclination of 1 inch in 24 ft and the columns deviated from vertical by the same degree. This resulted in the east end of the building being 6 ft lower than the west (213).

At 24 ft intervals on the outer skin, structural cast-iron columns supported the floors and roof above. Each 24 ft bay was divided by two wood columns shaped to look exactly like their cast-iron counterpart. A decorative cast-iron frame held the columns together and produced three visually unified 8 ft wall modules per bay. Behind this exo-frame, there were prefabricated panels of glass, or wood boarding, or doors to suit the functional requirements of the interior or of visual harmony. A 3 ft band of louvred ventilation ran around each tier at the top of the

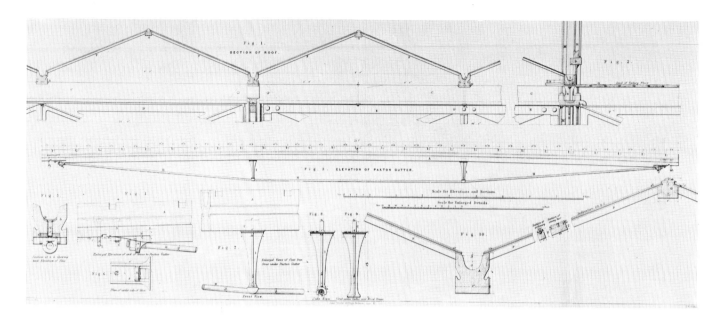

210, 211 Above, details of the Paxton gutter; left, the laminated wood arches, designed to allow the elms to remain within the building, were the same width as the area they were to cover, making them difficult to place. Fastened together, they formed a structural pre-assembled unit that was lifted up at an angle and dropped into place.

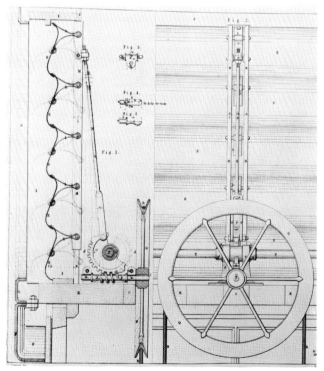

212 The galvanized sheet-iron louvres on the upper level were opened with a wheel and cord attached to the operating gear at ground level. It was possible to open a 216-ft run of louvres from one point.

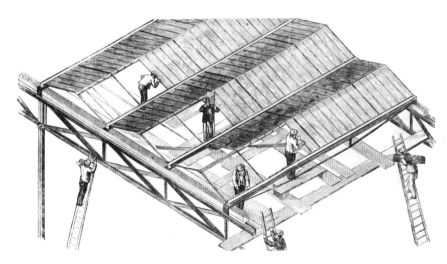

213   Cast-iron base plates and short columns, which varied in height depending on the slope of the site, were set on concrete pads. Hot lead sealed the joint between the vertical column and the horizontal pipe system that transferred the rainwater from the hollow columns down the natural slope to the east.

214   Glazing the roof on the lower areas without the aid of the glazing wagons clearly shows the notches in the gutter and ridge that the sash-bars were fitted into and the temporary sash bars supporting the ridge-bar. The two holes in the end of the Paxton gutter received wooden dowels.

wall. The ground floor had a band of ventilation at ground level, and the whole system was operated by a series of wheels, rods and gears, enabling an operator to open or close 108 ft of sheet metal louvre on each side of the mechanism. Plans were originally made to hang coarse canvas soaked with water in front of the louvres as a kind of crude cooling system (212).

The ground floor boarding, resting on sleepers, was spaced with a ½ in gap* to facilitate easy cleaning with a machine devised by Paxton involving water sprays and revolving brushes. This machine was not required, for the female Victorian attire performed this function admirably. The floor boards brought to the site at the beginning of construction were first used as a fence to protect the construction. When the building was enclosed, flooring was needed and the fence was dismantled, and used in the building. Paxton was said to have devised a way to make the fence without nails so that the boards were not damaged—such was his ingenuity (see 215).

Paxton had first used his sash-bar machine in August 1838 to groove the thousands of feet of wood for the Great Conservatory at Chatsworth. He had previously visited various workshops in London, Manchester and Birmingham to pick up information on woodworking techniques. The sash-bar machine was combined with a Boulton and Watt steam engine, which was also used for other tasks around Chatsworth. The whole cutting apparatus, including the table, cost him £20, and he

estimated that by the end of construction he had saved £1,400 in manual labour for grooving the 48-in bars. No doubt having previously contrived many mechanized techniques in their railway work, Fox and Henderson and their subcontractors used all the labour-saving devices they could on the Crystal Palace—both for cost and speed. Most of the machines were designed by Edward Alfred Cowper who was at that time working for the contractors.

At the Phoenix works, Birch had a number of machines for the large amount of wood used on the building. The rough timber was first worked with an adzing and planing machine or a circular planing machine. The square stock was run through a gutter-cutting machine which grooved the wood and cut it off at the required 24 ft length. Planks were run through a sash-bar machine and the bars painted with a painting machine. The majority of the roof glazing was done from glazing wagons that moved on wheels in the Paxton gutters. Holes were punched through the wrought-iron bars with a machine powered by steam at the Hyde Park site. These bars were used to assemble the huge iron trusses for the larger spans. The 24 ft cast-iron girders were all weighed and tested with a hydraulic press to detect any defect in the casting before being lifted into position. The building was designed so that it was made of few large pieces, the largest casting being the 24 ft girder weighing under a ton. This enabled a system of block and tackle, horse-drawn or hand-winched, to manipulate and lift the elements (215–220).

The Palace of the Great Exhibition was allowed to remain in Hyde Park through 1851 and into the next year,

* A cigarette falling into a similar gap at Sydenham was suggested as the cause of the fire.

215   As each 23 ft 3 in cast-iron girder arrived at the site, it was weighed, because of the possibility of air pockets in the casting causing structural failures. At the rear of the site is the fence made from the floor boarding of the building.

216   The sash-bar machine enabled a whole plank to be fed through a series of circular saws and cutters to groove the bar. Three hundred planks were fed in a typical 10-hour day, allowing ten minutes each hour for sharpening the cutters. Each plank produced three strips of bar that were cut to proper lengths, or about 2¾ miles of bar per day.

for Paxton influenced Parliament to vote for its retention until May 1852. Meanwhile, controversy was raging over what should be done with the great glass building that had proved so popular (221; 222). W. Bridges Adam had anticipated the debate when he wrote in 1850:

A rumour has reached us—but we are unwilling to believe that it is entitled to credit—that the Commissioners, while making preparations for an outlay exceeding £100,000, contemplate nothing beyond the immediate end for which it will be raised; and that they propose that the building which is to cost this large sum shall be pulled down at the close of the Exhibition, and the materials sold!

He then proposed a use that became popular for the great empty glass building in 1852:

Why should the inhabitants of the metropolis not be enabled to command between the months of October and April of every year, the facilities a winter garden would afford for healthful enjoyment; and especially that large and invalid class of our population whom the first breath of a north-easterly wind now consigns to the imprisonment of their own dwellings?

Paxton also suggested it for a People's Winter Garden, enclosing winding promenades, equestrian exercise areas and carriage drives among trees and greenery of perpetual summer. He proposed that the whole ground floor façade be removed in summer to create a continuous uninterrupted vista of Hyde Park. But more important, Paxton discussed in a pamphlet the maintenance and operation cost for such a winter garden, which demonstrated its potential profitability. Other proposals were to move

parts of the building to Battersea Park or Kew, but estimates of cost made these seem impractical. A Commission was formed by the government to review the matter. This was an opportunity for Paxton and another partizan of the Crystal Palace, Henry Cole, to demonstrate their own schemes for converting it into a Winter Garden much finer than the one standing in the inner circle of Regent's Park. With all the evidence collected, Paxton's statements were unfortunately misconstrued by the Members of Parliament, who inferred that a new Winter Garden could be built for less money than the conversion of the existing structure* this, and Prince Albert's wishes that the building be not retained, influenced the Commons to vote in April 1852 for its removal.

Paxton, not to be outdone, formed a public company in May, backed by half a million pounds in capital, to take over, relocate, and run the Crystal Palace for the benefit of the people and, of course, profit. Samuel Laing, of the London, Brighton, and South Coast Railway was appointed Chairman and Paxton, Francis Fuller, Scott Russell, and Matthew Digby Wyatt were among the directors. The Crystal Palace Company secured 349 acres of wooded parkland, including the east slope of Sydenham Hill and contracted Fox and Henderson to re-erect the Palace where it would have a commanding view of the surrounding Surrey and Kent Countryside. The company then sold 149 acres, and were left with a 200-acre pleasure ground conveniently sited along Laing's

* See George F. Chadwick, *The Works of Sir Joseph Paxton,* chapter on the Sydenham Crystal Palace, for an account of this episode.

217–19 Above: Wood stock was drawn through a gutter-cutting machine that milled the gutter and the side condensation channels, cut to the desired 24-ft length and drilled ready to receive wooden dowels at the site. Centre: sash bars were immersed in a tub of paint and then drawn through a set of fixed brushes, the paint being brushed off, instead of on. Below: the glazing waggon moving along in the Paxton gutter. The boys behind are mixing putty and preparing sash bars.

220 Below: the trusses were raised with poles, block and tackle.

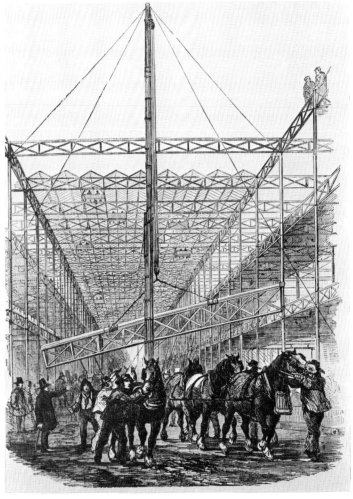

NATIONAL DISGRACE.

221 One architect's proposal was to convert the Crystal Palace into a tower looming 1,000 feet over London.

222 John Leech's cartoon in *Punch* of the 'National Disgrace' in 1853.

London to Brighton railway line within easy reach of London (223).

The Hyde Park Crystal Palace provided some of the components for Paxton's more grandiose design at Sydenham, that began construction in August 1852. Paxton added many extravagances in the new building and gardens which kept the company far from realizing any profit. The Sydenham site sloped so steeply that a basement floor had to be built to give a level plateau for the iron and glass construction. Remembering Barry's earlier suggestion of an arched roof over the main nave, Paxton adopted the idea for his 1,608 ft long Sydenham Palace nave. A huge, raised, 384 ft long central transept was sprung from the summit of this arched roof, adding an additional two storeys to the construction, so that what had once been a three storey building became six. Two more 336 ft long transepts were constructed at each end of the nave to balance the composition. The new structure nearly doubled the glass area of the original Hyde Park building. Inside, the side aisles were divided into courts representing the architecture of various epochs. The court idea gained the support of Ruskin, adding credibility to the historic venture. Architects Digby Wyatt and Owen Jones scoured Europe for maps, drawings, models, or casts to authenticate the Assyrian, Greek, Roman, Byzantine, Moorish, Egyptian, Chinese, and Renaissance courts built alongside Pugin's English Medieval Court which had been brought to Sydenham with the Hyde Park components. Paxton filled the nave with full-grown trees, exotic shrubbery, fountains and pools, all at enormous expense. In the central transept a

gigantic organ was built with a tiered concert platform large enough for 4,000 performers (224; 225, 226).

The new building, though a great technical achievement, was indeed much more complex than the original structure at Hyde Park and with its 843,656 cubic feet, nearly half again its predecessor's size. Paxton introduced heating with 22 boilers paired and distributed along the basement under the nave and serviced by an internal roadway. These low-pressure hot water systems combined with the special boilers for the tropical and aquatic plants had nearly fifty miles of pipe.** This extra heating added greatly to the operational cost when compared to the unheated Hyde Park palace.

It was Paxton's idea that the gardens and fountains around the Sydenham Palace should rival even those of Versailles. In order to maintain the required water pressure for the fountains, the Company commissioned I. K. Brunel to design two 282 ft high 300,000 gallon water towers which they later built at each end of the great nave, conforming to the symmetrical composition and also acting as chimneys for the boilers under the nave, and for the steam-engine pumps located at their base.

Queen Victoria opened the building on 10 June 1854, and for a period of time the Sydenham Crystal Palace enjoyed enormous popularity with London day-trippers. Besides the permanent displays and activities, the special

* A pictorial history is to be found in Patrick Beaver, *The Crystal Palace,* 1970.

** A more specific description can be found in George F. Chadwick, *The Works of Sir Joseph Paxton,* p. 148.

223 The Sydenham Crystal Palace and grounds during the Festival of Empire, 1911. The north transept and wing were destroyed by fire in 1866.

224 Preparing the stage for the Royal Opening in the central transept.

225 The Open Colonnade at Sydenham. The details are similar to those at the Hyde Park Palace. Paxton stands on the left.

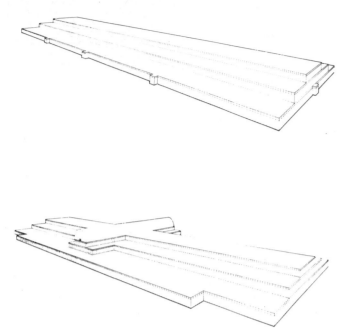

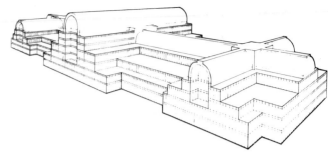

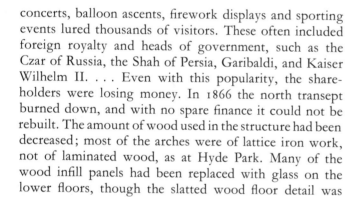

226 Top left: the design first proposed by Joseph Paxton. Left: the Crystal Palace as built in Hyde Park in 1851 and above, as it was rebuilt on Sydenham Hill in 1854, before the fire of 1866. The structure stood until the final fire of 1936.

227 Re-glazing a transept of the Sydenham Palace in 1899. ▷

concerts, balloon ascents, firework displays and sporting events lured thousands of visitors. These often included foreign royalty and heads of government, such as the Czar of Russia, the Shah of Persia, Garibaldi, and Kaiser Wilhelm II. . . . Even with this popularity, the shareholders were losing money. In 1866 the north transept burned down, and with no spare finance it could not be rebuilt. The amount of wood used in the structure had been decreased; most of the arches were of lattice iron work, not of laminated wood, as at Hyde Park. Many of the wood infill panels had been replaced with glass on the lower floors, though the slatted wood floor detail was retained in the new building. The glazing was still held in Paxton's wooden ridge and furrow construction, 21 oz glass being substituted for the 16 oz used before.

On 30 November 1936, when a fire broke out, a strong wind from the north west turned the central transept into a giant conflagration and the flames soon scaled the highest galleries out of reach of the fire hoses. It was visible to all of London and for miles around (as far as Cambridge), a spectacle that was the last anyone saw of the great Sydenham Crystal Palace. It was still remarkable that this structure, clad in glass thinner than horticultural glass used today, had stood for eighty-two years (227).

The Crystal Palace caused an immediate glass mania, albeit perhaps a minor one, in England. Small palaces were proposed for Manchester, Bath, Plymouth and London.* Engineers and cast-iron manufacturers saw the marketing potential of prefabricated construction. Glass arcades, markets and Winter Gardens, were built all over England throughout the sixties and seventies; the arcades

in Birmingham, Manchester, Newcastle to name a few, being the shopping centres of the day. An international impact resulted in exhibitions throughout the world.

Sir Joseph Paxton was a very popular figure in the fifties at the height of his glass building career.** Besides the Sydenham Palace, he proposed several glass constructions modelled on components from his previous work. Two of these were the Royal Exchange roofing and a Crystal 'Sanitarium'. Both were to be constructed from wood arches patterned on the transept covering of the Crystal Palace. Paxton knew how to exploit his ideas as well as his popularity. In 1851 he presented the design for a glass roof to the merchants who marketed in the court of the Royal Exchange (228). The design was rejected however by the governing committee. Another unbuilt project was a sanitorium in Victoria Park for the City of London Hospital for Diseases of the Chest (229). Paxton outlined his proposal as a prototype for all city hospitals. The building, with a 72 ft arched span (same as the Crystal Palace), would be 200 ft long and connected by two ridge and furrow corridors to the hospital, affording a large enough space for patients to exercise without being exposed to the open air. He went on to describe the variableness of the English climate, its humidity and the murkiness and impurity of the air, which could aggravate respiratory ailments, especially during London's winter months. Inside the huge health conservatory, the climate would be temperate, pure, sunny without undue humi-

* See George F. Chadwick, *The Works of Sir Joseph Paxton,* p. 156.

** Paxton was elected M.P. for Coventry in 1854.

144

228   The proposed Royal Exchange roof by Paxton.

229   The 'Crystal Sanitarium' by Joseph Paxton.

dity. Another of Paxton's ideas for the hospital anticipated complete air conditioning as we know it today.

> The ventilation should be constructed to afford a free circulation of air without direct currents; and no cold outer air should enter the building until it has been warmed, purified, and rendered fit for easy respiration.

Nor was Paxton content to confine these glass health resorts to the infirm:

> I advocate their general adoption as promoters of public health, combined with pleasing instruction; and by this means some of the squares of London might, by being covered, form the most delightful and interesting places of resort at all seasons.

In 1855, Paxton put forward a proposal, 'The Great Victorian Way' to the Committee on Metropolitan Communication.* Though an interesting glass-roofed structure, it was more important from a city planning point of view and represents Paxton's railway interests and urban concern. A similar idea, 'The Crystal Way' was submitted by William Moseley (1855) and followed a part of the route of London's present underground.

Paxton was to propose his finest and final great glass building in 1861, to be erected as an exhibition building at St Cloud, near Paris (230). Dr G. F. Chadwick thinks it was an early proposal for the 1867 International Exhibition, which Paxton would have wanted to show to Louis Napoleon when they met in 1862. Professor Hitchcock suggests that Owen Jones, the authority on Saracenic style, who was to propose a separate design for St Cloud, influenced Paxton's design with its three great glass domes that bulged from the side of the 1,952 ft long by

146

304 ft wide building, whose dimensions were reminiscent of Paxton's Palace in Hyde Park, the central dome being 328 ft in diameter and 360 ft high and the end domes, 216 ft in diameter and 250 ft high.

Architect Owen Jones had contributed greatly to the visual clarity of the Crystal Palace, for it was he who selected light blue for the structure, red for the underside of the girders, yellow cross-bracing and yellow and blue for the columns. He also designed the decoration on the gallery balustrades and stairs and suggested hanging oriental carpets over the galleries. Jones, because of his flair for decoration and his interest in Moorish art, became a major proponent of the Saracenic Style, so much so that he was often referred to as 'Alhambra' Jones.

Jones was also a proponent of Paxton's glass architecture. He designed and built the Crystal Palace Bazaar in Oxford Street using iron and glass and proposed his own glass exhibition building for St Cloud, Paris. His most exciting project was the 1859 design for the People's Palace to be sited in the north London suburb of Muswell Hill (232). The Palace straddled the top of the hill surrounded by a gently undulating wooded park with artificial gardens in the Italian, French and Old English style. Its high position allowed the site to include a large railway terminal which was to be served by the London and North-Western, the Eastern Counties and the Great Western railways, as well as the Great Northern, which was sponsoring the project with its subsidiary, the

---

* An illustration of the Victoria Way appears in *Country Life*, 9 Dec. 1965.

230 Joseph Paxton's St Cloud project.

Great Northern Palace Company. The link with the railways was to enable the 'visitors from the manufacturing areas of all Britain to participate in the instruction and amusement, being transported by excursion trains without the annoyance, delay and expense of working their way through the crowded streets of London'. Though sitting in the country, the Palace was to be connected to the National transportation network, a link to this nineteenth-century vision of the workers' paradise.

A two hundred foot diameter raised Winter Garden was to be in the centre of the Palace (233), positioned between four viewing towers and connected to the two upper galleries. There had been difficulty at the Sydenham Crystal Palace in keeping the right temperature for tropical plants. Here the Winter Garden was isolated from the rest of the building, so that its heat and moisture could not damage the other displays.

The 1,296 ft by 492 ft Modern English and Moorish-styled building was to be completely covered with glass, either with Paxton's ridge and furrow roofing used in the most inventive way, or as flat sheets in the walls and ornamental domes. Though the People's Palace lacked the visual clarity of the Crystal Palace, had it been built it would have been one of the most exciting amusement complexes in the nineteenth century and would have made its designer, 'Alhambra' Jones, as noted as Paxton.

The Royal Italian Opera House was destroyed by fire in 1856. The same site was leased from the Duke of Bedford to Frederick Gye. A new theatre (Covent Garden Opera House, still in existence today) was begun in 1857 following the designs of architect E. M. Barry, Charles

Barry's other architect son. In 1858 the Piazza Hotel, adjacent to the new theatre on the south side, was demolished and the site prepared for a new Floral Hall (231). Gye intended to lease stalls in the Hall for the sale of flowers, plants and seeds. Building began in 1858, the architect was also Barry, the contractors C. and T. Lucas, and the ironwork from Henry Grissel. The Hall extends some 230 ft back from Bow Street and ended in an iron and glass dome. The north side of the long nave abuts on the Opera House. Another entrance faces the Covent Garden Square. Each point in the interior cornice above the columns had a gas jet providing a romantic light to the activity below. The columns were perforated, and provided ventilation for the 18 ft deep cellars beneath.

For many years Gye and his successors tried to get permission from the Dukes to use the Hall as a market, but with no success. Licences were granted occasionally for concerts, exhibitions and as a drill hall. The West London Industrial Exhibition was held at the Floral Hall in 1865. The Ninth Duke of Bedford finally bought the Hall in 1887, and turned it into a foreign fruit market which relieved some of the congestion of the Covent Garden area. The Floral Hall exists today, at least up to the brackets above the columns, for the arched iron and glass roof and dome were destroyed by fire in 1956.

The 1851 Crystal Palace made an immediate impact on those who saw it in Hyde Park, and the technical achievements displayed so dramatically on Sydenham hill astounded contemporary observers and architectural critics. The Palaces' bare unadorned modular bones, however, countered the accepted decorative thinking too

231   Main entrance, Floral Hall, built at the same time as the Covent Garden Opera House, 1857–8. E. M. Barry.

232, 233   Above: design for the Palace of the People, 1859, at Muswell Hill, by Owen Jones. The north front, showing the railway terminus beneath. Below: the central winter garden, a beautiful, delicate structure.

strongly, and even Paxton considered the framed structures built in glass limited to special circumstances.

Paxton, as had Loudon before him, made enormous contributions to horticulture as well as architecture. The two men designed and improved glasshouses with scientific and functional purpose that also made for magnificent structures, at least to us today. They were also architects with no formal training. Loudon designed villas, farm buildings, inns and furniture; Paxton, Italian and Tudor villas, Norman cottages, mock Elizabethan ⁄ country houses and utilitarian train stations. From both, much is mediocre architecture, with very little environmental understanding and little experimentation in new materials. A utilitarian use of iron, wood and glass was reserved for industry, transportation and exhibition buildings. What they considered permanent buildings were constructed of masonry or carved stone in the style of the time. Even utilitarian structures, bridges, railway stations, when the budget could afford it, were covered with Gothic, Greek, Egyptian or Saracenic decoration (234–6). Architect and engineer were really in the same camp, accepting simplicity and utilitarian buildings, but not in architecture. The Crystal Palace of 1851, as we have seen, was built with techniques as sophisticated as those of today. They resulted from step by step discoveries that Paxton made empirically as early as 1828. They were cunningly used by a sophisticated building industry, nurtured with railway expansion, which required new methods and materials. We consider those results marvellous. But to the powerful legislator of style, John Ruskin, the Crystal Palace was no more than a feat of engineering. He wrote in *Stones of Venice:*

> The quantity of bodily industry which that crystal palace expresses is very great. So far so good. . . . The quantity of thought it expresses is, I suppose, a single and very admirable thought of Sir Joseph Paxton's, probably not a bit brighter than thousands of thoughts which pass through his active and intelligent brain every hour—that it might be possible to build a greenhouse larger than ever was built here. This thought, and some very ordinary algebra, are as much as all that glass can represent of human intellect.

In 1860 Paxton proposed a Winter Garden for Queen's Park, Glasgow, which could hardly be called a glass building, with its neo-Classical stone façade. The contrast between this building and his finest design, the exhibition building in St Cloud in 1861, represents the confusion and no doubt the controversy among architects and engineers over materials. The 1862 Exhibition building at Kensington, though with two bubble-like Saracen-styled domes, was of massive brick, not unlike the 1850 Building Committee's abortive design. The freshness of the Hyde Park Crystal Palace was only an interlude in the battle of styles.

234 Above: behind Sir George Gilbert Scott's Gothic Midland Grand Hotel is St Pancras Station (1866). This long glass and iron roof towered 100 ft above the centre rails below. The original plan of William Henry Barlow, consulting engineer to Midland Railways, was to have two or three short spans across the space, however it was decided to cover the area with one huge span to allow for vaulted storage below the concourse area, to be rented directly to a large beer company. Barlow left the detailing of the magnificent glass covered roof to R. M. Ordish who had developed an expertise in iron roofs and suspension bridges. The lattice ribs each weigh 55 tons and are 29 ft 4 in on centre and span 245 ft 6 in. Barlow later designed the second Tay Bridge and the famous Forth Railway Bridge.

235 Centre: Paddington Station (1853–4) has a direct link to the Crystal Palace of 1851. The engineer, I. K. Brunel, and the architect, Matthew Digby Wyatt, played a major role in the Crystal Palace by serving on the Building Committee that finally accepted Paxton's design. Brunel produced the first large station roof structured in metal which covered a 240 ft 6 in × 700 ft area with three spans. Wyatt contributed new decorative patterns in a Moorish style for the columns and iron ribs. Covering half the ribbed structure was a Paxton ridge and furrow glass roof, not surprising, for Paddington was constructed by Fox and Henderson, more noted for their railway work than for the Crystal Palace in 1851. The Great Western Hotel, opened in June 1854, covered the end of the great shed some distance away.

236 Below: King's Cross Terminus, the Great Northern Railway's main station, was completed in October 1852. Lewis Cubitt's design was not influenced by Paxton's Crystal Palace as it was built at the same time. Two semi-circular roofs, two thirds covered with plate glass, each span 105 ft along the 800 ft shed. The roofs are structured with laminated wood arches similar to Paxton's Palace. Wood purlins at 8 ft centres support plate glass of that length and 2 ft 6 inches wide held in rebated iron glazing-bars.

10 *The Great Exhibitions*

INDUSTRIAL EXHIBITION, DUBLIN—NEW YORK INDUSTRIAL EXHIBITION—LONDON EXHIBITION, 1862—UNIVERSAL EXHIBITION, PARIS, 1867—PARIS EXHIBITION OF 1889

The great world exhibitions, held with increasing frequency throughout the nineteenth century and into the twentieth, were preceded by national exhibitions. One of the first was in Paris on the Champs de Mars in 1798. As Walter Benjamin has said in *Paris, Capital of the Nineteenth Century,* this was the result of the desire to amuse the working class by holding festivals of emancipation.

The Exhibition of the Industry of All Nations, the brain-child of Prince Albert and Sir Henry Cole, was intended to marry industry with the arts, for Cole was in a sense one of the first theorists in industrial design. Prince Albert considered this 1851 Exhibition as a bid for universal peace which, because of the dropping of trade barriers, would allow the industrialization of the earth. W. Bridges Adam gives a sympathetic account of the Exhibition's gradiose scheme, which, he went on to claim, called for an equally grandoise and unique design:

> And last came Prince Albert to proclaim that England should no longer be misunderstood; that from the ends of the earth foreigners should come to an universal jubilee of the arts of peace; that they should hear with their own ears, and see with their own eyes, the works of all mankind, wrought for the welfare of mankind, side by side with their makers; that unmistakably should be exhibited the results of many varying races: the artistry of the Celts and dark skins, and the mechanism of the fair-haired Saxons.

Such was the spirit of the whole era of great exhibitions. Pilgrimages were made from all over the world to view this 1851 Exhibition, which emphasized the imperial and the imperialized, the civilized and the un-civilized, the haves and the have-nots. It glorified the exchange of commodities, hoping to create new markets in the land of the have-nots. The exhibitions did promote international travel, for a delegation of French workers went to London in 1851 and in a second group in 1862. Victor Hugo published a manifesto for the Paris World Exhibition of 1867—'To the Peoples of Europe'.

The international exhibition was a place of distraction —distraction with commodities and experiences not necessarily mundane and certainly not useful. The London Exhibition of 1851 was a show-case filled with useless and bizarre objects, from an eighty-blade sportsman's knife to a floating Church for seamen.* The visitors entered a phantasmagoria supposedly divorced from the realities of the real world.

Before 1850, glass had been used with restraint, except for in the private buildings of the rich mainly because of the exorbitant tax to which it was subject. In 1851 it was one of the cheapest cladding materials, which did not keep out the cold but did keep out the rain and provide the required illumination for displays. Iron, as a structural material, had received a tremendous boost from the building of the railways. Large building firms that developed from this transport expansion were willing to consider any grand structure. But iron was not yet trusted in the architecture of the dwelling and the permanent public building. It was reserved for buildings of transitory purpose—arcades, railway stations, conservatories and temporary exhibition halls. Even in exhibition

* See Christopher Hobhouse, *1851 and the Crystal Palace.*

237 Industrial Exhibition Building, Dublin, Sir John Benson, 1853. The opening by the Lord Lieutenant.

buildings, glass and iron (and later steel) were only gradually adopted. The development of exhibition buildings in Paris demonstrates the bitter struggle between the architect and the engineer, the decorator and builder. With iron and glass, architecture outgrew art. The Galerie des Machines and Eiffel Tower of 1889 attest to the supplanting of the Ecole des Beaux-Arts by the Ecole Polytechnique. However, the plaster neo-Classic halls of the 1893 Chicago Columbian Exhibition had the last word—at least for the Americans.

Competition among rival cities produced a number of international exhibitions (238); each strove to outdo the others in size and cost. There was, indeed, a lot to compete with, including London 1851, Cork 1852, Dublin 1853; New York 1853; Munich 1854, Paris 1855, Manchester 1857, Toronto 1858, London 1862, Paris 1867, Vienna 1873, Philadelphia 1876, Paris 1878, Sydney 1879, Melbourne 1880, Amsterdam 1883, Antwerp 1885, New Orleans 1885, Barcelona 1888, Copenhagen 1888, Brussels 1888, Paris 1889, Chicago 1893, Paris 1900 and Edinburgh 1903.

The Irish had held an architectural competition for the Great Industrial Exhibition in Dublin in 1853. John Benson, later Sir John Benson, from Cork, won the competition with a structure covered mainly in wood with a huge glazed skylight over the centre of the principal nave. This great hall was proudly acclaimed 17 ft longer and 28 ft wider than the transept of the London Exhibition Building. The wooden arches, spanning the hall (237) were supported on iron columns cast in Edinburgh and transported to the Merrion Square site

152

where the building was erected in two hundred working days between mid-August 1852 and May 1853. Richard Turner, the Dublin engineer and contractor, received third prize in the competition, but his only consolation was an order that his Hammersmith works in Dublin got for the wrought-iron trusses to support the upper galleries. Two smaller halls without apses ran parallel to the great hall. These were filled with examples of the four categories of the exhibition—Raw Material, Machinery, Manufactures and Fine Arts, similar in content to the 1851 exhibition in London, except that here oil paintings and watercolours were permitted entries. Several countries were represented, including Belgium, France and Prussia, with a major attraction being the side building with machinery in motion, again duplicating London. The Dublin Exhibition had too much wood to be in any real sense a glass building, but like the 1857 Manchester Exhibition and the 1876 Philadelphia Exhibition, it owes a great deal to Joseph Paxton and Charles Fox's prototype.

Not to be outdone, New York City invited designs in 1851 for its industrial exhibition. Joseph Paxton took part in the competition, but the prize was awarded to New York architects George Carstensen and Charles Gildemeister, even over an exciting entry by James Bogardus, the American master of iron skeleton construction. The entries from Paxton, Bogardus, and the winning entry did not carry roofs of glass, most probably because of the heavy falls of snow which are current along the eastern seaboard. Carstensen and Gildemeister's designs were, however, completely walled in glass, a derivative of the

238 The opening day Souvenir of the North, Central and South American Exposition, held in New Orleans 1885–6, claimed 1,656,30 ft of enclosed space, larger than any previous Exhibition.

239 The New York Crystal Palace erected in 1852 for the United States first World Fair in 1853. It stood on the present site of Bryant Park, east of 6th Avenue between 41st and 42nd Street. The Croton Distributing Reservoir, seen on the left, is now the site occupied by the New York City Public Library.

240 The New York Crystal Palace was reputed to be fire proof, but wood and other combustible materials caught fire in 1858 and the building collapsed almost instantly. In the true American spirit, Mrs Richardson, one of the unfortunates burnt out in the fire, obtained permission from the Mayor and the Receiver to sell vitrified masses of glass and metal as relics of the large iron building.

London Crystal Palace (239). The ground floor plan, a huge 355 ft diameter octagon was crossed by two main avenues with a 103 ft diameter dome over the centre. The 111,200 sq.ft main floor, combined with two gallery levels above, provided 179,000 sq.ft for display, considerably less than the Crystal Palace. The construction was mainly iron and glass, but a quantity of timber was also used, accounting for the spectacular fire that destroyed it in 1858 (240).

The following years saw other exhibitions in Europe and Britain. In 1854 a Glas Palast was built at Munich by the engineers Voit and Werder. In Paris, a huge glass and iron structure had been planned by Cendrier and Barrault for the 1855 French Universal Exhibition. It was decided, however, to surround the building with a covering of masonry. Behind this architectural façade, Alexis Barrault built the largest known iron span over a 47-m wide hall, known as the Palais de l'Industrie, sited on the Champs Elysées and in use until 1906 when it was replaced by the Grand Palais. The roofs of the three long galleries were covered with so much glass that they dazzled spectators unused to such interior light intensity.

Meanwhile back in Britain, Midlands industry, the backbone of British manufacturing, demanded an exhibition of their own. It was held in Manchester in 1857.

The building for the London Exhibition of the Works of Industry of all Nations (1862) would have pleased the 1851 Building Committee, for here was a design in masonry similar to the Committee's own of twelve years earlier. Wide interest in Saracenic decoration had generated a number of designs with Moorish domes, others being Owen Jones's proposed People's Palace at Muswell Hill and Joseph Paxton's proposed Exhibition Building at St Cloud. The 1862 Exhibition building had two glass bubbles rising above the brick façades (243). A considerable quantity of glass was used over the upper galleries and in the clerestory. Behind the masonry, a system of cast columns, iron girders and a delicate triangular truss supported an immense glass roof (241). The building was the design of Captain Fowke, an inventor and engineer who built many provincial galleries. He also designed the Royal Horticultural Society's large conservatory, which was sited on the Gore House estate, now occupied by the Victoria & Albert Museum and Albert Hall (see *Industrialization and Mass Marketing*).

The second Paris Universal Exhibition was to be housed in a huge circular building symbolizing the globe, but it would not fit on the Champs de Mars, so the design was changed to an oval 386 m by 490 m (242). The Second Empire, then at its height, and Paris then at the height of luxury and fashion, attracted exhibitors from around the world who felt compelled to be represented in this artificial and temporary world of iron and glass. Seven concentric galleries formed a fantastic elliptical earth; the large outer gallery was devoted to machines and the other galleries, in decreasing size, and in strict order, were devoted to clothing, furniture, raw materials, liberal arts, fine arts and the history of labour. In the centre was an open garden with a pavilion for coins, weights and measures. The building was divided into wedge-shaped segments occupied by the various nations, so that it was

241   Interior of the Exhibition building in London, 1862.

243   The 1862 Exhibition of the Works of Industry of All Nations, London, is attributed to Captain Fowke.

242   Below: the Universal Exhibition, Paris, 1867: bird's eye view of the whole.

244 Palais d'Horticulture, Paris Exposition Universelle, 1900. Architect Albert Gauthier. Built at the same time as the Grand Palais, it was dismantled in 1909.

possible to circumambulate the various galleries to compare similar commodities among different participants or meander from the outer gallery to the inner garden to see all the goods of one country. The original intention was aptly described in the official publication of 1867:

> To make the circuit of this place, circular, like the equator, is literally to go around the world. All peoples are here, enemies live in peace side by side. As in the beginning of things, on the globe of waters, the divine spirit now floats on this globe of iron.

The outer gallery, the Galerie des Machines, had a span of 35 m supported on iron arches. Outward thrust was eliminated by extending the pillars above the roof making an exo-structure. This façade, bedecked with pennants and flags, was criticized by the Parisians, for they were used to a more monumental style. The inner galleries were iron-trussed with glass-covered gable roofs. Designed by J. B. Krantz, the temporary building had a metal framework made in the works of the young engineer Gustave Eiffel (1832–1923), the major contributor to the detailed design.

In 1873 an exhibition was opened in Vienna in a building with a huge cone-shaped rotunda designed by the English architect, Scott Russell (cf. 238). In 1876 the United States celebrated a hundred years of independence with an international exhibition in Philadelphia. Erected in Fairmount Park, the largest municipal park in the world, the main buildings were reminiscent of the Crystal Palace of twenty-five years earlier. The large aisles were covered with triangular iron trusses supporting a wood roof, and iron lattice girders held up the galleries, the

whole resting on cast-iron columns. The walls were extensively glazed, giving a delightful open feeling to the space. One of the lesser buildings, the Horticultural Hall, exists today and functions as park police head-quarters.

The most important exhibition from the point of view of structural engineering and glasshouse design was the exhibition in Paris in 1889, which commemorated the centenary of the storming of the Bastille. Organized again on the Champ de Mars, it consisted of a complex of inter-connected buildings and Eiffel's famous tower. The Galerie des Machines, designed by the architect Dutert (1845–1906) and the engineers Contamin, Pierron and Charton, was the culmination of engineering confidence in steel structure and glass enclosure. Its great hulk dominated the exhibition complex, with a main hall measuring 115 m by 240 m surrounded by smaller vaulted side aisles parallel to the major space (245). The main hall was spanned by rigid trusses, with pin connections at the top and at each base. The largest span attempted until this time had been the 73 m of W. H. Barlow and R. M. Ordish's St Pancras Station in London, where the arched trusses had been firmly secured at the foundations. These new pin connections disturbed many visitors familiar with structures securely planted into the earth; the gallery seemed to float above them. The north and south ends were enclosed with transparent glass walls supported by structural steel decoration that doubled as wind structure. From inside, one could see through the glass wall to the sky, a sensation of space never achieved in the halls of the past. This gave a disconcerting sensation of

245   Galerie des Machines, Paris, 1889.

immensity, especially since the low-pointed arches obscured the exact height. The roof was a design of translucent white and blue glass. There are recorded com-
ments of visitors who found it disconcerting to see such a
delicate skin of light purlins, glazing bars and glass supported by the massive trusses, 3 m in depth. The smaller
arched side aisles and the two mobile trolleys that travelled the length of the space above the machines and
exhibitions added some human scale to this vast volume.
The exhibition was too large to be walked around, and
the travelling cranes carried as many as one hundred
thousand visitors on a busy day. This marvellous structure was unfortunately dismantled in 1910, though it
remained much longer a prototype of the exhibition
halls and field houses later built in the United States.
Eiffel's three-hundred-metre tower still remains, a tribute
to what must have been a magnificent exhibition.

246 Glass tower project by Mies van der Rohe, Berlin 1920–21 (model). Contrast the masonry construction in the background with Mies's new material, glass.

11   *The Expressionists*

PAUL SCHEERBART—BRUNO TAUT—HOUSE OF HEAVEN—TROPICAL HOUSE IN THE ROYAL BOTANIC GARDENS BERLIN-DAHLEM—BRUCE GOFF

This book would not be complete without a discussion of the writings of Paul Scheerbart (1863–1915) and the work of Bruno Taut (1880–1938) in Berlin between 1910 and 1920.

Paul Scheerbart was a writer of extravagant and fantastic novels and stories that might be considered early science fiction; he was the German Expressionists' Jules Verne. Architect Bruno Taut described him as the 'only poet in architecture' and was greatly influenced by Scheerbart's utopian phantasmagoria. Scheerbart had a fanatical love for glass architecture, and his moral views on it are idealistic and full of joy. In the same vein he hated bricks.

> Colourful glass destroys hate
> Without a glass palace life is a burden
> Only colour-happiness with glass culture
> Light permeates everything and is alive in crystal
> Glass brings us the new era; brick culture is a burden
> Bricks pass away; coloured glass endures*

Scheerbart evoked the lofty dreams of the young German architects (246) of the Expressionist period with his ideas of glass architecture; light, crystal clear, colourful, mobile, structures floating, soaring to change the European, to liberate him from his brick boxes into the new light.

* Paul Scheerbart, *Glasarchitektur*.

** Paul Scheerbart, 'The Architects' Congress', excerpt from *Frülicht*, I, p. 26.

† The Glass Chain was an exchange of circular letters, utopian sketches and essays instituted by Taut and Adolf Behne that linked the group together.

Technically Scheerbart's glass visions were not impractical: in fact they were prophetic. He saw the problems of heat loss, heat gain and condensation with glass materials but suggested that several skins of glass combined with air-conditioning units could provide a successful environment.

> Glass is also useful in the tropics. There, one requires only three-ply or four-ply glass walls and a few sheltering walls of white canvas. Cooling units can easily be installed in the walls. Air is a poor conductor of heat.**

Scheerbart saw the familiar glass conservatory expanding until it became detached from the dwelling, sitting alone in the garden. The new citizen would then leave his masonry house and move into a world of coloured double glass walls held in reinforced concrete frames, ceramic floors, glass furniture, glass fibre cloth, and glass lamps.

In 1914 Bruno Taut built his famous 'Glass House' at the Werkbund Exhibition in Cologne (247, 248). That same year Scheerbart's 'Glasarchitektur' was printed in *Der Sturm*. Excerpts from this prophetic work capture the spirit that stirred the young architects of the *Glaserne Kette* (chain of glass)† who were looking for some salvation from the trying times before World War I. *Der Sturm* provided the communicative link between the young architects, artists, and writers embroiled in the unreal but utopian world of Expressionism, and Scheerbart was one of their prophets.

We live for the most part within enclosed spaces. These form the environment from which our culture

247, 248 The Glass House, Bruno Taut, 1914. Built for the glass industry at the Werkbund Exhibition in Cologne, it was a concrete lamellar structure, 'to demonstrate the use of glass in all its varied aesthetic charm'. Exterior and (right) interior '. . . the variegated shining glass prisms of its glass envelopments, its glass ceilings, glass floors, glass tiles and the cascade, lit up from beneath, and a giant kaleidoscope, which was intended to illustrate by its illumination at night all that glass might achieve towards the heightening of intensity in our lives.'

grows. Our culture is in a sense a product of our architecture. If we wish to raise our culture to a higher level, we are forced for better or for worse to transform our architecture. And this will be possible only if we remove the enclosed quality from the spaces within which we live. This can be done only through the introduction of glass architecture that lets the sunlight and the light of the moon and stars into our rooms not merely through a few windows, but simultaneously through the greatest possible number of walls that are made entirely of glass—coloured glass. The new environment that we shall thereby create must bring with it a new culture.

Scheerbart accurately predicted the light zoning restrictions that formed most of New York City's wedding-cake sky-scrapers.

No doubt a terrace formation is necessary in taller glass buildings and with several storeys, since otherwise the glass surfaces could not reach the free light-conducting air, to which they aspire. . . . This terrace formation of the storeys will of course quickly replace the dreary frontal architecture of brick houses.

It was the steam railway that produced the brick metropolis culture of today from which we all suffer. Glass architecture will come only when the metropolis in our sense of the word has been done away with.

Even if we cannot for the present assume that our sense organs will evolve further from today to tomorrow, we shall nevertheless be justified in supposing that to begin with we may attain that which is accessible to us—to wit, that part of the spectrum which we are

able to perceive with our eyes, those miracles of colour which we are capable of taking in.

The only thing that can help us to do this is glass architecture, which must transform our whole life—the environment in which we live.*

In an article** about *Glasarchitektur,* Adolf Behne, secretary of the Work Council for Art, an arch-propagandist of the modern movement and colleague of Taut's, demonstates the faith shared by the Glass Chain group in Scheerbart's word.

The idea of a glass architecture is perfectly simple and is to be understood just as Scheerbart presents it . . . in the light of gayest optimism. It is not the crazy caprice of a poet that glass architecture will bring a new culture. IT IS A FACT! New social welfare organizations, hospitals, inventions or technical innovations and improvements—these will not bring about our new culture . . . but glass architecture will.

Glass architecture is going to eliminate all harshness from the Europeans and replace it with tenderness, beauty and candour.

The most ardent proponent and interpreter of Scheerbart's message was perhaps Bruno Taut. Taut, besides producing great quantities of the best German mass-housing, was an outstanding figure of the so-called Expressionist period, particularly after the War. In 1919 he published *Die Stadtkrone,* a treatise on town planning emphasizing residential layouts on the lines of garden

* Paul Scheerbart, *Glasarchitektur.*

** Published in *Wiederkehr der Kunst,* 1919.

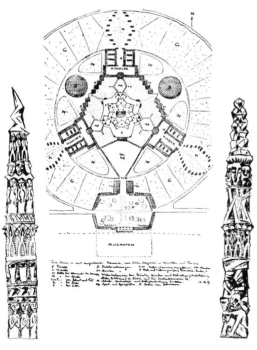

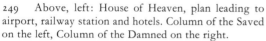

249　Above, left: House of Heaven, plan leading to airport, railway station and hotels. Column of the Saved on the left, Column of the Damned on the right.

250　Above, right: 'A valley as a flower—walls are erected on the hillsides, out of coloured glass in rigid frames—light shining through creates a variety of changing effects, as much for those in the valley who walk within them, as for the pilots of aircraft overhead.

251　Right: a superstructure, primarily of glass, atop Monte Resegone near Lecco on Lake Como.

252　Below, left: House of Heaven, interior. Inscription reads 'Brückner's 9th Symphony, 3rd movement'.

253　Below, right: House of Heaven, an Utopian cathedral by Bruno Taut, made of electrolytically joined glass roofs and poured glass walls.

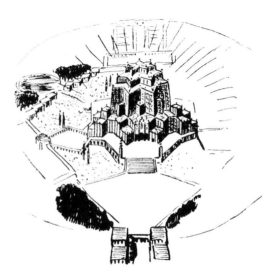

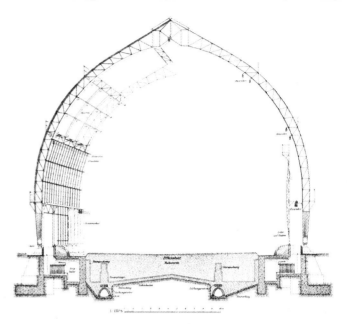

cities with the *Stadtkrone* as public buildings visible to all around, full of utopian glass imagery. His *Alpine Architektur,* a utopian project consisting of thirty drawings done in 1917 and 1918 and published in 1919, was divided into six sections: The Crystal House; Architecture of the mountains; The Alpine Structure; Earthcrust Architecture; Star Architecture; Cathedral Star. The fantastic drawings are of imaginary glass projects, nestled between and crowning the mountains of Southern Europe (250, 251) and crystal-domed buildings on the Riviera. As Scheerbart was the prophet, Taut was the disciple trying to bring some of the dream into reality. He made the drawings and held the material. It was Taut's Glass House at the Deutsche Werkbund exhibition in Cologne that made a lasting impression on his colleagues. Built to demonstrate the new uses of glass, it was 'proof of the new art of architecture', according to Taut in his book, *Modern Architecture* (1929), in which he described his pavilion as:

> The lightest possible concrete structure, destined to demonstrate the use of glass in all its varied aesthetic charm, the variegated shining glass prisms of its glass envelopments, its glass ceilings, glass floors, glass tiles, and the cascade, lit up from beneath, and a giant kaleidoscope, which was intended to illustrate by its illumination at night all that glass might achieve towards the heightening of intensity in our lives.

In 1920 Taut found new media for expression in every issue of the periodical *Stadtbaukunst Alter und Neuer Zeit* (Urban Architecture Ancient and Modern), for he ran a series called *Frühlicht* ('Early Light') (1920–2) in which he

could carry on the spirit, publishing articles of his favourite architects and friends. There were two *Frühlicht*s, the first being discontinued with an apologetic letter from the publisher explaining that Taut had used too much freedom in airing the younger architects' radical views.

Perhaps the most exciting theoretical project for Taut was the House of Heaven, a huge all-embracing sacred structure in which all the arts merge into one. The House of Heaven was conceived as a temple of the *Zeitgeist* that united the views of the *Glaserne Kette* members. Just as Walter Gropius saw painters and sculptors under the arm of the great art architecture, so, too, did Taut design the cathedral of the future, a truly twentieth-century structure in which all arts work together, perhaps modelled on the great Gothic cathedrals (249, 252, 253).

> Between the inner and outer glass skins is the lighting. It will be switched in and out, changing from lighting the proceedings in the room, to creating an effect outside. Both inside and outside will be lit through richly coloured glass walls. If one approaches by night from the air, it appears from far off like a star. And it sounds like a bell.
> To build the roofs, prisms of coloured glass will be electrolytically joined, and for the walls, the prisms will be poured. In a very stable structure the glass prisms of the roof could also be poured as one. Roofs and walls will echo the crystals of the outer structure in a subdued manner, like bas-reliefs, crisp and stylish, and in their glittering richness they will absorb the deepest colours of the sparkling glass windows. In

254–56   Far left: Tropical House at the Royal Botanic Gardens in Dahlem, Berlin. Construction photograph. 1905–7. Left, section: hot water pipes were hung under the roof structure and radiators heated the vaults below. The glass skin was hung under the exo-skeleton steel construction. Various catwalks enabled canvas to be draped for sun control and maintenance. Right: the Tropical House was partially destroyed in 1943, losing most of its glass. Between 1963–8 it was enclosed with 1,650 vacuum-formed acrylic panels, fitted with hot-air heating and ventilating equipment that maintains an average day temperature of 18°–20°C. Below: one of the plant chambers with a delightful exposed structure and suspended glass roof.

257   Below: Royal Botanic Garden glasshouses in Dahlem, Berlin. The complex was designed by the Royal Building Office under the direction of A. Koerner and was constructed in 1905–7. The Tropical House is the largest of the many environmental chambers.

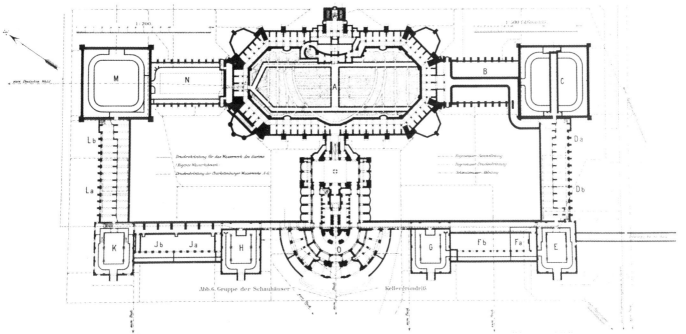

258 Above: glass house over the Seine at the International Exposition of Decorative Arts, Paris, 1925. Peter Behrens, architect.

259 Left: interiors of the glass house at the International Exposition of Decorative Arts, Paris, 1925. Peter Behrens, architect.

260 Interior perspective of a projected residence for a musician, Urbana, Illinois, 1952 by Bruce Goff showing helical access ramp enclosed in transparent tube. To the right, a partial view of the dining globe; below in the background, a music space.

261 An aluminium structure supports transparent walls and roof. Large aluminium globes, supported with tubular frames are connected by the helical ramp. The globes house living, sleeping and dining areas and receive air directly from outside, as seen in this view from the garden.

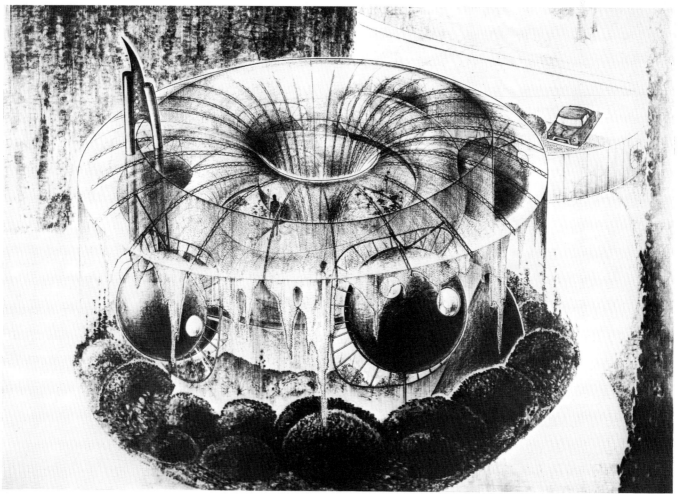

262　View of Goff house from the street.

fact they are not glass 'windows', since walls and roof are all bright and colourful. The windows will therefore be like colourful carpets, somewhat darker and even more colourful than the walls and roof.

All the forms climb, struggle and grow upwards, pulled on by the roof star. Steep and harsh, weak and delicate in the manifold flux of form, the colours are deep and glowing, mysteriously luminous, each arm of the star being one of the colours of the rainbow.

The verticals of the columns bind the whole together. Flashing and sparkling, the sun catches the glittering colours, the grey day speaks earnestly through them, and the moon and stars twinkle their light through the coloured glass like little silver bells.*

To sum up Bruno Taut's exuberant attitude at this time, the introductory page in the first *Frühlicht* entitled 'Down with Seriousism' provides the following:

In the distance shines our tomorrow. Hurray, three times hurray for our kingdom without force! Hurray for the transparent, the clear! Hurray for purity! Hurray for crystal! Hurray and again hurray for the fluid, the graceful, the angular, the sparkling, the flashing, the light—hurray for everlasting architecture!

A huge complex of glasshouses, designed by A. Koerner of the Royal Building Office, was under construction in 1905–7 in Dahlem, Berlin, and must have attracted the

eye of Scheerbart** and Taut. The complex was made of several glass chambers (257) providing different climates, and in the centre was the great tropical house 61 m long, 30 m wide, and a dramatic 26 m high (254–256).

Few buildings have been built that would have pleased Scheerbart. Perhaps Lloyd Wright's Wayfarer's Chapel above the Pacific at Palos Verdes, California, built in 1951, or Peter Behrens' glasshouse above the Seine in Paris, 1925 (258; 259), would have met his ideal. Most certainly he and Taut would have thrilled to the architecture of Bruce Goff. Goff infilled the hard coal masonry walls with large glass cullets in the Ford house at Aurora, Illinois, 1949, and the Price studio in Bartlesville, Oklahoma, 1957. Exotic glass furniture in the Price house fits Scheerbart's description. It is Goff's unbuilt house for a musician which is to be made from aluminium structure, transparent plastic, and aluminium globes, that fulfils Scheerbart's prediction of building with plastics (260–262).

... and one is going to try to invent materials that can compete with glass. I am referred to materials that are as elastic as rubber but also transparent.†

* From *Frülicht,* translated by James Read.

** See *Glasarchitektur* for an account of the gardens by Scheerbart.

† Paul Scheerbart, *Glasarchitektur.*

12 *People in Glass Houses*

MINIMAL PLANNING—FULLER'S GEODESIC DOMES—THE GLASS HOUSE—CAMBRIDGE MAXIMUM SPACE HOUSE—OTHER GLASS HOUSES—RASMUSSEN HOUSES—MYERS HOUSE—OTTO HOUSE—THE ECO-HOUSE—GLASS STUDIOS

A house is basically a shell around environmental servicing, like a tepee or igloo around its fire. We have been and are experiencing a gradual shrinking of the shell and an expansion of the mechanical servicing inside with little area left for the dweller. A traditional small house often contains the same expensive servicing as a large house, and a similar number of joints and corners in its construction. It is difficult and expensive to integrate mechanical systems into tight spaces. Fitting the small compact house puzzle together results in such a dramatic increase in cost per unit area that designers tend to apply only minimal space planning principles based upon arduous anthropometric studies. Phrases like 'the smallest kitchen for a family', 'the minimum bathroom', 'the minimum bed chamber for a child', 'space for a pram', have crept into the designers' language. Low space standards have resulted in 'multi-use' and all the costly complications that 'flexibility' implies. The most pathetic results have been produced by the misconception that house costs are directly related to the area enclosed. The irony of the supposedly affluent consumer society is that equipment, furniture and games are readily available, but there is nowhere to put them, with a resultant limitation of lifestyle. If the future holds a shorter working week and the home has to function for recreation, then the minimal concrete cellular houses built now will be the slums of the future; too small to adapt to changing requirements and practically indestructible.

The challenge is to find a way to make a large inexpensive and high-performance shell to house the dweller's partitioning, mechanical and recreational equipment and his furniture. In the early 1950s, Buckminster Fuller described* a 'super-camping structure', a double-skinned dome with variable optical controls to cover the service mechanisms that 'make us masters of our environment'. In 1952 a group of M.I.T. graduate students assembled a house design incorporating Fuller's Geodesic Dome and 'Standard of Living Package', combined with a 'Utility-Energy-Package' for all the mechanical systems (263). This mini-Garden-of-Eden attitude has been recently restated by Reyner Banham,** and theoretically illustrated with Francois Dallegret's environmental bubble (264).

Domestic sized domes are difficult to adapt to existing needs and conditions.† The hemispherical shape, with so much volume above the ground, requires multilevels, resulting in difficulties with air stratification and heating. But perhaps the greatest limitation of the dome enclosure is integrating windows, doors, and insulation into a curved tegument supported by a myriad triangulated structural members. Site planning is not particularly easy outside an idyllic American wood, if domes are to be integrated with other houses.

In deference to Fuller, one must say the horticultural glasshouse, though a visually crude substitute for the elegant dome, embodies some of the principles he has promulgated—mass-production, low labour content, light

* 'The Autonomous Dwelling Facility', *Perspecta,* 1, Yale University Press, 1952, p. 30.

** 'A home is not a house.' *Architectural Design,* Jan. 1969, p. 45.

† See Dome Cook Book, Portala Institute, Inc., Menlo Park, California.

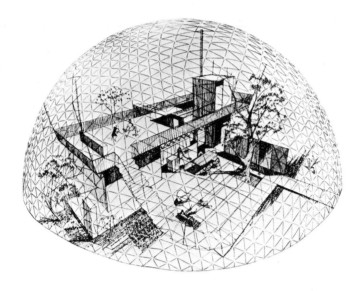

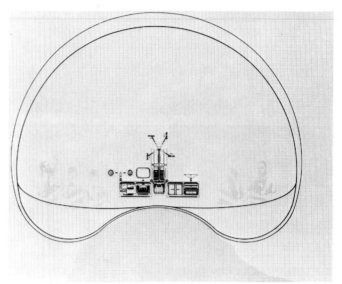

263 The 'Industrialized House' incorporating R. Buckminster Fuller's 'Geodesic Dome' and 'Standard of Living Package'. Designed by graduate students at M.I.T. in 1952.

264 The Environmental Bubble as a plastic dome inflated with conditioned air from the 'Standard of Living Package' it shelters. A restatement of Fuller's domes by Reyner Banham.

weight, minimum materials—in short a simple enclosure for a 'Standard of Living Package'. The idea of using a glasshouse was introduced to me by architects Ib and Jorgen Rasmussen whose mock-up glasshouse of canvas and wood was such a success at the 1967 Ideal Home Trade Fair in Copenhagen (265). Their elegant design demonstrated the principle of a maximum space zoned into functional areas and 'houses within a house'.

The glass house is covered by a skin of stick and panel construction; readily adaptable to varying internal requirements. A whole range of skin panels can be used, transparent or opaque, with operable doors and windows in any position, and the pitched roof performs its job without generating too much interior volume. Side by side, glass houses can cover vast areas the way Joseph Paxton's exhibition building of 1851 covered nearly eighteen acres of Hyde Park with a ridge and furrow roof. Their rectangular shape allows easy packing into terraces (270). Compared to a dome, its gable form is mundane and uninspiring, but to the conservative housing market, this can be an asset and a graphic challenge to Robert Venturi's idea of the 'decorated box'. Infill the pediment with vacuum-formed panels, add ornamental architrave and column panels in any vernacular from Neo-Greek to French Provincial Ranch Style, and every owner would be pleased. Anyway, a house is designed for its interior, the making of good spaces and rooms to live in and their fit relation to outside places.

The Charles Eames home (1949) in Los Angeles is an enclosure assembled from existing components; steel columns, trusses and an assortment of infill panels. Ex-

tending further the ideas of assembling these marketed products, the purchase of whole marketed enclosures that can be readily adapted and upgraded is a next step. For example, enclosure systems exist for farm animal shelters, grain storage, warehousing, container packaging and horticulture—in England the commercial glasshouse. Manufacturers who market enclosures have established methods of transportation and delivery, and can readily adapt themselves to a new product. This eliminates the major difficulties in the mass production of housing: the amortization of new plant and the establishment of a market large enough to keep production moving.

Horticultural glasshouse manufacturers have developed a technically sophisticated product over a period of time and have cost-engineered their enclosures in view of competition with others. This efficiency is not usually available to the architectural profession, which deals in one-off expensive building.

Most architects' industrialized designs have produced specific building types with a specific system—the industrialized house, the industrialized school, the industrialized factory. The market is limited to specific use requirements—living, learning, or working, with a specific building for each. But manufacturers could concentrate on the production of one enclosure that would be adapted to the specific use by the nature of the tegument and the equipment that it has to shelter. Move a juke box into a warm shed and you have a place to dance; replace the juke box with a computer, a typewriter, add more lighting, make more openings in the skin and you have an office; the shed can be readily transformed.

265   Architects Ib and Jorgen Rasmussen's elegant canvas and wood mock-up glasshouse in Copenhagen, 1967.

I have myself attempted to develop this basic idea with the readily available horticultural glasshouse marketed in Britain. The temperate maritime climate of Britain obviously makes the adaptation easier, but the concept can of course be applied to other climates with other indigenous structures, like the laminated arched barn in the Midwest United States or the California schools component system making houses, hospitals, offices, and factories, in addition to schools.

I have made several drawings of the glasshouse to demonstrate its adaptability. The shell can be considered as a stage and the partitions and equipment, the stage-set for the activity, not unlike the Assyrian, Egyptian, Moorish, and even Pugin's English Medieval Courts housed in the neutral background of Paxton's Sydenham Crystal Palace. In the drawing of houses and a nursery grouped in the countryside, plots are divided by walls and glasshouses constructed in between (270). Inside, each dwelling suits the dweller's needs and life style. The house shells are built to their projected maximum size. Any space that is not immediately required can be partitioned off and used for storage, a workshop, or children's play room. The Maximum Space House is based on the idea that difficulties with neighbours or planning permission make it easier and better to 'build-in' instead of 'build-on' a new addition to one's house. With a house that is initially 'bigger than we dreamed of', rooms made from non-structural walls and independent insulated-ceilings can be added or subdivided much more efficiently than old houses gutted to meet new life styles.

The Maximum Space House in Cambridge, England, built by students in the summer of 1969, demonstrates the principles of this simple enclosure for housing. A later, refined version now houses the Carter Design Studios in Foxton near Leicester (266–69) and a garden sales centre has been built in Hertfordshire. Other uses that have been proposed include a factory extension, a printing works, a farmhouse and an open-plan school (271, 272).

The Cambridge Maximum Space House was the outcome of a project run by the Cambridge University School of Architecture in 1969. The aim was to make a prototype low cost dwelling which would incorporate current ideas of planning flexibility, build- or change-it-yourself. The project was made possible by a grant from the University and by donations of materials from the building industry. Design and background research were carried out by a group of eight students under the direction of John Hix and the house was built by seven students[*] inexperienced in construction, over six weeks, in the summer vacation. The completed building is used by the School of Architecture for conferences, exhibitions and as studio accommodation for research students. But, most importantly, it was a working model in which the initial ideas could be tested (273–81).

As its name implies, one of the main features of the house is its space standards, which are far in excess of current practice, and ones which would be thought economically impossible in the public housing sector. The prototype MSH has a ground floor area of 2,100 sq.ft

* B. Vale, C. Frankl, M. Goulden, J.-P. Porchon, D. O'Neil, R. Vale, Murdah.

266–69 Carter Design Group Studios, Foxton, Leicestershire are housed in an horticultural glasshouse, costing one third of normal construction. The polyethylene tubes distribute hot air to the rigid polyvinylchloride down tubes. The roof is glass and lined with expanded polystyrene. The south wall is infilled with pre-finished panels. The sliding door can be installed in any position along the façade, as can ventilation panels. Scaffolding supports platforms between the roof trusses, providing extra work and storage space above. The floor is of tongue-and-groove chipboard lying on expanded polystyrene and concrete slab.

270–272 Below, this page and facing: group of glass houses in the countryside. The trend toward an agro-urban community puts the people in the country and the cows in the city. Facing, left: house project for a horticulturalist with suites of rooms for parents and children surrounding the large living room which has a kitchen and dining area. Around the house a thicket is planted as protection from the wind. Right, an open-plan landscape school is enclosed with standard 30-ft span glasshouse system. The partitioning and equipment is based on designs by Jacob Bakema.

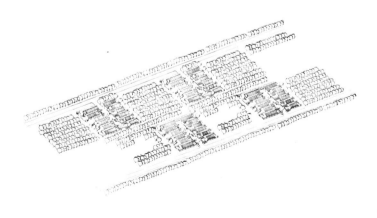

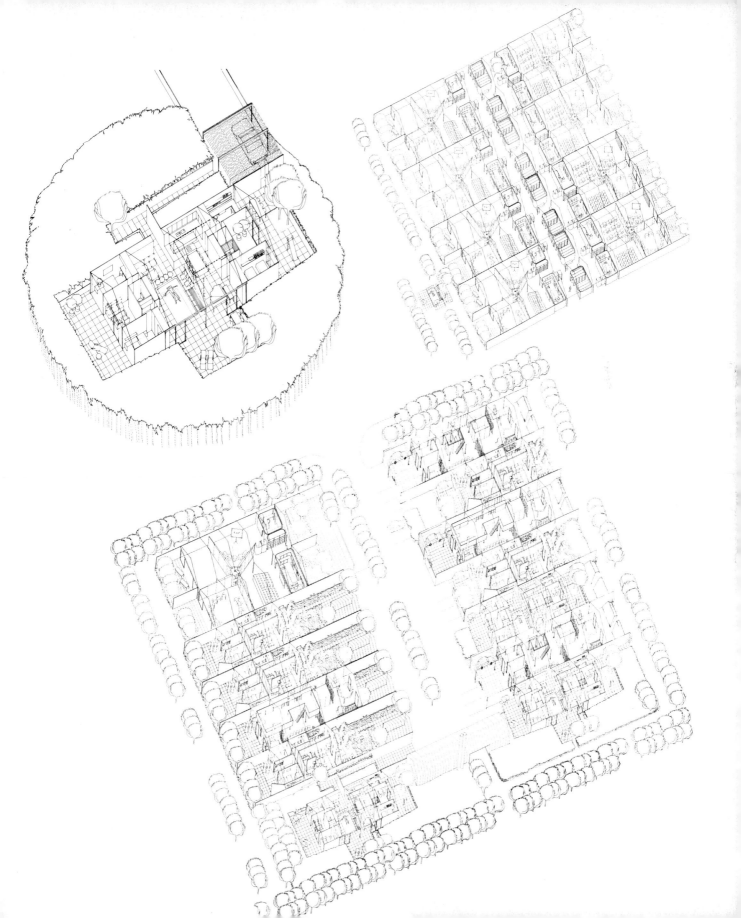

273, 274 Cambridge Maximum Space House built by architecture students, 1969. Section, upper level, ground level:

1. vent fans
2. 30″ summer vent fans
3. storage and desk units
4. 13″ polyethylene hot air duct
5. wc, basin, shower and sauna
6. hot-air upflow furnace
7. garden
8. lounge
9. vines
10. dining area and discussion area
11. kitchen unit
12. entrance patio

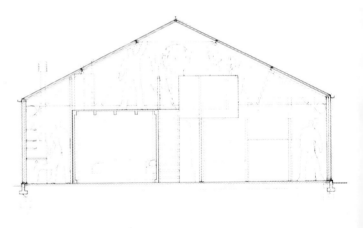

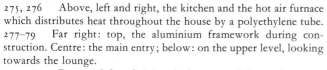

275, 276   Above, left and right, the kitchen and the hot air furnace which distributes heat throughout the house by a polyethylene tube.
277–79   Far right: top, the aluminium framework during construction. Centre: the main entry; below: on the upper level, looking towards the lounge.
280, 281   Bottom, left and right: the lounge and the garden.

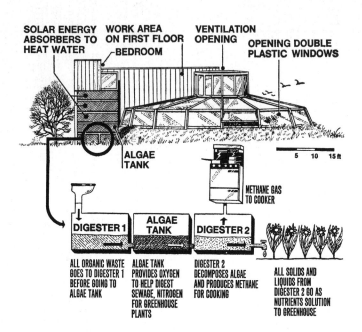

SOLAR ENERGY ABSORBERS TO HEAT WATER — WORK AREA ON FIRST FLOOR BEDROOM — VENTILATION OPENING — OPENING DOUBLE PLASTIC WINDOWS

ALGAE TANK

METHANE GAS TO COOKER

5 10 15 ft

DIGESTER 1 | ALGAE TANK | DIGESTER 2

ALL ORGANIC WASTE GOES TO DIGESTER 1 BEFORE GOING TO ALGAE TANK

ALGAE TANK PROVIDES OXYGEN TO HELP DIGEST SEWAGE, NITROGEN FOR GREENHOUSE PLANTS

DIGESTER 2 DECOMPOSES ALGAE AND PRODUCES METHANE FOR COOKING

ALL SOLIDS AND LIQUIDS FROM DIGESTER 2 GO AS NUTRIENTS SOLUTION TO GREENHOUSE

282   The Eco-House, designed by Grahame Caine, to demonstrate the possibility of self-supporting, independent living units. Waste is re-cycled to provide gas for cooking and fertilizer; solar energy is employed.

283   Architects Ib and Jorgen Rasmussen of Copenhagen have designed terrace glass-roofed houses with summer all year round. Masonry party walls support wood trusses and the ventilated, double-glazed roof. A swimming pool and portable kitchen unit complete the living area.

and an upper level area of 600 sq.ft. Our belief was that however conditioned and adaptable the minimal house tenant is proved to be, and however much design in-genuity is expended on humanizing the orthodox home, no radical improvements could be made without breaking out from the limitations of minimal planning.

The problem was to achieve this within current cost limits and in a form that the owner could build himself. Experience has shown that the use of new constructional systems has resulted in houses costing ten per cent to fifteen per cent more than ones built by traditional methods to the same space standards, for a new system designed for industry almost inevitably means a large initial investment in re-tooling and this passes on a financial burden that most housing contracts cannot afford to carry. Furthermore, the product of these systems is essentially the industrialized cottage (cf. 'the horseless carriage') and seemingly offers few opportunities for significant life style changes. These findings suggested an approach which utilized existing industrial products and not necessarily those usually associated with housing construction. With this approach the house made at Cambridge cost around £1.50 ($3.60) per square foot taking materials and labour at current market prices.

The structure is that of a standard aluminium horticul-tural greenhouse. The only modification made was to change the compression struts in the roof trusses to meet statutory loading requirements. Clearly the poor thermal characteristics of glass would necessitate enor-mous expenditure on heating and cooling. Taking this into consideration, and the uncertain psychological effects

of excessive exposure, we modified the enclosing skin. The glass in the roof (32-oz in place of the 24-oz glass used in horticultural models) was augmented by a secon-dary internal skin of expanded polystyrene which allows the light to come through it. In the side walls most of the glass was replaced by an outer skin of asbestos panels and an inner one of commercial partitioning. Glass remained only where lateral views were required and in the end gables. These changes gave U values of 0.18 and 0.15 respectively for the roof and the walls. A smaller house of 1,300 sq.ft was computed for running cost, and the esti-mated heat bill was £60 ($144) per year. As the basic cost for the envelope was low, a larger amount of the budget could be spent on more sophisticated heating and ventilating equipment. Heating is by thermostatically controlled, upflow, fan-driven, gas-fired furnace, and is distributed round the perimeter of the envelope in a perforated polyethylene tube. Summer ventilation is by means of a 30-in fan mounted in one of the end gables. This is also thermostatically controlled and on a regulator.

But it was not only the economic advantages that recommended the greenhouse as a basis for the project. The use of the roof as a primary source of daylight implied the feasibility of combining large usable internal spaces with reasonable planning densities. It suggested the exciting possibility of bringing the garden into the house. Moreover, it was lightweight and easily assembled, affording opportunity for unskilled erection.

External maintenance is inexpensive. Though the aluminium will oxidize initially, the house simply needs washing once or twice a year.

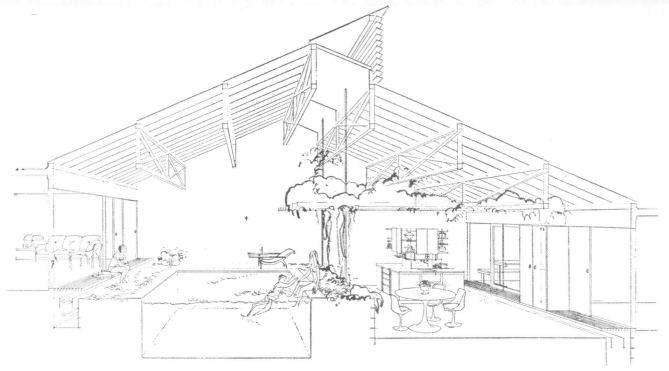

Other fascinating glass houses are being lived in. Two of these provide ad hoc solutions to housing and show refreshing initiative on the part of the owners. A Dutch artist has built his house in Boskoop, Holland, from a proprietary Dutch glasshouse system, infilling the roof with opaque insulative panels and using glasshouse hot-water piping. In Ireland Mrs Harry Bewick has been living for over twelve years in a small glasshouse she purchased at an auction. Mrs Bewick, whose house rests in the quiet privacy of Glenda Lough, lives a refreshingly simple life, in contrast to most of the western world today (286).

Architects have also proposed and built glasshouse homes recently. Japanese architect Makoto Suzuki's 'Bubble Space Project' suggests a minimal enclosed house with an attached transparent 'spatial unit', showing that though the conservatory has maintained its size since Victorian times, the house has shrunk. The Danish architect brothers Ib and Jorgen Rasmussen have designed six terrace glasshouses (283) providing a temperate climate, while increasing the internal volume which they see as a necessary environmental solution to the trend of decreasing space standards. A precisely detailed steel framed terrace house, with a huge fibreglass roof, designed by architects A. J. Diamond and Barton Myers, has recently been built in Toronto. The interior is zoned into two suites of rooms on each side of the main space, one for children and the other for the parents. The house demonstrates the possibility of deep terrace planning with good internal natural lighting conditions. In climates of heavy snows, like Toronto, the covered internal court provides well tempered sunny space in the winter (287, 288).

Perhaps the most informal and environmentally satisfying glasshouse is Frei Otto's own private house situated on a hillside facing south above a village near Stuttgart. Movable radiant heaters make the huge glass space habitable in the winter. In the summer, the roof slides upward providing maximum ventilation. The house is in two units, the lower a multi-level glass-enclosed studio with attached garage, and the upper, the main glass house with flat-roofed rooms pushed into it at two levels. On one side are the parents' rooms, with kitchen, a small living room, bedroom and the mechanical equipment house. The other side is for the children, with a guest suite downhill. In the centre, behind the sliding glass roof, is a small wading pool surrounded by warm-climate plants—fig, orange, and eucalyptus. Frei Otto has created a temperate micro-climate in Stuttgart where these plants, native to the Mediterranean area, hundreds of miles south, attest to its success (284, 285).

The present and rightful concern about pollution and the depletion of natural resources and the world's fuels has nurtured many schemes for living involved with waste recycling, hydroponics horticultural systems, methane production for cooking, and solar heat storage. These are all dependent on the sun's energy and the glasshouse effect. Such ecological houses have been proposed by students at the University of Cambridge, England, and one has been built in London by Architectural Association student, Grahame Caine. With it, Caine hopes to demonstrate, as would other Eco-enthusiasts, that man can

284　Frei Otto House: main house above and part of the studio to the left.

285　Frei Otto House: section through hillside. Left: the lower studio and garage. Right: the main glasshouse with multilevel rooms and guest suite.

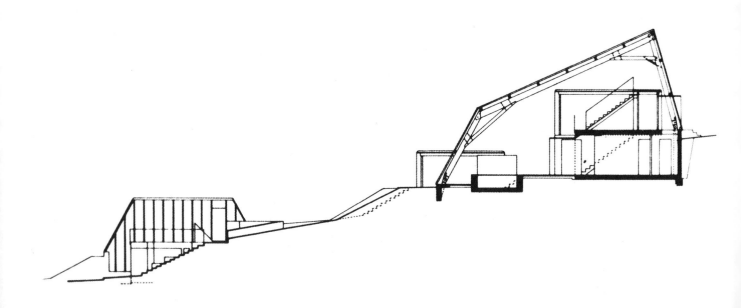

286   Purchased at an auction in 1960 for £28, this Dutch frame greenhouse is home for artist Mrs. Harry Bewick of Laragh, Glenda Lough, Eire. Mrs. Bewick's clothes and larger possessions are kept in a nearby cottage. She puts a kettle on the fire for privacy.

287, 288   Left: Myers House, Toronto, Ontario. View toward entry. Canvas curtains shade the area in summer. Below: section. To the left of the central winter garden are entry, garage and above, two bedrooms and a bath; to the right the kitchen and low dining room and above, a bath, master bedroom and study. A standard steel and fibreglass greenhouse roof spans the 40-ft central area.

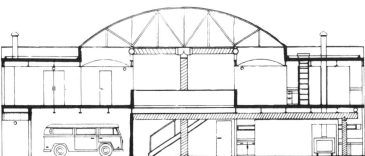

289 Ford Foundation, New York City. Kevin Roche, John Dinkeloo and Associates.

290 Metropolitan Museum of Art, American Wing. Kevin Roche, John Dinkeloo and Associates.

291 Méliès' glasshouse Cinema Studio, Paris.

292 Study for Stefansplatz, Vienna, Austria. Gruppe M.

293 Student Union housing, University of Alberta. An internal arcade filled with shops and student facilities connects the major university buildings enabling pleasant walks to class during the extreme winter climate. Diamond & Myers, Architects and Planners.

flourish without the dependence on organized power sources and can also reduce pollution in the environment with human-scaled techniques (282).*

The glasshouse has traditionally provided natural light for studio work. Otto Wagner's design for the Academy of Fine Arts in Vienna, 1910, included twenty-three glasshouses for painters and sculptors similar to Méliès' cinema studio in Paris (291).

In North America, transparent roofs are becoming more popular because of the introduction of plastics. The University of Alberta in Canada has a new student housing arcade by Diamond & Myers that connects most of the campus buildings, providing protected walks to classes during the winter (293). The Regency Hyatt House in Chicago has a giant acrylic and glass covered tree-filled court. In the centre is the main circulation tower and its transparent lifts. To one side is the tinted acrylic covered swimming pool typical of those so popular in the United States. It is the firm of Kevin Roche and John Dinkeloo that have proposed major transparent projects like the National Fisheries Center and Aquarium in Washington D.C., a computer museum also in the nation's capital, large transparent covered courts unifying the buildings at the Metropolitan Museum of Art (290) and the proposed Centennial Exposition buildings for Philadelphia. Their completed buildings include the Rochester Institute of Technology and the interesting Ford Foundation building in New York (289).

* See *The Observer,* 27 Aug. 1972 and *Architectural Design,* July 1972.

294 The Climatron in the Missouri Botanical Garden 1960. This
zoned-climate environment hovers behind a pool of Victoria Regia.
Designed by architects Murphy and Mackey and Synergetics, Inc.

13 *The Garden of Adonis*

Buckminster Fuller's proposed two-mile diameter dome over Manhattan (295) in the 1950s was a daring solution to environment control that would have pleased the nineteenth-century visionary J. C. Loudon. Today we are able (should we want) to carry out Loudon's desire to cover vast tracts of land with an artificial climate. The horticultural engineers, as we have seen, have the necessary expertise to develop the environmental equipment that would control such large man-made space. We shall also see that the technology exists to enclose vast tracts of land in huge teguments. Combining the two, environmental control and structural systems, it is possible to enclose a Garden of Adonis climate. Inside the Garden, building as we know it today would be unnecessary.

It is rather doubtful that in the immediate future we shall resort to such technical dependence. However, the pressure of population growth or pollution may eventually force communities into areas of the world previously considered uninhabitable, and then we will turn to the Garden of Adonis as a place of refuge and survival.

The world's extreme climates in deserts, jungles and polar regions are bound to be the first to have large-scale controlled environments, as already projected in the work of Frei Otto and Ove Arup Associates on Arctic City. On the other hand, cities with seasonal climates could be enveloped in an artificial climate during months of extreme conditions. Large recreational envelopes like Japan's Summerland demonstrate a way of creating more habitable climate during the seasonal extremes. The glasshouse effect of the thin skin alone can do a great deal to trap the sun's energy, keeping away winds, and so tempering nature. Add to this nuclear power, and an Arctic region can be transformed.

It is instructive to discuss recently-built or proposed projects that embody the artificial climate on a large scale. The enclosure's large size is fundamental to the Garden of Adonis concept, for the building must be large enough to present itself as a sky vault rather than just a large room. The sky vault is experienced in large indoor exhibition halls like McCormack Place, or enclosures like the United States pavilions at Montreal and Osaka. Man's activity goes on around display areas, with little awareness of the gigantic enclosing backdrop. The same sensation exists in the huge glass and plastic conservatories of the nineteenth and twentieth centuries, like the Kew Palm House, the dramatic Climatron in St Louis, the Berlin Botanic Garden Tropical House in Dahlem, or the Horticultural Conservatory in Milwaukee.

In 1960 the Missouri Botanical Garden (Shaw's Garden) in St Louis built the first plastic-domed conservatory on Buckminster Fuller's geodesic principles (294). The Climatron is a huge space, 175 ft (53 m) in diameter and 70 ft (21 m) high, spanned by a hexagonal grid of aluminium tubes supporting an internal lining of quarter-inch acrylic plastic. The structural loads are supported by five concrete piers rising from a peripheral concrete base that also houses two independent air circulation systems. Temperature and humidity are automatically controlled by a complex of pneumatic switches, monitoring fans, dampers and water sprays. Without partitions, the Climatron maintains several climates within its large area by using water sprays to heat or cool the air in different

295 Two-mile diameter tensegrity dome over Manhattan. The Empire State Building is at the centre. The structural members would be the size of the masts on the s.s. 'Queen Elizabeth', but too far from the ground to be seen. R. Buckminster Fuller.

296 Pyramid Research Project. Each pyramid contains a different activity: solarium, hotel, conference centre, ballroom. Each has its interior floor levels separate from the glazed skin. Gillinson Barnett and Partners.

locations in the dome. During the day, a temperature gradient from East to West is maintained, whereas during the night the temperature gradient is from South to North. This produces the warmest area in the south-east segment of the Climatron, corresponding to a tropical lowland jungle. Here an 'Amazonian forest', with a bog and pool with a transparent underwater tunnel enables visitors to see the Victoria Regia and other tropical water plants, growing in their normal habitat. In the south-west segment, cool days and warm nights imitate an oceanic climate, making a 'Little Hawaii' area where the most colourful tropical flowers are grown. The north-east area, with its warm days and cool nights, is typical of the dry tropics such as India, and in the north-west segment, a tropical mist forest is planted. These different eco-systems, with their indigenous plant life and climate, are all monitored and programmed from a control panel located at the entrance to the complex. The varied climates within the Climatron, though covering only a half acre and enclosing 1,300,000 cu.ft, have significant implications for larger structures. Taking advantage of internal orientation and relationship to the sun to vary climates within the enclosure suggests the potential of creating varied climates for people living in them, who can choose the atmosphere to match their needs and mood. It also suggests that climate can be zoned without physical barriers, making partitions and sealed house enclosures unnecessary. The Climatron's transparent roof allows visual contact with the outside world. It sometimes produces a play of light and atmosphere reminiscent of Scheerbart's poetry.

184

A tradition of glass-enclosed recreation buildings was begun in England with Paxton's Crystal Palaces and the conservatories of the rich. This tradition reappeared on a grand scale again in 1946 with Clive Entwistle and Ove Arup's huge glass-covered pyramid entry in the 1946 Crystal Palace Competition* held to find a replacement for the destroyed Sydenham building.

Entertainment centres have been proposed by English architects Gillinson Barnett and Partners in the same spirit as the early glass pavilions that reach out on piers into the sea along England's south and west coasts. A pyramid research project (296) to study the problems of solar gain, natural and powered ventilation, winter heating, glazing and cleaning techniques was initiated.

The proposed Hunstanton, Norfolk sea-side Entertainment centre (297) is a total environmental package designed to cope with England's unpredictable climate. Besides the aluminium-clad hall designed for a wide variety of activities, the main attraction is the tempered climate of a 250 ft diameter geodesic dome covered in acrylic similar to the St Louis Climatron. The dome houses a man-made lagoon with water slide, pools for board and skin diving and a wave-making machine. Positioned next to the solarium, bathers may lie in an artificial sun even on a grey and windy east-coast day.

To duplicate a holiday trip to Spain, Yugoslavia and Italy in England can mean a sizeable expenditure in climate equipment. The Derby Castle Entertainment

* Maxwell Fry, 'Report on the Crystal Palace Competition', *Architectural Journal,* 23 May 1946.

Centre, Isle of Man, off the west coast of England (299), was the first such large facility, designed for the local government of Douglas.* The architects programmed the solarium to be as large as possible, so that its enclosing skin could be forgotten while it provided a warm and sunny atmosphere whatever the weather. This centre was recently destroyed by fire with a considerable loss of life, putting into grave question the use of acrylic plastic as an enclosing membrane.

The Garden of Adonis milieu is best represented in Summerland,** a popular all-weather recreational environment outside Tokyo, Japan (298). Thousands of people enjoy an eternal summer in the plastic enclosed space. The 3-acre room is filled with tropical vegetation, swaying in the artificial breeze. There is a restaurant area circumscribed by a circuitous boating canal, an amusement terrace, garden theatre, and huge swimming pool complete with a wave machine producing artificial surf. Under the tubular steel covered space, near the entrance, is a four-storey building with administrative offices, guest rooms, conference halls, restaurant, banquet hall, party rooms, shopping halls and hot baths and showers. The steel roof is 531 ft long, spanning 266 ft and covered with acrylic domes and fibre-glass panels. Sprays to water the plants and clean the roof are housed within the truss depth. Summerland can accommodate the population of a

* Designed by J. Phillips, Lomas & Partners with Gillinson, Barnett & Partners.

** Ishimoto Architecture and Engineering Firm, Tokyo.

small town or village. Its average daily attendance is eight thousand visitors but the building can house up to twelve thousand—the size of a small town.

Milwaukee, Wisconsin, is on Lake Michigan, north of Chicago, and has a natural climate that is hot in summer and extremely cold and often windswept in winter. Drifts of snow as high as a man are common in the countryside after a blizzard. The Milwaukee County Parks Commission opened their new Horticultural Conservatory in 1965 to give people who could not visit other climates the ecological experience of arid desert, tropical or temperate conditions, all housed in three 140 ft diameter conoid domes (300). Building separate enclosures ensures positive differences in climate, in contrast to the more subtle variations of the St Louis Climatron. The arid dome containing cacti, succulent plants and acacias is maintained at 75°F and 35 per cent humidity. The tropical dome, with its palms, ferns, orchids, citrus, papaya and a 25 ft water fall is also maintained at 75°F, but with 85 per cent humidity. The precast concrete hexagonal and triangular units are fastened together to form a complex lattice structure. Over this is an elaborate system of aluminium and neoprene gasket glazing, combined with a system of ball joints and connection tubes. The glazing holds quarter-inch wire plate glass and the tube system carries condensation to the bottom of the dome. If the Sydenham Crystal Palace with its wood glazing bars and 21 oz glass lasted over eighty years, then this structure must be indestructible.

The Exhibition Plant House in the Royal Botanic Garden in Edinburgh was opened in 1967. The external

297   Above: entertainment centre proposed for Hunstanton, Norfolk, England. Gillinson Barnett & Partners.

298   Left: Summerland: The tubular steel structure clad in acrylic domes forms a background to the activity. The ventilation ducting has an effective sculptural expression independent of the structure. Ishimoto Architecture and Engineering, Inc.

299   Below: the Derby Castle Entertainment Centre, before its destruction by fire. The swimming pool is on the left. The large solarium was the Isle of Man's answer to its uncertain climate. J. Philipps Lomas & Partners, Gillinson Barnett & Partners.

300 Above: Milwaukee County Horticultural Conservatory, Milwaukee, Wisconsin, 1965. The tropical dome is in the foreground, the arid and temperate showhouses behind. Architect, Donald Grieb.

301 Right: Hamburg Botanical Garden: A beautiful steel exoskeleton supports a glass envelope housing six different climates tempered by sophisticated mechanical equipment in cellars below. Designed by B. Hermkes; Botanic Consultant, K. Renard; Director of Gardens, J. Apel.

302 Below: Tropicarium at the University of Tübingen, West Germany. A cluster of six hexagonal inverted umbrellas of various heights ensures perfect conditions for every plant height. The central supporting columns also function as ducts for the heating and cooling ventilation system.

suspension structure* provides a relatively inexpensive unobstructed space divided into six different climates. Visitors can don sound-guide equipment and follow a path connecting the environments laid out with plants to create an illusion of being in diverse exotic landscapes (303). Suspension structures for glasshouses are not new to Scotland. In 1853 Charles McIntosh published two designs in his *Book of the Garden* that could, according to a 'high engineering authority' he quotes, span up to 150 ft.

Contemporary suspension buildings demonstrate the potential for creating huge structure-free spaces enclosed in glass or plastic. Suspension bridges are familiar ever since I. K. Brunel and John Roebling (1806–69) popularized them in the nineteenth century. The Verrazzano Narrow Bridge in New York City has a span of 4,260 ft, carrying relatively heavy dynamic loads when compared to a glazed roof covering.

Frei Otto has proposed a suspension project for a transparent and translucent roof over the parks at Montreal's Expo' and an enclosure for the Medical Faculty at Ulm. A research project** at Illinois Institute of Technology is proposed as an exhibition hall 2,000 ft (668 m) in length with plate-glass walls and plastic-domed roof with a span of 1,000 ft (334 m) (304). A quick calculation reveals that the 2,000,000 sq.ft enclosure covers some forty-six acres, fifteen times the area of Tokyo's Summerland. If we can imagine fifteen interconnecting Summerlands with diverse activity areas in diverse micro-climates, then we can see the possibility of total landscape living.

Buckminster Fuller has for many years been an advocate of thin-skinned enclosures developed from his geo-metric studies. The repetition of building elements, like the stick, the joint and the skin, takes advantage of mass production and mass marketing. The enclosure, which could be used for all purposes, would enjoy a large market. Levels, partitions, equipment, and climate determine the activity inside. His attitudes, like Scheerbart's prophetic musings, were summed up in an interview on the United States pavilion at Montreal's Expo '67:

> From the inside there will be uninterrupted visual contact with the exterior world. The sun and moon will shine in the landscape, and the sky will be completely visible, but the unpleasant effects of climate, heat, dust, bugs, glare etc. will be modulated by the skin to provide a Garden of Eden interior.†

At Expo '67 (308–310), mechanical failures thwarted the original intention of creating a skin that reacted dynamically to modulate the interior climate. The building skin would have changed as the intensity and position of the sun changed. A solar-activated motor was mounted over the centre hub of each group of three interior hexagonal frames that formed the skin structure. Each of these six hundred motors was programmed to start when the

---

* A similar suspension house has recently been built at Chatsworth. Its relatively small span does not take advantage of the suspension potential.

** Project by Peter Pran, MNAL, with advice from Myron Goldsmith and Fazlur Khan, Illinois Institute of Technology.

† *Architectural Forum*, 1967.

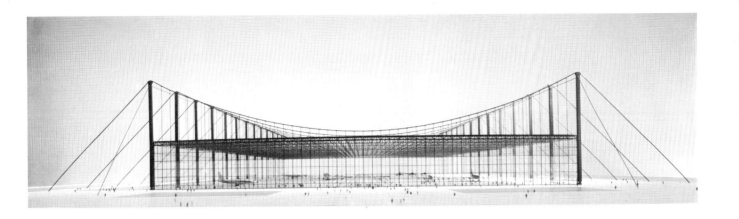

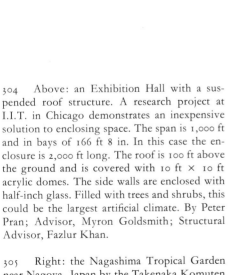

303   Left: Exhibition Plant House, Royal Botanic Garden, Edinburgh, 1967. Ministry of Works.

304   Above: an Exhibition Hall with a suspended roof structure. A research project at I.I.T. in Chicago demonstrates an inexpensive solution to enclosing space. The span is 1,000 ft and in bays of 166 ft 8 in. In this case the enclosure is 2,000 ft long. The roof is 100 ft above the ground and is covered with 10 ft × 10 ft acrylic domes. The side walls are enclosed with half-inch glass. Filled with trees and shrubs, this could be the largest artificial climate. By Peter Pran; Advisor, Myron Goldsmith; Structural Advisor, Fazlur Khan.

305   Right: the Nagashima Tropical Garden near Nagoya, Japan by the Takenaka Komuten Co., a vast steel and fibreglass complex housing gardens, shops and public baths.

306 New York Botanical Garden Conservatory, Bronx, N.Y., was built in 1901 by Hitchings & Co. who merged with Lord and Burnham.

307 Palace of Plants at Meise, Belgium (1947–59) near Brussels. The huge steel and teak structure (73 m × 154 m) covers some 2½ acres under double glazing. Thirteen halls are devoted to the display of plants to the public and twenty-two others are for scientific study.

308–10   Above: United States Pavilion, Expo. '67, Montreal.
R. Buckminster Fuller, Geometrics Inc. and Cambridge Seven Associates Inc. Right, top: escalators connect the elevated platforms. The
monorail could pull into the station. The highest acrylic domes have
vents so that the skin can breathe. The sun shades are in a beautiful
disarray. Right, below: platforms provide landings for houses and
shops of the past, during a United States Craft Exhibition. The contrast
between the two architectures is humourously prophetic. The ground
area covered is only one acre; this necessitated multilevel development.

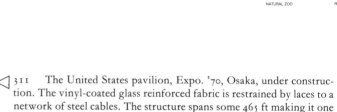

RING TRANSPORTATION ARCTIC ZONE NATURAL ZOO RESEARCH C

◁ 311   The United States pavilion, Expo. '70, Osaka, under construction. The vinyl-coated glass reinforced fabric is restrained by laces to a network of steel cables. The structure spans some 465 ft making it one of the largest pneumatic spans and a landmark in large enclosure design. Architects, Davis, Brody and Schwartsman; designers, Chermayeff, Geisman and de Harak.

sun's rays struck them at a given angle. As the sun moved across the sky and struck each motor, it would close eighteen silvered plastic roller blinds within the three hexagonal frames, shading the building during the day and reducing radiation heat loss and some conduction heat loss at night. Fuller's pavilion has a spherical diameter of 250 ft and is 200 ft high. The ground area covered is only about an acre, which necessitates multi-level development. Each level could enjoy a different climate because of its elevated position within the space. Bruno Taut often suggested that exhibitions in Europe should be banned, to be replaced by demonstrations of architecture and its potential. Fuller's 1967 pavilion at Montreal is just such a construction.

The future lies with pneumatic structures, or traditional construction allied to pneumatic principles. Hundreds of prototypes have demonstrated that small air pressure will support large areas with both single spans and patterns of multiple spans. Some enclosures have already been provided with double skin construction, bettering the environmental performance of a single thin skin. However, the inflated enclosure is dependent on power sources which up to now have been unreliable, and in the field of pneumatics safety factors and collapse times still have to be investigated. Recently-proposed pneumatic structures are too small to take advantage of their ultimate potential, for inflatable environments must be very large to recreate the sky vault and, more importantly, to contain enough air so that internal air pollution is not a problem.

There are two interesting proposals in environmental control that are unfortunately too small and too un-

sophisticated. Both are related directly to housing and educational facilities. The Student Housing Co-operative at Princeton University are using a design by Gus Escher and John Ringel to house fifty people in a self-constructed living accommodation under a half-acre air-structure. Antioch Columbia College has built a one-acre inflatable campus in the new town of Columbia, Maryland, which houses lecture rooms, offices, accommodation for three hundred students, plus a college green. Unsophisticated projects such as this will not encourage the acceptance of large, open-planned enclosures.

At Osaka, in 1970, the United States made a contribution to the pneumatic age with the low-profile pavilion that claimed to be the largest single-spanned air structure. A 274 ft by 465 ft super-elliptical bowl was dug, and the earth mounded around. A concrete ring made to sustain the steel cables was poured at the top of this peripheral berm. The cables were laid out in a diamond pattern, and a vinyl-coated glass-fibre fabric was laced to the supporting cables through a transition rib system. The internal air pressure of 20 mm water gauge on the skin was transferred to these ribs and then to the sustaining cables holding the roof down (311).

Designers may discuss air structures and draw and build models of them; but it is not until experimental environments are built that we will derive the kind of empirical information that can develop confidence for the future. For this reason the low-profile United States pavilion with its large span was an important constructional landmark. In architecture and building engineering, in contrast to automobile and aircraft production, the

192

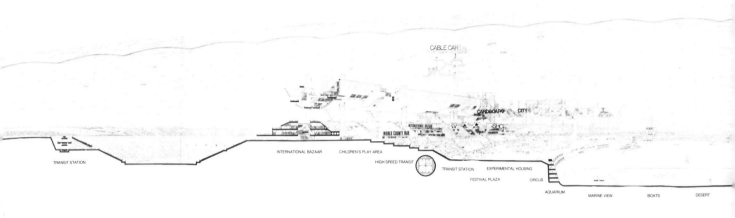

Labels on image: CABLE CAR, CARDBOARD CITY, SHOP, WORLD COUNTY FAIR, INTERNATIONAL BAZAAR, CHILDREN'S PLAY AREA, HIGH SPEED TRANSIT, TRANSIT STATION, EXPERIMENTAL HOUSING, FESTIVAL PLAZA, CIRCUS, AQUARIUM, MARINE VIEW, BOATS, DESERT, TRANSIT STATION, FOOD

312 World Environmental Laboratory, a proposal for an 8000 ft span enclosing an Arctic city. Davis Brody.

feed-back from prototypical experiment is very slow, mainly because most buildings are one-shot endeavours. Without empirical information, far-reaching and often good ideas are rejected by slide-rule, code book and at the drawing board. International pavilions or constructions that test ideas make an important contribution and should be encouraged in future. The architects of the Osaka pavilion—Davis, Brody—are now proposing its use as an Arctic city (312).

Vast tracts of the earth's surface are uninhabitable because of severe climate even when tempered by normal buildings. The search for natural resources necessitates development in these extreme climates of the Arctic and the Antarctic, Alaska, Lapland, Siberia and Greenland. An international design team, led by Frei Otto, has been working on a project to erect a city in the Arctic under a transparent inflated skin which without supports covers an area of 3 km^2 and encloses an artificial climate corresponding to European conditions (313–17).*

The main object of the plan is to make life in these pioneer exploration cities as bearable as possible and to demonstrate that they can even be attractive. Also the transparent environments could be used for covering

open-pit mines and whole exploration areas. The plan therefore was not to cover a specific city but to develop a realistic conceptual model, a prototype for cities built under large climate-regulating roofs.

The making of the enclosure is simple in concept, but there are many details to be worked out. A circular foundation is built around the city to take the thrust of the roof. A preassembled skin is laid flat on the ground and inflated. After this the construction of the city proceeds as if under normal conditions. The enclosure dome has a free span of 2 km (1.24 miles) and a height of 240 m (790 ft), and is made with a double-layered plastic skin within a strong cable net of specially prepared and impregnated high-strength polyester fibres. The dome shape will be able to resist severe storms and its form prevents snow accumulations. The city can accommodate between fifteen thousand and forty-five thousand people. The residential areas are interspersed with kindergartens and schools around the inside periphery of the dome. The main street of the city begins at the main traffic insersection on the outside, crosses the business section, and ends at the city centre with its municipal auditorium, theatres, city administration, churches, hotels, apartments, tourist and shopping centre and high schools. A pedestrian system connects administration, residence and recreational areas. The administration, located at the entrance to the city, is the headquarters for land exploration and development.

There are special provisions for ventilation, and protection against fires and catastrophes. Two interconnected ground levels join all of the buildings in the city. All

* The calculations for the supporting structure were made by Structures 3, Ove Arup & Partners in London. Kenzo Tange with Urtec in Tokyo are solving urban planning problems. The Warmbroon Studio in Stuttgart with Frei Otto and Ewald Bubner are responsible for central co-ordination. Scientific work is also done at the Institute of Lightweight Structures of the University of Stuttgart. The client for the project is Farbwerke Hoechst AG who are handling all the materials research problems.

193

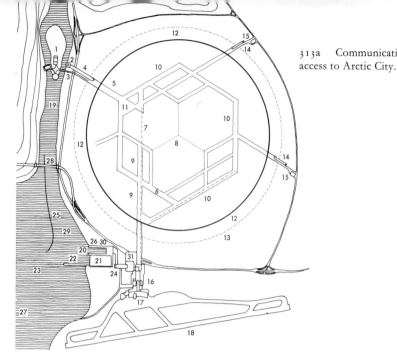

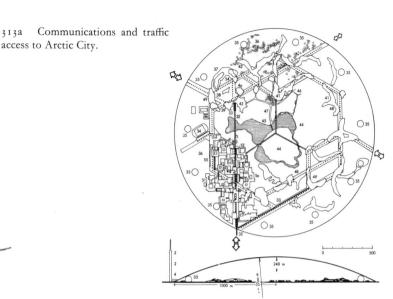

313a   Communications and traffic access to Arctic City.

313b   Plan and elevation of the city.

313d   Below: the construction process of the skin. 1. The site is levelled. 2. The foundation holes are dug. Balloons to assist inflation are placed and anchored. 3. The protective net is laid out. To erect the constructive net the cables of the lower layer are drawn in a straight line with low pretension. The cables of the upper cable layer are then laid on at right angles. Both layers are bound together into a single net with 10 cm mesh width. 4. The transparent skin is fixed to the cable net. 5. The foundations are closed and the support balloons inflated. 6. The inflation with heavy-duty auxiliary blowers takes approximately 50 hours. 7. Inflation is complete. The middle support balloons are inflated. The giant hull serves as a roof over the construction site. 8. The ventilation tower is constructed and the air exchange system installed. 9. The first buildings are complete. Construction of the city begins.

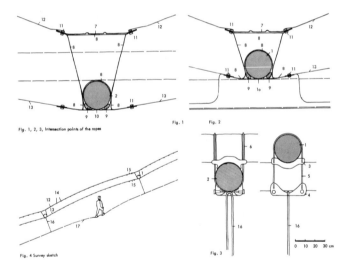

Fig. 1, 2, 3, Intersection points of the ropes

Fig. 4 Survey sketch

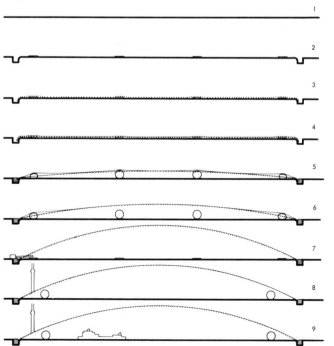

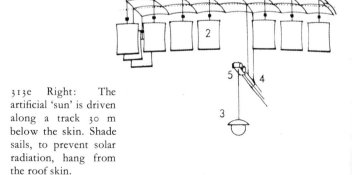

313e   Right: The artificial 'sun' is driven along a track 30 m below the skin. Shade sails, to prevent solar radiation, hang from the roof skin.

314–16   Above: the covered harbour basin and external traffic terminal and on the left, the air circulation tower. Right: view through the skin to the civic centre below, the traffic axis and moving pavements leading through park to the business centre. Below: view across the park.

313c   Facing, centre: Constructional details of the skin. 1. Cable in the upper cable layer φ 270 mm polyester fibre bundle (Trevira Heavy Duty) without air gaps, impregnated with PVC. 2. Cable in the lower cable layer of the net, design as in 1. 3. Saddle-shaped element made of Hostaform 30 × 30 × 7 cm. 4. Tension element of Hostaform 32 × 32 × 12 cm. 5. Intersection cable φ 15 mm of polyester fibre pretensioned with tension collars (aluminium) and nuts. 6. Girdle support for 5. 7. Walk-on opaque skin of PVC-coated, heavy polyester fibre with knobs. 8. Chamber, bonded from PVC-coated, heavy polyester fibre. 9. Sealing cord of foam rubber. 10. Interlacing. 11. Erection joint, screwed on metal leaves, exchangeable with 12 and 13. 12. Upper transparent skin with girdle reinforcement every 50 cm. 13. Lower transparent skin. 14. Girdle reinforcement for transparent skin. 15. Air lock made of textile, exchangeable with transparent skin 12 while maintaining air pressure in the hull. 16. Suspension cable for protective cover 17. 17. Protective cover, knotless fish net, 60 mm mesh width, 4 mm web thickness.

317 The traffic axis leading from the civic centre to the business district and on to the terminal buildings for airport and harbour.

intake air and exhaust air is directed through these levels. A street network for the supply of goods is located in the hermetically sealed air-exhaust level. An atomic plant provides electricity and its warmed cooling water keeps the harbour free from ice and warms the fresh polar air which is taken at a height of 300 m (984 ft) and distributed into all buildings in the city and across all open surfaces. This air is also the load-bearing element of the dome structure.

The scale of the city's buildings is kept small so that the dome appears as a great limitless horizon. The dome should be invisible so that the weather outside the shell, the sun, the moon and the nights can be experienced. The city does not have a sterile indoor climate, for the influence of the external climate can be felt everywhere.

196

Interior conditions are altered by raising the temperature only as much as necessary, and both the temperature and humidity fluctuate. A bright electric sun lamp is moved across the dome in accordance with the daily rhythm, producing daytime during the long polar winters. The continuous sunlight of polar summers is screened with movable sails. Air in the city is healthy and fresh, for used air is vented into the atmosphere. The city is quiet, the moving sidewalks glide noiselessly, and all walking surfaces are covered with carpeting; the evergreen trees in the landscaped areas dampen the sound. Vegetation covers all open spaces and all roofs that do not need to be walked on. There is a lake and a botanical garden with birds and animals. The Garden of Adonis is complete.

Abercrombie, J., *The Hot-House Gardener* . . . . London 1789

Adams, M. & Godwin, E., *Artistic Conservatories*. London 1880

Adanson, M., *Familles des Plantes* (2 vols.). Paris 1763

Ames, W., *Prince Albert & Victorian Taste*. London 1967

Anderson, Dr J., *A Description of a Patent Hot-House* . . . . London 1803

Architectural Design, Jan. 1969

Auger, B., *The Architect and the Computer*. London and New York 1972

Banham, P. R., *Theory & Design in the First Machine Age*. London and New York 1960

Banham, P. R., *The Architecture of the Well-Tempered Environment*. London and New York 1969

Bean, W. J., *The Royal Botanical Gardens, Kew*. London 1908

Beaver, P., *The Crystal Palace*. London 1970

Benjamin, W., *Paris, Capital of the Nineteenth Century*. Berne 1935 (reprinted *Perspecta* 12)

Blunt, W., *The Compleat Naturalist*. London 1971

Bradley, R., *The Keeping of Exotics*. London 1718

Bradley, R., *A Philosophical Account of the Works of Nature*. London 1724

Bradley, R., *New Improvements of Planting and Gardening*. London 1724

Buckley, F., *Old London Glasshouses*. London 1915

Builder, The, 38, 1848; 18, 31, 1852

Canham, A. E., *Air-Supported Plastic Structures, Materials and Design Factors*. Reading 1967

Casson, H., *An Introduction to Victorian Architecture*. London 1948

Chadwick, G. F., *The Works of Sir Joseph Paxton*. London 1961

Civil Engineer and Architectural Journal, v, 1851

Cobbett, W., *The English Gardener*. London 1829

Collins, P., *Changing Ideals in Modern Architecture*. London 1965

Commeleyn, J., *Nederlantze Hesperides*. Amsterdam 1676

Conrads, V. & Sperlich, H., *Fantastic Architecture*. London and New York 1963

Dale, A., *Fashionable Brighton*. Newcastle upon Tyne 1947

de Caus, Salomon, *Hortus Palatinus*. Frankfurt 1620

de la Court van de Voort, P., *Lanhuren Lusthaven, Plantagien*. Leyden 1737

Desmond, R., ed. *Kew Bulletin*, vol. 26, 3, 1972

Dingwall, R. and Lawton, B., *The Climatron*. nd

Downes, C., *The Building for the Great Exhibition*. London 1852

Downes, K., *Hawksmoor*. London 1959

Drewitt, F., *The Romance of the Apothecaries' Garden at Chelsea*. London 1928

Evelyn, J., *Kalendarium Hortense or, The gard'ner's almanac*. London 1691

Exposition Universelle, *Rapport Général*, vol. I, Paris 1891

Fairchild, T., *The City Gardener*. London 1722

Fish, D., *Cassell's Popular Gardening* (4 vols). London 1884–6

Fletcher, H. & Brown, R., *The Royal Botanic Gardens, Edinburgh*. Edinburgh 1970

Fletcher, H., *The Story of the Royal Horticultural Society*. London 1969

Florist, The, XI, 1855.

Garden, The, IV, 1872; IV, 1875

Gardener's Chronicle, The, 1850; 1860; 1877; 1880; 1885; 1886; 1896

Geretsegger, H. & Peintner, M., *Otto Wagner 1841–1918*. London and New York 1970

Giedion, S., *Space, Time and Architecture*, Cambridge, Mass. 1963

Gloag, J., *A History of Cast-Iron in Architecture*. nd

Gloag, J., *Mr Loudon's England*. London 1970

Gloag, J., *Victorian Taste*. London 1962

Gorse, P. A., *Wandering through the Conservatories at Kew*. nd

Groen, J. van der, *Der Nederlantsten Hevenier*. Amsterdam 1669

Hesse, H., *Neue Garten-Lust*. Leipzig 1696, 1714, 1734

Hibberd, S., *The Floral World and Garden Guide*. London 1871

Hibberd, S., *The Amateur's Greenhouse and Conservatory*. London 1873

Hitchcock, H. R., *Architecture: Nineteenth and Twentieth Centuries*. Harmondsworth 1971

Hitchcock, H. R., *Early Victorian Architecture in Britain*. London 1954

Hitchings & Co., *Greenhouse Heating and Ventilating Apparatus*. New York 1889

Hobhouse, C., *1851 and the Crystal Palace*. London 1937

Hyams, E. & MacQuitty, W., *Great Botanical Gardens of the World*. London 1969

Illustrated London News, VIII, 1848; XI, XII, 1850; VII, 1851; VIII, 1852; VI, 1853; VII, 1854; III, 1859

Institute of Horticultural Engineering, *Annual Report,* Wageningen, Holland, 1965

Institution of Civil Engineers, *Minutes and Proceedings,* 9, 1849–50; 10, 1849–50; 19, 1851

Jackson, A., *London's Termini*. London 1969

Journal of Horticulture, 1871

Kerr, R., *The English Gentleman's House*. London 1871

Knight, C., *Cyclopaedia of London*. London 1843, 1851

Langford, T., *On Fruit Trees . . .* London 1681

Langley, B., *The Principles of Gardening*. 1728

Lemmon, K., *The Covered Garden*. London 1962

Lightoler, T., *The Gentleman & Farmer's Architect*. London 1762

Lindeboom, G., *Boerhaave, the Man and His Work*. Leiden 1968

Linnaeus, C., *Hortus Uppsaliensis*. Uppsala 1748

London & Wise, *The Retired Gardener*. London 1706

Loudon, J. C., *Short Treatise on Several Improvements recently made in Hot-Houses*. Edinburgh 1805

Loudon, J. C., *Remarks on the Construction of Hothouses*. London 1817

Loudon, J. C., *Sketches of Curvilinear Hothouses*. London 1818

Loudon, J. C., *Comparative View of the Common & Curvilinear Modes of Roofing Hothouses*. London 1818

Loudon, J. C., *Encyclopaedia of Gardening*. London 1822, 1835

Loudon, J. C., *The Different Modes of Cultivating the Pineapple . . .* London 1822

Loudon, J. C., *The Greenhouse Companion*. London 1824

Loudon, J. C., *Illustrations of Landscape Gardening & Garden Architecture*. London 1830

Loudon, J. C., *Encyclopaedia of Cottage, Farm and Villa Architecture and Furniture*. London 1833

Loudon, J. C., *The Suburban Gardener & Villa Companion*. London 1838

Loudon, J. C., *The Derby Arboretum*. London 1840

Loudon, Mrs (ed.), *Encyclopaedia of Gardening*. London 1850

Loddiges, Conrad & Sons, *The Botanical Cabinet*, I, 1817

Lord and Burnham, *Some Greenhouses We Have Built*. New York 1929

McCracken, E., *The Palm House and Botanic Garden, Belfast*. Belfast 1971

McDonald, C., *Gardeners' Dictionary*. II, 1807

MacFarlane, W., *Catalogue of Cast-Iron Manufactures*, 6th ed., II. Glasgow 1882

McGrath, R. & Frost, A., *Glass in Architecture*. London 1937

McIntosh, C., *The Greenhouse, Hothouse, & Stove*. London 1838

McIntosh, C., *The Book of the Garden*. Edinburgh 1853

Markham, V., *Paxton and the Bachelor Duke*. London 1935

Matheson, E., *Works in Iron*. Handyside & Co., London 1873

Messenger & Co., *Artistic Conservatories*. London 1880

Miller, P., *The Gardeners' Dictionary*. London 1731

Moore, D., *Botanical & Horticultural Tours*. London 1860

Musgrave, C., *The Royal Pavilion*. Brighton 1951

Nicol, W., *The Gardener's Kalendar*. Edinburgh 1810

Oosten, H. van, *The Dutch Gardener*. London 1703

Perspecta, Vol. 1. New Haven, Conn. 1952

Pevsner, N., *Pioneers of Modern Design*. Harmondsworth 1960

Platt, H., *The Garden of Eden*. London 1654

Punch, London 1851

Repton, H., *Sketches and Hints on Landscaping*. London 1796

Repton, H., *Observations on the Theory and Practice of Landscape Gardening*. London 1803

Repton, H., *Designs for the Pavillon at Brighton*. London 1808

Repton, H. & J. A., *Fragments on the Theory and Practice of*

Landscape Gardening. London 1816

Revue Générale de l' Architecture et des Travaux Publiques. Paris 1849

Robinson, W., *The Garden*. London 1872

Robinson, W., *The English Flower Garden*. London 1883

Rohault de Fleury, C., *Dessin pour un Jardin des Plantes au Musée National d'Histoire Naturelle*. Paris 1856

Rowan, A., *Garden Buildings*. London 1968

Rowley, W., *The Garden under Glass*. 1914

Saunders, A., *Regent's Park*. London 1969

Scheerbart, P., *Glasarchitektur*. Leipzig 1914

Shaw, C., *London's Market-Gardens*. London 1880

Shaw, J., *Forcing Houses . . .* Whitby 1794

Sheppard, R., *Cast-Iron in Building*. London 1945

Sweet, R., *Hot-House & Greenhouse Manual*. London 1825

Switzer, S., *The Practical Fruit Gardener*. London 1724

Taut, B., *Alpine Architektur*. Leipzig 1919

Taut, B. (ed.), *Frühlicht*. Magdeburg 1920

Taut, B., *Modern Architecture*. London 1929

Taylor, G., *Some Nineteenth-Century Gardeners*. nd

Texier, E., *Tableau de Paris*. Paris 1853

Thornbury, G. W., *Old and New London*. 1873–8

Thompson, J., *A Practical Treatise on the Construction of Stoves and Other Horticultural Buildings*. London 1838

Tod, G., *Hothouses, Greenhouses . . . Aquaria etc.* London 1812

Transactions of the Horticultural Society, II, 1817; IV, 1822; V, 1824; VI, 1826; VII, 1829; Second series, I, 1835

Veitch, J., *Hortus Vechii*. London 1906

Webber, R., *The Early Horticulturalists*. Newton Abbott 1968

Webber, R., *Covent Garden*. London 1969

Wright, W., *Greenhouses, their Construction and Equipment*. London 1917, 1931

References in *italic* are to illustrations